TELEPEN

UNIVERSITY OF NOTTINGHAM
60 0337085 4

WITHDRAWN
ROM THE LIBRARY

DATE DUE FOR RETURN

This book may be recalled
before the above date

90014

D1580355

The
North Eastern
Railway

Cecil J. Allen

M.Inst.T., A.I.Loco.E.

LONDON

IAN ALLAN

© *Ian Allan Ltd.*

First published 1964

337086
X760353874

385.0942   104032 B

LEICESTERSHIRE AND RUTLAND
WITHDRAWN FROM STOCK
LIBRARY

Made and printed in England by
STAPLES PRINTERS LIMITED
at their Rochester, Kent, establishment

Contents

Author's Preface

MOST of the great British railways of former years began as main lines radiating from London, or from cities such as Liverpool, Manchester, Edinburgh and Glasgow; the throwing-off of branches in various directions was a later development. With the North Eastern Railway, however, this was not the case. Long before there had been any serious thought of the trunk route from south to north which today forms a part of the East Coast main line, the County of Durham and the south of Northumberland had become criss-crossed by numerous wagonways which had been laid down to carry coal from the inland mines to the sea for shipment.

It is the story of these early constituents, from the beginning of the century onwards – their unique engineering through the rugged *terrain* of North-Eastern England, the fierce rivalries that produced formidable groups of competitors, the obstruction and rapacity of powerful landowners in the matter of 'wayleaves', and the unceasing warfare waged in later years by the North Eastern Railway in and out of Parliament to resist threatened invasions of its territory by envious rivals – that makes this so fascinating and at the same time so complex a history. Not until the middle of the book do we come to the incorporation of the North Eastern Railway in 1854; ultimately, no fewer than 53 public and 21 private companies had been absorbed in the North Eastern system, not to mention lines built jointly with other railways.

Doubtless this complexity until now has deterred railway authors from the formidable task of compiling a history of the N.E.R. – with one notable exception. This was the late William Weaver Tomlinson, who exactly fifty years ago produced his monumental 820-page treatise, *The North Eastern Railway, Its Rise and Development*. So meticulously detailed a history is this that any later historian would be foolish indeed if he were to neglect Tomlinson as his main source for the facts and figures of these early times; for myself, I have been under a considerable debt to my predecessor in writing this book. I am also very grateful to the book's publishers, Messrs Andrew Reid & Company of Newcastle, for their permission to reproduce many of the admirably clear maps and one or two diagrams from the Tomlinson volume, now long since out of print.

In undertaking the compilation of the present book I am fortunate in having spent a large part of my life in North-Eastern England, mainly among the steelworks of Tees-side, Tyneside and up to the 1,000ft altitude of Consett. Travelling constantly to and from this area, and between it and other steel-producing districts, such as Sheffield, Manchester, West Cumberland, and Clydeside, together with many exploratory journeys that unlimited pass facilities made possible, I gradually acquired an intimate acquaintance with the whole of the North Eastern system, which has proved invaluable in putting the story together.

In its vaults at York, the North-Eastern Region of British Railways possesses what are probably the most complete archives of any portion of British Railways, right back to Stockton & Darlington days, and all most carefully indexed; and my warm thanks are due to the Curator, Mr E. H. Fowkes, not only for verifying certain obscure facts, but also for reading through my manuscript and making a number of valuable suggestions. This is a part only of my indebtedness to York; Mr G. S. Knox, Public Relations and Publicity Officer of the North-Eastern Region, and his staff have been most helpful with information and photographs, and especially my friend Mr J. Norman Stainthorpe, Public Relations Assistant, with whose kindly assistance in many ways this book has been brought to completion. I trust that it may prove worthy of the notable railway whose history it describes.

CECIL J. ALLEN

CHAPTER I

The Cradle of Railways

MANY claims could probably be advanced as to the precise date and site of the birthplace of railways. North-Eastern England is often given the credit, but for the actual place of birth we must look elsewhere. In his book *The Evolution of Railways* Charles E. Lee produces evidence to show that the first mention of a wagonway – a track laid with wooden rails to provide a smoother passage for wagons carrying coal than the dirt tracks of the period – appears to be in documents of 1597 and 1598, which mention such a wagonway laid from mines at Wollaton and Strelley to the River Trent in Nottinghamshire. An agreement of 1609 has a reference to 'Wollerton lane end at the new rayles end'. It was Huntingdon Beaumont, member of a Leicestershire family with interests in the coalfields of this area, who took the idea of wagonways up to Northumberland, and was responsible about ten years later for laying a similar short wagonway between pits at Cowpen and Bewley and the River Blyth near Bedlington.

As to public railways, a claim might be put in for the Leeds and Middleton wagonway as the first of its kind to be sanctioned by Parliament in the Act of 9th June, 1758. But well before the opening in 1825 of the Stockton & Darlington Railway the Surrey Iron Railway had secured its Act of Incorporation, in May, 1801, and had opened for horse-drawn traffic on 26th July, 1803; and the Oystermouth Railway, between Swansea and the Mumbles in South Wales, began the conveyance of passengers in its horse-drawn vehicles on 25th March, 1807.

As to steam traction on rails, Richard Trevithick by 1804 had produced the first steam locomotive to run on a railway track, and in February of that year was trying it out over the Pen-y-Darran tramway at Merthyr Tydfil in South Wales. In 1808 his *Catch Me Who Can*, another primitive steam locomotive, was hauling passengers round a circular demonstration track near the Euston Road in London, and by 1809 yet another engine had been built at Gateshead to Trevithick's design to work on the Wylam tramway, though it never appears to have started active service. In any event, however, Trevithick preceded Blenkinsop's 1811 locomotive for the Middleton Colliery at Leeds, Hedley's locomotive of the following year for the Wylam tramway, and George Stephenson's first Killingworth locomotive of 1814.

But if the distinction of having seen the birth of railways and steam locomotives belongs to other parts of the country, there can be little question that North-Eastern England provided the cradle in which the railway idea was fostered and developed to the point at which it was realised that railway transport would become a necessity over the entire country. And, as we shall see later, it was to the brilliant and versatile George Stephenson, self-educated son of a poor pump-engineman at Dewley Colliery on Tyneside, that the major part of the credit was due. After Stephenson, at the early age of 31 and easily the youngest man to hold such an appointment, had been appointed in 1812 engine-wright at Killingworth High Pit in Northumberland, under an enlightened management which gave him a free hand to develop his ideas, there began the work which was to have so profound an influence on transport, not only in Britain but all over the world.

It was the vast development of the coal measures of the County of Durham and those in the southern part of the adjacent County of Northumberland that provided the greatest of all incentives to railway construction in North-Eastern England. As new pits were opened, the transport of their coal to the towns, and above all to the sea for shipment, was the major difficulty; and the early wagonways proved to be the salvation of the coal owners. The first pits opened for the most part were near the Rivers Wear, Tyne and Blyth, and short wagonways between the collieries and tidewater facilitated the movement of coal.

But as more pits were opened farther inland, difficulties began to arise and chief among them the exorbitant 'wayleave' charges exacted by landowners for the mere passage of coal over their lands, which in many cases made it impossible to work the coal at a profit. This problem was not grappled with successfully until five prominent men, all owners of large estates and of mines in the County of Durham, came together in 1726 and formed the most powerful partnership ever known in the coal trade. Indeed, this group, known as the 'Grand Allies', established what was practically a monopoly of coal production over the entire district. In all the pits controlled by the group the coal was to be produced on a joint basis, but worked down to the same separate staiths as before for loading.

Four of the partners in the 'Grand Alliance', the Hon. Sidney Wortley Montagu and his son, with Sir Henry Liddell and Col. George Liddell, already had begun the construction of the most ambitious of all the early wagonways to carry coal from their Burdon Moor Colliery, and other pits which they planned to open on the Causey estate, down to the Tyne at Dunston Staiths, opposite Elswick. Durham is a rugged county, with many of its streams flowing down deep valleys. But whereas a number of the wagonways used rope-worked inclined planes to cross such obstacles, the Tanfield wagonway scorned any such expedients. The Beckley Burn was diverted through a channel blasted in the solid rock and over its valley there was tipped an embankment which at its maximum was 100ft high and 300ft broad at its base, and which still carries the Tanfield Mineral branch of the North Eastern Region.

Higher up the line, the same valley was spanned by the famous Causey Arch, a notable engineering work indeed for the period, across the deep valley of the Houghwelburn a mile to the north-east of Tanfield village. The Causey Arch, or Dawson's Arch as it was sometimes known, was designed and built by a master mason named Ralph Wood, and in planning a freestone arch on this scale he could have had little previous experience to guide him. The excellence of his work, however, is evident from the fact that after more than two centuries and a half the arch still stands, now rightly regarded as a monument of national importance. It is in the form of a slightly flattened arc, of 105ft span, rising 35ft from the springing level, the arch having three rings or voussoirs with a total thickness or depth of 7ft; it is 22ft 7½in wide. It was completed in 1727. Above it ran a double wagonway of 4ft gauge, the 'rails' being 6ft lengths of timber from 6 to 7in wide by 5in deep, carried on timber sleepers spaced from 2 to 3ft apart. Nothing but horse-drawn traffic ever passed over it; in later years, when steam locomotion had been introduced, it was over a diversion which avoided the arch. The total length of the wagonway laid down by the 'Grand Allies', from Tanfield Moor to Dunston Staiths, was about seven miles.

In course of time the Tanfield wagonway was extended south-westwards to the Pontop collieries and threw off branches to Beamish South Moor and Marley Hill, so that all the coal from a large area passed over it. By 1732 it is recorded that an average of some 400 wagons – or 'chaldrons' – each holding some 2½ tons, was moving over it daily. By the beginning of the nineteenth century the whole of the northern part of the County of Durham was criss-crossed by wagonways, at least seven of considerable size and importance making their way north to the Tyne between Blaydon and the east side of Gateshead, while a maze of lines came down to the navigable stretch of the Wear between Chester-le-Street and Hylton. There were many wagonways in South Northumberland also, a number to the Tyne and some to the Blyth, while the historic Wylam wagonway skirted the north bank of the Tyne from Wylam through Newburn to Scotswood.

Considerable developments took place in wagonway construction also. Whereas in South Wales the early tramroads first developed from the wooden rail era into 'plate-ways', when the change began in North-Eastern England it was in general to the use of rails. The plate-ways, which appear to have originated with John Curr for laying in colliery lines at Sheffield in 1776, consisted of cast-iron angles, with the ordinary road wheels of the wagons running along the flats of the angles, but in the north the use of flanged cast-iron wheels had come in at a comparatively early date; the wagons on the Tanfield wagonway certainly were of this type. Charles E. Lee, in his book previously mentioned, gives it as his opinion that the name 'waggon' originated to distinguish the vehicles with flanged wheels from the 'wagons', which had cast-iron wheels with flat treads only.

With the increasing production of iron, it was soon realised that iron could be used both to give a harder running surface and also to prolong the life of the timber. Such protection appears to have been used first in 1758 at the Whitehaven collieries in Cumberland; next, in 1767, the Coalbrookdale Ironworks in Shropshire, having a surplus of cast iron in the form of 'pigs,' laid these down as rails on their works lines, intending later, if the demand for pig iron should increase, to take them up and sell them. Between 1768 and 1771, however, the Coalbrookdale Company produced some 800 tons of cast-iron rails, and this was the beginning of manufacture on a more extensive scale.

Early in the nineteenth century production also had begun, at the Bedlington Ironworks in Northumberland, of malleable or wrought-iron rails, with a wearing quality far superior to cast iron, and, as we shall see in Chapter III, at the time of the building of the Stockton & Darlington Railway there was some controversy as to which of these two alternatives should be chosen. George Stephenson strongly favoured the wrought-iron type, and though outside influences compelled him to use some cast-iron rails, the lengths of wrought-iron track were considerably in the majority.

One other type of rail, of cast iron, needs to be mentioned, because it had an integral connection with one of the earliest steam locomotives brought into use in North-East England. As mentioned already, a steam locomotive of Trevithick's design was built in 1805 at Gateshead, similar to his first locomotive used on the Pen-y-Darran tramway at Merthyr Tydfil, though the Gateshead product never ran on rails and eventually was converted into a stationary engine. The next steam locomotive in the north, however, was the one which John Blenkinsop designed for the Middleton Colliery Railway at Leeds. This remarkable machine did not depend for adhesion on the grip between ordinary driving wheels and the rails, but its two cylinders worked pinion wheels which engaged with semi-circular projections cast on the outer sides of the rails. In effect, Blenkinsop was the father of the rack-and-pinion mountain railways of much later years.

Completed in 1811 by the firm of Murray, Fenton & Wood, Blenkinsop's 'patent steam carriage' proved itself capable of hauling no fewer than 110 tons of train, at 3½ m.p.h., as compared with the 25 tons capacity of Trevithick's 'travelling engine' on the Pen-y-Darran tramway. Indeed, on an experimental run early in 1829 one of the Blenkinsop engines actually moved a 38-wagon load of 140 tons at from 2 to 3½ m.p.h. The *Prince Regent* was joined by the *Salamanca* and both worked for years over the short line across Hunslet Moor. One or two similar engines were in service from 1813 to 1815 over the Kenton & Coxlodge wagonway near Newcastle. Against the Blenkinsop system there was the 30 lb per yard added by the projections to the weight of the rails, which increased track construction costs by £352 per mile, and explains why the system did not find general favour.

Christopher Blackett, owner of the Wylam tramway, was much impressed with the performance of Blenkinsop's engines, but having recently relaid his lines with rails of the plate type could not face the expenditure of £9,000 which would have been needed for relaying again with Blenkinsop's cogged-edge rails. It was the quest for adequate adhesion that caused William Hedley, Blackett's 'viewer', to design his strange locomotive of 1813, carried on four axles, with two vertical cylinders driving a beam engine arrangement which worked a shaft between the two middle axles, and communicated the motion to all the axles by means of gear wheels. Little is known of its work. One or two other curious designs were evolved on Tyneside at about this period, but it was not until George Stephenson had been appointed engine-wright at the Killingworth High Pit in 1812, as we have seen already, and (after an inspection of what was going on over both the Wylam tramroad and the Middleton Railway), had begun to apply his mind to the most economical way of carrying his own colliery's coal, that steam traction began to emerge in a reliable form.

Stephenson's first locomotive, completed and first tried at the end of 1814, was based largely on the Blenkinsop design; it worked regularly over the West Moor wagonway, some two miles long, and was capable of hauling 16 loaded chaldron wagons, with a total weight of 56 tons, up a slight gradient at 3 m.p.h. It was sufficiently effective in use to make it possible for Killingworth High Pit to reduce the number of horses used up to then in loading coal from 50 to 30.

Before his second locomotive took the rails, in March, 1815, Stephenson had patented various improvements. For the first time his connecting-rods drove the wheels directly by means of a pin on one of the spokes and a ball-and-socket joint; the two cylinders were vertical, above the two ends of the boiler, and worked horizontal beams high above the boiler to which the connecting-rods on both sides of the engine were attached. Chains passing round toothed wheels on each axle performed the same function as coupling rods.

A little while later, before the advent of springs, in order to avoid the shocks to which his engines might be subjected by the rough tracks of the period Stephenson fitted additional cylinders below his boilers, the pistons of which were made to bear on the axles; the steam admitted to these cylinders thus had a cushioning effect. As the news spread of these locomotive developments, not to mention various other inventions of Stephenson's directed towards the improvement of rail transport, many engineers of note made their way to Killingworth Moor to gain personal impressions of what was going on. Among these visitors was Edward Pease, accompanied by other members of what had now become the Stockton & Darlington Railway Committee, as described in Chapter II, who visited Killingworth in 1821. Four years later there was an important deputation from the Liverpool & Manchester Railway Committee, with results which will be referred to later.

Mention has been made earlier of the many wagonways which by the early years of the nineteenth century had come into use all over the northern part of County Durham and also in South Northumberland, for the movement of coal from the mines to tidewater for shipment. Included in their number were, in addition to the Tanfield line, wagonways from the Rainton and South Hetton districts to Seaham Harbour, the Londonderry wagonway from Pittington and West Rainton down to the Wear near Penshaw, the Beamish and Pelaw Main wagonways from Stanley to the Tyne at Poulter's Close, between Newcastle and Jarrow, and various others.

But probably the most notable was the Hetton Colliery Railway, because from its opening on 18th November, 1822, steam locomotives of Stephenson's design were used. He himself also had been entrusted with the task of engineering this 7½-mile line, from Hetton Colliery to the River Wear at Bishopwearmouth, so that it was in the nature of a trial ground for the working out of his principles. These were that locomotive engines should be used on track that was level, or on no steeper inclination against the load than 1 in 300; that on gradients steeper than those which could be climbed with locomotives or horses rope haulage by fixed engines should be employed; and that gradients steeper than 1 in 30 should be operated on the funicular principle, with the descending loaded wagons pulling the empty wagons up. Stephenson had now to show his skill as a civil engineer as well as an engine-wright, for the country over which the Hetton line was laid was very hilly and a limited amount of money only was available, but the success with which he carried out this task, and of his five Killingworth locomotives that he put into service, had no small influence on the Stockton & Darlington Committee decision to use steam traction.

The new means of transport that was thus being evolved was bringing to a head public dissatisfaction about the slowness of travel by road, which even in the best stage-coach conditions could not expect to exceed some 12 m.p.h., while moving freight in bulk in lumbering wagons drawn by relays of pack-horses was a costly business. In the closing decades of the Eighteenth Century various canal schemes were being brought forward, some on a considerable scale, to ease the situation; but the extent to which the movement of coal was now being expedited by the wagonways of North-Eastern England already was applying the brake to the expenditure of capital on grandiose canal proposals.

The advent of steam traction proved to be the turning-point. As will be described in the next three chapters, while canals were first proposed to connect Stockton-on-Tees with the Auckland coalfield, and Newcastle with Carlisle, it was railways eventually that were built. Moreover, by 1825 some vastly more ambitious railway schemes were in the air; indeed, from 1824 onwards there broke out a kind of 'railway mania' quite comparable with the more notorious outbreak of twenty years later. In his book *The North Eastern Railway – Its Rise and Development*, W. W. Tomlinson calculated that in 1825 agitations were in progress for some twenty railway schemes, representing a total outlay of £13,950,000, including two lines to link London with Edinburgh and a 'London–Northern Railroad', with a capital of £2,500,000, 'to connect Birmingham, Derby, Nottingham, Hull and Manchester with each other, with the parts adjacent and with the Metropolis'. But at the time little money was available, and the actual beginnings of public transport by railway were on a considerably more modest scale.

CHAPTER II

The Stockton & Darlington Railway

On 18th September, 1810, the Tees Navigation Company gave a dinner in the Town Hall, Stockton-on-Tees, to celebrate the opening of the 'New Cut'. This waterway, though no more than 210 yards in length, had eliminated a great bend in the river, thereby reducing by no less than $2\frac{1}{4}$ miles the water distance between Portrack and Stockton-on-Tees. At this dinner a resolution was moved by Leonard Raisbeck, the Recorder of Stockton, that a committee should 'inquire into the practicability and advantage of a railway or canal from Stockton, by Darlington, to Winston, for the more easy and expeditious carriage of coals, lead, etc.' Later it turned out that the main purpose was to provide an outlet to the sea for coal from the Bishop Auckland area, where expansion of the mining industry was impossible otherwise. Such, then, was the genesis of the Stockton & Darlington Railway, but fifteen years were to elapse before the projected railway was actually opened for the conveyance of traffic.

The famous engineer, John Rennie, was engaged to examine and report on the two alternatives, waterway or railway, but it was not until August, 1813, that he presented his findings. They were in favour of a canal, of which he estimated the cost of the main section, between Stockton and Winston, at approximately £179,600. If branches to Yarm, Croft Bridge and Piercebridge, all at different points on the Tees, were to be included, the cost would be increased to £205,600. But such a figure was prohibitive, at that time, with money very short owing to the wars with France and the United States, so that the matter lay dormant until 1816; moreover, Rennie had damped the ardour of the promoters by declaring that they might have to wait many years to receive any return on their capital.

A new proposal was then made, for a canal from Stockton to Darlington and a railway from there onwards, which would reduce the cost to £141,460. By this time the idea of canals was much in the ascendant, and it was in this atmosphere that another engineer, George Leather, financed by Christopher Tennant of Stockton, prepared an estimate for a $29\frac{1}{2}$-mile canal from Portrack on the Tees through Norton, Whitton and Stillington, and then, crossing the Skerne near Bradbury, on past Shildon and Brusselton to the River Gaunless at Evenwood Bridge, so tapping a considerable part of the Durham coalfield. The idea was for the Tees to compete with the Tyne and the Wear in coal export. Fifty locks would have been needed and the estimated cost was £205,300, or, with a branch from Bradbury to the City of Durham, £241,100.

While Stockton welcomed this proposal with enthusiasm, Darlington and Yarm, which would be left out in the cold, took a very different view.

In Yarm a strong movement was set on foot in favour of the southern route, through Darlington, by Jonathan Backhouse, a man of considerable influence, Richard Meynell and his steward, Jeremiah Cairns, and Thomas Meynell, with the support of Leonard Raisbeck in Stockton. Their meeting in the George and Dragon Hotel at Yarm is sometimes regarded as the true promotion date of the Stockton & Darlington Railway.

Cairns was connected by marriage with a Welsh engineer named Overton, and wrote to him about the canal, with the result that he received back a series of letters strongly advising a tramroad in preference to a canal. Miles, who was very active in the matter, having seen the letters, communicated their contents to Meynell, and convinced him of the desirability of a railway rather than a canal. Also a letter published on 22nd August, 1818, in the *Durham County Advertiser*, over the *nom-de-plume* 'Alexis' – actually John Grimshaw – carried a good deal of weight. It criticised the estimates of the canal advocates, and maintained that those who found capital for a canal could not expect a return of more than 1 per cent on their holdings for at least thirty years.

The railway advocates promptly convened a public meeting, which was held at Darlington on 4th September, 1818; no time was to be lost, as Christopher Tennant a fortnight before had got his canal scheme approved at a meeting at Bishop Auckland. Overton, the writer of the letters which had stressed the greater advantage of a railway, was brought up from Wales to go over the route and give his opinion, and completed his survey by 20th September. The course that he proposed was from Stockton by way of Fighting Cocks to Haughton, just north of Darlington, then by Denton to its highest level at Hilton, continuing through Shildon and by the Brusselton incline to the Etherley and Witton Collieries. There would be a branch northwards from Shildon to serve collieries in the Coundon area. Including branches to the River Tees at Yarm, Croft and Piercebridge, there would be 51 route miles of line, 20 miles double and the rest single, to be built at an estimated cost of £124,000.

At this stage 'Alexis' weighed in with some further letters to the *Durham County Advertiser*, pointing out, *inter alia*, that a railway had the great advantage of carrying coal from the pit to the shipping staith without breakage; Nesham Main coal, he claimed, had suffered so much by transfer from wagon to lighter and from lighter to ship that its export price had declined badly, whereas the best price of all coal shipped from Sunderland had been for that brought down by the Newbottle wagonway to the Bishopwearmouth staiths. He also pointed out that the 23-mile Sirhowy tramway in South Wales had been earning 18 per cent, whereas the earnings of the parallel canal had been 8 per cent only. He considered that the proposed Stockton & Darlington Railway – as the scheme by now was being called – would benefit farmers as much as coal owners, and might be expected to pay at least 15 per cent.

But it was the advocacy of the renowned Edward Pease of Darlington, in a public meeting at Darlington on 13th November, 1818, that carried the day. This shrewd and straightforward Quaker held out no prospects

Right, the Causey Arch, on the Tanfield wagon-way, with its span of 102ft, built about 1726.
[*N. Wilkinson*

Below, George Stephenson's bridge over the River Gaunless, on the Stockton & Darlington Railway, built in 1825 and believed to be the first metal railway bridge in history.
[*British Railways*

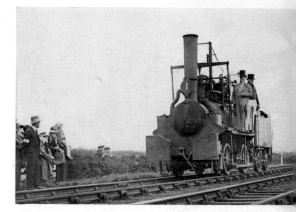

Above, Locomotion No. 1 and replica train of chaldron wagons and the coach *Experiment* in the Railway Centenary procession of 1925 over the former Stockton & Darlington route.   [*British Railways*

Right, Stephenson's Hetton Colliery locomotive in the 1925 Centenary procession.
                    [*F. R. Hebron*

Left, Locomotion No. 1 and tender. The engine is now on permanent exhibition on a pedestal at Bank Top Station, Darlington.
                    [*British Railways*

of astronomical profits; his estimates were based on road traffic that existed already, and which by transfer to the railway could be relied on to give a certain return of at least 5 per cent on the capital invested. Convinced by these arguments, the meeting decided to apply for an Act of Parliament to sanction the construction of the Stockton & Darlington Railway, on the basis of Overton's plans and estimates, and also to authorise the surveying of possible branches to Richmond, Northallerton and Guisborough.

Things were not to proceed too smoothly, however. One of the promoter's solicitors discovered that Overton's proposed route would pass over part of Lord Eldon's estate and, worse, through one of the Earl of Darlington's fox covers; with two such powerful opponents the Bill would have slender prospects in Parliament. It was, therefore, decided to ask a Scottish engineer named Robert Stevenson, who was already regarded north of the Border as an authority on railways, and also the eminent John Rennie, to meet Overton and examine his survey. Although by now the opinions of Rennie, shortly before his death, were veering towards railway construction, he declined to play second fiddle in this way, but Stevenson accepted, and by the end of January, 1819, he was said to have made a favourable report. The matter was now becoming urgent, for distrust of what Darlington might exact in dues for the carriage of coal over its land had caused the Stockton party to turn its attention to a considerably shorter route between the Bishop Auckland mining area and the north side of the Tees, which was to materialise later as the Clarence Railway.

The promoters had been allowed up to 12th March, 1819, to present their Bill to Parliament, but it had been ill prepared, and defects in the plan gave no small help to its opponents. In the House of Lords the two peers whose property was to be affected took precisely the line that had been expected. The solicitor Mewburn, in his *Larchfield Diary*, records how Earl Grey observed Lord Eldon, while on his knees in the House during prayers, busily making notes on his copy of the Bill; when the latter rose to speak, his criticism was directed chiefly against the compulsory purchase of land for the railway. If only the surface of the land were required, why not a wayleave for what the railway carried over it, leaving it in the possession of its owner?

The Earl of Darlington proved a more formidable opponent. Just before the second reading, a message reached him at Newton House from his solicitors, stating that the Quaker support of the Bill was much stronger than had been expected, and urging him to come to London at once. That day he was hunting, and a servant had to hurry across country to find his master, who at that moment was following 'a beautiful scent', and had to call off the hounds, with much abuse of the Quakers, dine in haste, and post up to town. Despite fifteen petitions in favour of the Bill from towns and villages in the North Riding, his opposition and that of the other peers was too strong and by 106 votes to 93 the Bill was thrown out.

It was now evident that a new route was essential, especially as scrutiny of Stevenson's report showed that he was not as enamoured of Overton's original route as had been thought; in any event, the whole scheme needed more careful preparation. Stevenson, therefore, surveyed a new route, from Stockton to Railey Fell *via* Middridge Grange, with branches to serve Yarm, Darlington, Witton Park, Cockfield Fell and other areas, by which he shortened the main line by some nine miles. Meantime plans were going ahead for a 'Northern Railway', which would have started from the north bank of the Tees at Portrack or Billingham, with a branch to Stockton, and would have pursued a more direct course than Overton's line. But eventually the two parties came together and agreed on the southern route. They had placated Lord Eldon by undertaking to pay handsomely for his land, and the threat to the sporting activities of the Earl of Darlington had been eliminated by avoiding his fox covers altogether, though at the expense of arousing the opposition of yet another peer, Lord Barrington.

As finally presented to Parliament, the Stockton & Darlington Railway Bill proposed a main line a little over 26¼ miles in length; with the 3¼-mile Black Boy branch from Shildon to the Coundon Collieries, another 4¼ miles long from St Helen's Auckland up the Gaunless valley to the Evenwood and Norwood Collieries, terminating at Hagger Leases Lane, and shorter branches to Yarm and Darlington, the total length would be 36¾ miles. A number of possible opponents had been appeased in various ways, but at the last moment the Bill nearly suffered shipwreck because it did not comply with the Standing Orders of the House of Commons. These laid it down that four-fifths of the share capital had to be subscribed before the Bill went into Committee; and the needed amount was £7,000 short. The solicitor, Mewburn, tried every possible means of raising the money, but without success, and the situation was saved only by Edward Pease, Jonathan Backhouse, the principal subscriber, and one or two others, agreeing to increase their subscriptions, the addition to rank either as a mortgage on the railway or as shares in it, whichever they preferred. So, on 12th April, 1821, the Bill had its third reading in the House of Commons; five days later it was passed by the Lords; and on 19th April it received the Royal Assent.

The Act laid down what the railway might charge for carriage. This was 4d. per ton per mile for coal, coke, limestone, road metal, ironstone, building stone, paving stone, bricks, tiles, slates and similar materials; 6d. per ton per mile for lead, bar iron, timber and merchandise generally; but no more than ½d. per ton per mile for coal shipped at Stockton-on-Tees. The smallness of this last charge was at the instance of the Earl of Durham, who feared competition with the coal-carrying wagonways farther north that he owned. Eventually, however, coal for shipment, even at this low rate, proved by far the most profitable of all the traffic carried by the Stockton & Darlington. Later, an extra 6d. per ton was charged for all coal hauled up the Etherley and Brusselton inclines.

Owners of land within 5 miles of the line were to be permitted to build branches effecting junctions with it, and subject to the dues laid down, any private owner would be allowed to run his own trains, provided that his wagons had been designed and built in accordance with the Company's regulations. No night operation was to be permitted; the use of the railway would be limited to between 7 a.m. and 6 p.m. from November to February inclusive; 5 a.m. to 10 p.m. from May to August inclusive; and 6 a.m. to 8 p.m. during the remaining months. One curious provision was that gates had to be provided wherever the railway crossed a road, and that a driver of any train must open them to allow the train to pass and close them after it had done so; if he failed in the latter duty he would be fined 40s., half of this sum going to the witness who informed against him and the other half to the poor of the parish where the offence was committed!

Powers were granted to raise £82,000 in shares and £20,000 by loan, and the time allowed to complete the construction was five years. It should be noted, however, that the Act merely authorised the haulage of wagons or carriages along the line 'with men or horses or otherwise'; no mention was made of the use of steam traction. Indeed, up to this date the steam locomotive had not greatly distinguished itself. By contrast, on the Surrey Iron Road, as the result of a wager, an exceptionally strong horse had succeeded in pulling a 12-wagon train of 38 tons weight over a distance of 6 miles in just under $1\frac{3}{4}$ hours, and had hauled no fewer than 16 wagons weighing 55 tons in the opposite direction, though in the latter case in a time not stated.

Edward Pease now lost no time in preparing for the line to be built; indeed, he took what was to prove a decisive step on the very day that the Act received the Royal Assent. Not altogether satisfied with the competence of Overton as an engineer, he had decided already to look elsewhere. So it was, on 19th April, 1821, that George Stephenson, whose all-round ability in all matters connected with railways – as seen already in Chapter I – was becoming well known in districts far removed from his native Tyneside, was summoned by a special messenger, John Dixon, to meet Pease in the latter's house at Darlington. The impression made by Stephenson on the older man was immediate; so also was Stephenson's advocacy of the use of locomotive power, which up till then had not been considered, on the new railway.

On 12th May the shareholders held a meeting in Darlington at which they appointed the Committee previously referred to. It included, of course, Edward Pease and his son Joseph, who from now on was to take a more prominent part than his father; Jonathan Backhouse, who provided most of the finance; Thomas Meynell, who was appointed Chairman and took a very active part; and ten others. Unfortunately Richard Miles, to whom Edward Pease paid the tribute that 'he was among the first in the kingdom who gave railways consideration as objects of public utility' and who had been the chief moving spirit in the Stockton & Darlington project, had fallen into financial difficulties and had had to dispose of his shares; otherwise he would certainly have been elected to the Committee. One of the Committee's first actions was to approve a design for a Corporate Seal, which showed a horse, not a locomotive, drawing four wagons, and bore the motto *Periculum privatum utilitas publica*, that is 'at private risk for public service' – a laudible conception indeed of private ownership!

By the end of July the Committee had made two important decisions. One was definitely to build a railway rather than a mere tramroad; and the other was to engage George Stephenson to make a fresh survey of Overton's route, in order to ascertain if any deviation within the authorised limits would be of advantage. It was realised that Stephenson might propose deviations outside those limits, in which event a new Act of Parliament would be needed. To this possibility Meynell was strongly opposed, but eventually Stephenson was given a free hand. His report, presented at the end of 1821, stated that a practicable line could be laid within the limits laid down in the Act, but that another route, shorter by three miles, would provide easier gradients and avoid the tunnels and deep cuttings which would be unavoidable on Overton's original route. It was decided to accept the amended route, and to proceed at once with those parts of the line which would still be within the authorised limits. Also it was decided to appoint George Stephenson as Engineer, at a salary of £660 per annum.

The decision to build a railway rather than a tramway meant that rails would be required rather than merely the angle-irons used for the plateways over which horses drew ordinary road wagons. There was a considerable difference of opinion as to whether the rails should be of the cast-iron type which were being produced at the Neath Abbey Iron Works, or of the malleable-iron type then in production by the Bedlington Iron Company and strongly favoured by Stephenson. Eventually it was decided to use some of both. An actual start on the work was made at Stockton-on-Tees on 13th May, 1822, amid much public rejoicing. From the Town Hall a procession, including the Stockton & Darlington Chairman, Thomas Meynell, the Mayor, Corporation, leading citizens and several hundred navvies, marched to St John's Well, the place appointed for the ceremony. Meynell himself laid several rails of the new line, and very significantly, at a distance of 4ft 8in apart, the same as Stephenson had used for his Killingworth Railway, and destined, with the slight modification to 4ft 8½in, to become the standard gauge of the major proportion of the world's railways.

Work at first progressed rapidly. By the autumn of 1822 six miles of the authorised route had been completed in the Darlington direction, together with a ¾-mile branch to Yarm. As the site of the deviations was approached, the new Bill had to be prepared, and though there was some opposition in Parliament, it was passed on 17th May. It also authorised an additional branch, to Croft Bridge.

More important, for the first time in history an Act of Parliament provided for the conveyance of passengers by steam power, as is shown by the following extremely wordy extract. 'It shall and may be lawful for any person or persons permitted by them, from and after the passing of this Act, to make and erect such and so many loco-motive or movable engines as the said company of proprietors shall from time to time think proper and expedient, and to use and employ the same in and upon the said

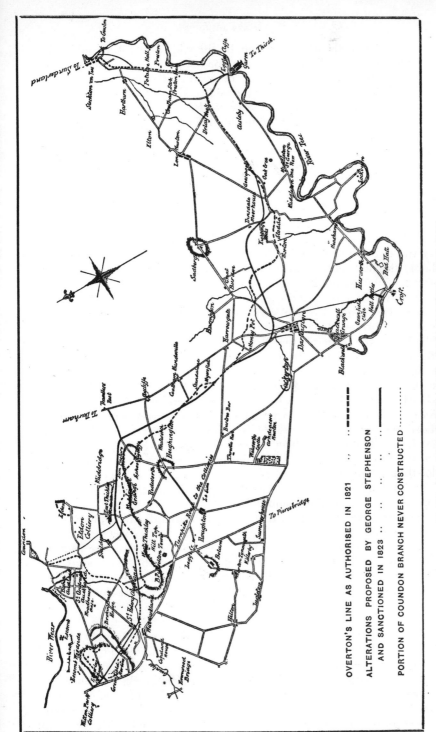

PLAN OF STOCKTON AND DARLINGTON RAILWAY

(Showing Overton's Line and George Stephenson's Alterations).

[Andrew Reid & Co., Ltd.

railways or tramroads or any of them, by the said recited Act, and by this
Act directed or authorised to be made, for the purpose of facilitating the
transport, conveyance and carriage of goods, merchandize and other
articles and things upon and along the said roads, and for the conveyance
of passengers upon and along the same roads.'

The work steadily progressed, though no general contract had been let.
The earthworks, some of which were of considerable magnitude – one
embankment was 48ft high – were let out to small contractors and even to
groups of navvies, at prices varying with the types of soil that had to be
dealt with; not a little trouble was caused when one group considered that
it was being less well-treated financially than another, and price adjust-
ments had to be made from time to time. Myers Flat, a swampy area at the
north end of the line, proved the most troublesome section, and many tons
of material had to be dumped before a stable foundation was reached.

For the crossing of the River Gaunless Stephenson designed what was
probably the first metal bridge in history. Each of its four 12ft 6in spans
consisted of two wrought-iron segments, one curving upwards and the
other downwards, united at the outer ends by cast-iron bosses; each pair of
segments was joined by five vertical ties which extended upwards to
support the bridge floor carrying the track. The whole in miniature
foreshadowed the principle that Brunel was to use years later in designing
for the Great Western Railway his vastly greater Royal Albert Bridge at
Saltash.

In the matter of the bridge over the River Skerne, Stephenson had a
brush with Edward Pease, who with other members of the committee
exercised a close supervision over all that was going on. It was, perhaps,
a reflection on Stephenson's ability that they asked him to consult Ignatius
Bonomi, a well-known architect in Durham, as to the design, and when he
failed to do so they called in Bonomi over his head. The handsome stone
bridge that was built was to an Italianate design, and appears to have been
mainly Bonomi's work, but Stephenson was broad-minded enough to
accept the situation without opposition.

Some four-fifths of the track had been laid with 12ft and 15ft wrought-
iron rails from Bedlington, weighing 28 lb per yard. They were fish-bellied
in shape, 2in deep at the ends and $3\frac{1}{4}$in deep in the centre; the width of
the heads was $2\frac{1}{4}$in. The remainder of the line, and all the turnouts, had
much heavier cast-iron rails from Neath, also fish-bellied, 4ft long only,
and weighing $57\frac{1}{2}$ lb per yard. Both types were held in cast-iron chairs, of
6 and 10lb weight respectively.

The chairs were secured by oak pins to sleepers which at the Stockton
end of the line were oak blocks from 18 to 24in long, 7in wide and 5in deep,
and at the Etherley end stone blocks from 18 to 21in long, 12 to 15in wide
and 7 to 10in deep. Stevenson would have preferred stone blocks throughout, but the cost of carriage to the Stockton end of blocks weighing any-
thing from $1\frac{1}{4}$ to $1\frac{3}{4}$ cwt each was prohibitive. In view of today's costs, it
is amusing to recall that the stone sleepers cost no more than 11d. per pair,
and those of oak 1s. per pair. The oak blocks had a link with the Royal

Navy, as they were cut from old warships – the 'wooden walls' of England – that were being broken up by a firm named Holmes & Rushman of Portsea. No tie-rods were used between each pair, and their firm bedding in the ballast was therefore a matter of prime importance for the maintenance of the gauge.

By 1824 the line was nearly finished, but the completion was held up by some exceptionally bad weather. So greatly had the estimates been exceeded that no work had been done on the Croft, Hagger Leases and Coundon branches. Nevertheless, when in that year a deputation came from Liverpool and Manchester to decide whether a railway between these two cities 'would best combine the essential requisites of speed, economy and despatch', their opinions, after visits to the Stockton & Darlington line and also to West Auckland, Bedlington, Killingworth and Hetton, were so favourable that a month or so later the Liverpool & Manchester Railway scheme was formally inaugurated; moreover, George Stephenson was appointed to make the preliminary survey.

The directors of the Stockton & Darlington had indicated to the deputation from Lancashire their definite intention to use steam locomotives, and the time had now come to place an order for the new power. In the previous year there had been opened at Forth Street, Newcastle, a locomotive works under the name of Robert Stephenson & Company – Robert being George Stephenson's equally famous son – with George and Robert, Edward Pease and two co-directors as the board, and the firm's tender for two locomotives at £500 each was accepted. They were to be to George Stephenson's design. Orders were placed with the firm also for the stationary engines needed to work the Etherley and Brusselton inclines, the former, of 30 h.p., to cost £1,983 and the latter, of 60 h.p., £3,483. These inclines ranged in steepness from 1 in 30½ to 1 in 33¼, but over the first 20 miles from Stockton there was no gradient steeper than 1 in 104.

CHAPTER III

The S. & D.R. Opens and Begins Operation

By the summer of 1825, matters were sufficiently advanced for a decision as to the opening date of the Stockton & Darlington Railway, which the directors realised would be an occasion of even national importance. Stephenson's 'improved travelling engine', the *Locomotion*, had arrived by road from Newcastle; and the stationary engines for working the Etherley and Brusselton inclines had been installed. It had also become urgently necessary for the line to start earning money at the earliest possible date, for £60,000 had had to raised by promissory notes to meet the excess of expenditure over the authorised capital, and the holders of the notes had given notice that they expected repayment within six months. So Tuesday, 27th September, 1825, was fixed for the opening ceremony – one of the most momentous dates in railway history. The lines that had been completed were the main line, 25 miles long, from the Phoenix Colliery at Etherley to College Row, Stockton; the ¾-mile branch to Yarm; and two ½-mile branches, one to the depots at Darlington and the other a part of the Hagger Leases branch.

There was no question as to the interest of the public in what was about to take place; an enormous crowd of spectators, brought thither by every conceivable type of conveyance, had assembled along the route from all the districts around. The proceedings began early, with 12 wagons of coal being drawn by the stationary engine up the 1,100 yard incline to Etherley Ridge, from which they descended by the self-acting incline to St Helen's, Auckland. Horses then worked the train, to which another wagon loaded with flour had been added, to Brusselton West Bank. Up the 1,850 yards of this incline the Brusselton stationary engine moved the 13-wagon train at 8 m.p.h., lowering it 825 yards down the succeeding incline to Shildon Lane End. Here *Locomotion No. 1*, newly painted in green, and with George Stephenson in person as the driver, was waiting with steam up.

A remarkable train was now put together. Behind *Locomotion* and its tender there came six coal wagons, the wagon loaded with flour, a wagon containing the surveyors and engineers, the coach *Experiment*, occupied by the directors and shareholders, 20 wagons packed to capacity with passengers, and six coal wagons at the rear – 35 vehicles in all. Tickets had been issued to some 300 people, but there was such a wild rush of would-be travellers that the total rose eventually to more than 450, packing every wagon, even including those loaded with coal. Fortunately at first the gradient was with the load, and soon after the start, down 1 in 144 and then 1 in 128, *Locomotion No. 1* was bowling along with its 100-ton train at from 10 to 12 m.p.h. On both sides of the line gentlemen on their hunters, having to negotiate hedges and ditches, found themselves unable to keep pace with the locomotive. There were only two mishaps. Rather ironically, the wagon carrying the surveyors and engineers twice came off the track, due to a wheel being out of gauge, and finally had to be cut out of the train; while near Simpasture *Locomotion* came to a standstill owing to some oakum having got into the feed pump.

Down the 1 in 135 from Burtree Lane to Darlington *Locomotion* attained its top speed of 15 m.p.h; from Shildon Lane, deducting the time spent in stops, the average had been 8 m.p.h. Between 10,000 and 12,000 people, it is estimated – almost the entire Darlington population – had assembled to greet the distinguished newcomer. The engine now took water, and the train was remarshalled, leaving behind the rear six wagons of coal but attaching two wagons carrying Meynell's Yarm band. The total number of passengers by now was quite certainly at least 550.

Over level track *Locomotion* could not manage much more than 4 m.p.h., but down the final 1 in 104, as the train neared Stockton, the 15 m.p.h. gait was reached once again. At one point, past the grounds of Preston Hall, the railway and the road ran parallel, and the train was raced by a great number of carriages, gigs, carts and horsemen. In view of the public enthusiasm and the vast number of spectators, it is surprising that no more than one case of injury was reported, to a brakeman who fell off one of the wagons and had a foot crushed under a wheel. So, three hours and seven minutes after leaving Darlington, the train drew up at Cottage Row, Stockton, with the Yarm band playing the National Anthem and a thrice-repeated salute fired by a row of seven 18-pounders on the Company's wharf nearby.

A procession was then formed to the Town Hall, where a company of just over 100 sat down to celebrate the occasion suitably; they seem to have had plenty of physical and vocal exercise, seeing that no fewer than 23 toasts were drunk, all with appropriate musical accompaniment and a number of them rounded off by 'three times three'. The day, fortunately fine, had been a brilliant success. This had not been the first railway over which steam power had moved a load, for that distinction belonged to the Pen-y-Darran tramway at Merthyr Tydfil; at that date also passengers were being carried regularly by horse traction over tramways, such as that between Swansea and the Mumbles. But, as the *Durham County Gazette* wrote, it proved that 'the facility of communication by railways had been fully established by the experiment of that day'.

It must not be thought that steam traction took over completely from the opening of the line onwards; far from it. The Robert Stephenson works delivered the second locomotive, *Hope*, in the month after opening; two others of the same type that had been ordered, *Black Diamond* and *Diligence*, appeared in April and May, 1826; but *Experiment*, a Stephenson locomotive of another type, though built in 1827, seems not to have been delivered until early in 1828. The first four were all of the *Locomotion* type, with two 10in by 24in vertical cylinders, mounted above the boiler, working vertically through parallel motions on the two coupled axles.

Their working pressure was in the region of 50 lb per sq in, but the single flues of their boilers afforded a very limited heating surface. Their weight is generally quoted as 6½ tons each, but subsequent investigation shows that this must have been the weight empty, and that the weight in running order must have been nearer 8½ tons.

The *Experiment* was of more advanced design. It was the first to be fitted with two horizontal cylinders, and special arrangements to improve the steaming included water-tubes in the firebox and a primitive form of feed-water heating. Another machine of rather curious design, built by Robert Wilson at Gateshead and acquired in 1826, had four cylinders; it was nicknamed the *Chittaprat* from the odd noises that it made while in motion. As it gave a good deal of trouble, however, a year later its boiler was used by Timothy Hackworth, who had been put in charge of the traffic arrangements, in the *Royal George*, designed by him and built at the Company's Shildon Works. This was the most successful of the locomotives that had been built to that date. It still retained vertical cylinders, but with a simpler form of motion than *Locomotion*, and was carried on six-coupled wheels. More important, the boiler had a return flue, which doubled the heating surface, so that steaming was improved. The weight had now gone up to more than ten tons.

After the formal opening the Committee had no experience of railway working, and everything had to be improvised. Haulage, both by horses and even by the locomotives, was let out to contract, and the superiority of rail transport over that by the rough roads of the period was apparent in the fact that soon after the opening the price of coal at Stockton had dropped from 18s. to 8s. 6d. a ton. Despite a constant shortage of wagons, due to the time taken in discharging their contents, in the first three months some 10,000 tons of coal were carried, and the Company received nearly £2,000 in dues.

At the time of opening London merchants were becoming interested in being supplied with coal by water from the Durham coalfield, and the Stockton & Darlington directors realised that they might profitably take a hand in this operation. Work had begun on a coal-shipping staith on the Tees at Stockton – a simple pile jetty with rails laid over its planking – and this was finished in January, 1826. On 24th January, the Tees Coal Company began loading the first ship, the *Adamant*, which two days later was towed out to the sea to the music of a band and more public rejoicing. A second staith was brought into operation later in the same year and a third and fourth in 1827. At first miscellaneous freight, such as colliery stores, was carried by the Company, but after a month or two the wagons were turned over to cartage contractors, which proved to be a worth-while transaction, as receipts immediately began to rise.

Before the railway was opened, the only passenger communication between Stockton and Darlington was a road coach which made a return journey three times a week. The railway Committee, armed with the necessary powers by their Act, decided to enter this business with their passenger coach *Experiment*; after some delay, due to their having overlooked the necessity to obtain a licence, the *Experiment*, horse-drawn, began to run on 10th October, 1925. The 12-mile journey was allowed two hours each way. On four days in each week it made a return journey, but on Tuesdays and Saturdays a single journey only. By the following February, as with coal and freight, tenders had been invited for the taking over of the coach and its working by outside contractors, the first of whom was Richard Pickersgill, and soon outside as well as inside passengers were being accom- modated, at a fare reduced from 1s. to 9d. As many as 158 passengers are reported to have been carried on a single day.

On the introduction in April, 1826, of a new and more comfortable coach, called the *Express*, the service developed to two double journeys daily. By July two hotel owners, one in Stockton and the other in Darling- ton, had combined to put two further coaches on the line – the *Defence* and the *Defiance* – and in October a fifth, the *Union*, started to run between Yarm and both Stockton and Darlington. Each coach was drawn by a single horse, which was able to make two round journeys in a day, of 48 miles in all, between Stockton and Darlington. The normal passenger complement was about 20 persons, but a record was reached on a Stockton race day in 1826, when no fewer than 46 passengers, many hanging on to any part of the vehicle they could, were seen on a single coach.

The normal running speed was about 10 m.p.h., increased to 14 m.p.h. on the falling gradients, and the journey time, including stops, had come down to just over $1\frac{1}{4}$ hours for the 12 miles. Fifteen months after the opening day, though the somewhat Spartan original coach *Experiment* had ceased to run, seven coaches were operating over the line daily. Such a passenger development from the three-times-a-week only road service before the advent of the railway gave a remarkable forecast of what might be expected in the future from railway communication.

The main line had been laid out with about four loops or passing-places to each mile; of signalling, of course, there was none. Coach drivers could be awkward, and sometimes when two coaches met on a single track section neither driver would give way and back his coach to enable the other to get by. It is on record that one driver coped with this awkward situation by getting his passengers to help him to lift his coach off the rails altogether, so letting his opposite number pass, after which his coach was replaced on the track in the same way. But gradually orders of precedence came into force. In general, locomotive engines with their trains had the right of way over all horse-drawn traffic, except that if a locomotive-hauled train was being overtaken by a coach, the former had to stop at the next loop and let the coach get ahead; and similarly when the driver of a loco- motive caught sight in the distance of a coach approaching, he was expected to stop at the next loop ahead to let the coach get by.

There were also the horse-drawn trains, usually comprising not more than four wagons, the working of which was greatly improved by an ingenious contrivance which first came into use in the summer of 1828. As mentioned earlier, from Shildon eastwards there were several gradients down which wagons would travel by gravity. It was realised that if the horses could be carried down these inclines, instead of hurrying down on their feet, a good deal of their strength would be husbanded, and more useful service would be got out of them each day. The contrivance referred to, which became known as a 'dandy-cart', was a light four-wheeled truck, open at each end and attached to the rear of the train.

On reaching one of the down gradients, the horse was unhitched from the front of the train, and was taught, after the wagons had passed him, to jump on to the dandy-cart. As soon as the animals realised that a bag of hay was kept for their consumption at the front end of the dandy-cart, they fell in with the idea with enthusiasm – to such an extent, indeed, that one day when the special vehicle had not been attached to the rear, a horse was observed attempting to get into a coal wagon! At the foot of the incline the horse would resume his place at the head of the train. The dandy-cart was of such benefit to the horses that whereas, before its introduction, a horse walked about 175 miles in a week with its train, the train mileage increased to 240 weekly and the horses' condition improved at the same time. Between Shildon and Stockton the dandy-cart came into use over four different stretches of the line, with the 17½ tons of the loaded train; but on the return, of course, with the 5½ tons of empties, the horse had to work all the way.

By comparison, the *Locomotion*-type engines could handle up to 19 wagons, and the *Royal George*, which was easily the most successful, 24. Indeed, the *Royal George*'s driver, Gowland, was much envied by his colleagues, for his earnings, averaging 25s. 8d. per day, were considerably greater than their 19s. to 22s, all the men being paid ¼d per ton per mile for their services. Very likely the *Royal George* burned more coal than the other engines, but as the cost of locomotive coal at the pithead at that time was at the almost unbelievably low level of 2s. to 3s. 9d. per ton, this was hardly of serious consequence. In the first year's working, the *Royal George* moved 22,442 tons of coal, at a total cost of £466.

But all did not go well with steam power in those early days. Failures were frequent; over the rough permanent way there were such casualties as the breakage of wheels; and careless handling by the inexperienced enginemen of the period resulted in 1828 in two boilers blowing up. These reports reached the ears of the Liverpool & Manchester board of directors, and prompted the visit of another deputation to Darlington to ascertain the true facts. The visitors appear to have been reassured, however, for no change was made in the plans to use steam locomotives on the Lancashire line. In the earlier days it was intended that each Stockton & Darlington locomotive should make two return journeys a day over the line, but with no more than four locomotives in a serviceable condition at one time, a journey on every second day became the more general rule, until the locomotive stock had been increased sufficiently to expand the service. In his book *The North Eastern Railway*, W. W. Tomlinson remarks on the odd fact of a management under strong Quaker influence showing in its accounts, beneath the heading 'Contingent Expenses', a sum of money for 'men's allowance in ale to stimulate them to greater exertion when repairing the engines'!

Another handicap to steam power was the mixed steam and horse traction which prevailed for so long. Even when the steam stock had reached 19 engines, 50 horses were still in regular use on the line. What happened when horse-drawn passenger coaches met on the single track has been described already; conditions were still worse with the horse-drawn trains of coal wagons. To improve line occupation, it was laid down that the horse-drawn trains must move in groups of four or five, but this method had its dangers. If drivers did not control their speed properly on the down-grades, it was no infrequent occurrence for one set of wagons to collide with the next set ahead.

Drivers often left the switches wrongly set, drove furiously across roads and lanes (which in those days had no gates), and ran after dark without lights, as a result of which there were numerous accidents, horses being lamed or killed and rolling stock damaged. The horse-drivers also had a rooted objection to taking their coaches or wagons into one of the sidings to let a locomotive-hauled train pass them. Worse still, from time to time a horse-driver would leave his train standing on the single line while he adjourned for refreshment to a neighbouring ale-house; there was a recorded case of a delay of two hours being caused in this way.

Bit by bit the Stockton & Darlington locomotive stock was increased until by 1839 the Company owned 30 steam locomotives, though it proved no easy matter to get rid of the horse-drawn trains and coaches. Eventually the colliery owners who were leading their own coal over the line gave way, and later on the coach proprietors also; from 7th September, 1833, a service of steam-hauled mixed passenger and goods trains began between Stockton and Darlington, extended to and from Shildon three months later, while the coal train working also was gradually turned over to steam power. As we shall see in Chapter XIII, however, many years were to elapse before the final disappearance of horse traction.

Now it must not be thought that the advance embodied in steam traction was universally appreciated; far from it. In 1831 an indictment was brought by a number of landowners against six of the Stockton & Darlington Railway directors and seven enginemen seeking for an abatement of the 'nuisance' caused by their locomotive engines. This indictment, Rex *versus* Pease and others, alleged that the engines emitted 'unwholesome and offensive smells, smokes and vapours', that they made 'divers loud explosions, shocks and noises', and that they exhibited 'terrific and alarming appearances when travelling at night', with a startling effect on horses.

There were doubts as to whether it would be possible to obtain an impartial hearing in the County of Durham, and the trial was held at York. Here highly coloured evidence described locomotives as 'those great snorting, roaring and mighty monsters, vomiting fire in all directions, which the horse by no means recognises as relations of his'. The case was later remitted to the King's Bench Division in London, where the Court sensibly decided that as Parliament had ruled that the use of steam locomotives should be sanctioned over the railway, the rights of the public must have been duly taken into account, so that there was no case to

answer. Judgment was therefore given in favour of the railway on 3rd
December, 1832.

Despite such handicaps, the Stockton & Darlington Railway was able
in its first year to pay a dividend of 5 per cent – precisely the figure that
the astute Edward Pease has promised. And when, as just described, steam
traction was coming under fire, and reports were being spread that
horses were beating the steam locomotives, the Company's own figures
showed that, whereas in the first half of 1828 the engines had moved
35,202 tons of coal and freight and the horses 31,886 tons, at the end of the
second half of the same year the respective figures were 39,349 and 23,349
tons. Thus it became clear that steam would eventually provide the sole
means of traction.

It was not long before the movement of coal for export became the main
activity of the Stockton & Darlington Railway, and with this expansion the unsuitability of Stockton as the port for shipment became more
and more apparent. The trouble was shoals in the Tees, which limited the
vessels moving up river to Stockton to those drawing not more than 7 to
8ft at a normal tide and possibly up to 11ft at a spring tide. Stranding was
not infrequent, and often the ships had to leave without having taken on
a full cargo. Another trouble was inadequate storage space for coal at the
staiths, so that if ships were delayed coming up river, the coal had to be
kept in the wagons, which thus remained out of service until they were
emptied.

At first a branch from Stockton to Haverton Hill, farther down the
Tees on the north bank, was considered; but later the attractive
plan of crossing the Tees and reaching Middlesbrough, on the south bank,
found greater favour, and was approved at a meeting of the shareholders
on 26th October, 1827. This decision was destined to meet with serious
opposition, from expected as well as unexpected quarters. As might have
been anticipated, the Tees Navigation Company, which was about to
spend a considerable amount of money in improving the river channel,
was much concerned about the probable loss of revenue from diversion of
the growing export trade from Stockton to Middlesbrough. But the main
opposition came from within the Stockton & Darlington ranks.

From the start there had been an influential body of men in Stockton
who had regarded their town as playing second fiddle to Darlington in the
development of the railway, and felt that Stockton could have benefited
by a considerably more direct route from the Auckland coalfield than that
which had been laid by way of Darlington. As mentioned already, a so-
called 'Northern Railway' had been mooted as far back as 1819, and matters
had gone further in 1823, when a Bill had been presented to Parliament
for a 26-mile Tees & Weardale Railway, to start from Willington in the
Wear Valley, and run 3½ miles south of Durham City and on past Mainsforth (Ferryhill) to Billingham Reach, on the Tees 4 miles below Stockton.
But the Bill did not comply with Standing Orders, and was thrown out.
Now, however, Christopher Tennant, a prominent Stockton citizen who
had been behind the two previous schemes, brought forward a new plan,

which in honour of the Duke of Clarence, later King William IV, he called the Clarence Railway.

Whereas the former schemes were to tap the coalfield in the Coxhoe area, the Clarence Railway prospectus boldly proposed to run from Haverton Hill on the Tees to Simpasture, and there to join the Stockton & Darlington, a distance of $11\frac{1}{2}$ miles from Haverton Hill as compared with the Stockton & Darlington's $17\frac{1}{2}$ miles from Stockton. Not only would this be an invasion of Stockton & Darlington territory, but the line would also serve the town of Stockton by a short branch. At two public meetings in Stockton called by the mayor, approval was given both to the Tees Navigation Company's scheme and also to the proposed Clarence Railway.

For the Stockton & Darlington the worst blow was the defection of its Chairman, Thomas Meynell, who shortly afterwards resigned his office, as well as of Leonard Raisbeck, the Recorder of Stockton, Benjamin Flounders and other prominent men, who felt that the prospects of Stockton would be gravely injured by the proposed Middlesbrough extension, and thus had decided to back the Clarence Railway. Nevertheless, despite violent opposition in the House of Lords, the Stockton & Darlington Bill passed through all its stages and received the Royal Assent on 23rd May, 1828. A few days later, however, the Clarence Railway Bill was passed also; the chequered career of that line will be dealt with later.

The principal obstacle in carrying out the Middlesbrough extension was, of course, the River Tees and also its old channel. The Tees Navigation Company insisted that both should be crossed in a way which would not interfere with the movement of shipping, though the railway at first had intended that only the main river should be dealt with in this way. Eventually the Tees Navigation was placated by the building of a drawbridge over the old channel; the river itself was crossed by a suspension bridge, with a clear span of no less than 281ft 4in, a total length of 412ft, and a height above water of 20ft. The floor carrying the track, 16ft wide, was suspended by 110 rods from 12 curved chains, arranged in sets of six on either side.

Graceful though this structure appeared, preliminary tests of it proved disappointing. A weight of 18 tons imposed on the centre caused a deflection of $9\frac{1}{4}$in; 28 empty wagons of 37 tons weight, drawn by an 8-ton engine, caused a maximum deflection of $5\frac{3}{4}$in. The passage of a heavier train of 16 loaded wagons of 66 tons affected the masonry of the towers on both sides of the bridge, and it was realised that no greater weight than this could safely be imposed on the structure, which it had been hoped would stand up to a weight of at least 150 tons.

The staiths erected at Middlesbrough were on so extensive a scale as to accommodate six vessels simultaneously. The coal wagons were hoisted by steam power some 18ft to an upper gallery 450 yards long. Horses were then used to pull each wagon to a point above the vessel which was to receive its contents, where a cradle lowered it in a curved line to a position immediately above the hold. Its attendant now unbolted the bottom board, dropping the coal into the ship; a counterbalance weight, which had been lifted by the descending wagon, brought it back to the gallery level. From here it was pushed to an opening on the opposite side of the gallery, after which steam power lowered it once again to the rails at ground level and gave it an impulse strong enough to propel it to a siding 100 yards away.

The usual opening ceremony took place, in the case of the Middlesbrough branch, on 27th December, 1830. A train of coaches and of wagons fitted with seats left Darlington in the morning behind Timothy Hackworth's new locomotive *Globe*, and after adding a party from Stockton, proceeded, first to view the new Tees bridge and then the shipping of coal at the Middlesbrough staiths. The proceedings concluded, needless to say, with a feast, to which some 600 guests were entertained in part of the upper gallery of the staiths prepared for the purpose. Such was the beginning, not merely of a branch railway, but also of the first town in Britain which it could be claimed owed its existence to railway communication. For a company called the Middlesbrough Owners had been formed to develop 32 acres of what until then had been waste land into a town which today, under the combined influence of coal, iron ore, the chemical industry and the railway boasts nearly 150,000 inhabitants.

Meantime other sections of the original Stockton & Darlington plan, held up previously for financial reasons, had been completed, the 3 miles from Darlington to Croft on 27th October, 1829, and the 4¾ miles from St Helen's, Auckland, to Hagger Leases Lane – including an interesting skew bridge in masonry over the River Gaunless – late in 1830. With a new office building at Darlington the Stockton & Darlington Railway was now complete and in working order, and, moreover, with its prudent Quaker direction, on a sound financial footing.

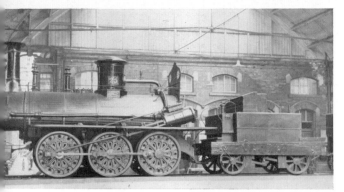

Left, *Derwent*, a Stockton & Darlington Railway locomotive built in 1845, preserved on a pedestal in Darlington Bank Top Station.

Right, Stockton & Darlington Railway chaldron wagons.

Above, an early Stockton & Darlington composite coach with one first and two second class compartments.

Right, a dandy cart in which horses drawing wagon trains rode down the falling gradients.
[All, *British Railways*

Brougham, a 4-4-0 of Bouch's design built in 1860 for the Darlington–Tebay line of the Stockton & Darlington, the first British type with a side-window cab.

One of Bouch's 4-4-0s nicknamed 'Ginx's Babies', built for the Stockton & Darlington in 1871–1874, with coupled wheels of no less than 7ft 1in diameter.

A Stockton & Darlington Stephenson 'long boiler' 0-6-0, with firebox in rear of the trailing coupled wheels.   [*All, Locomotive Publishing Co.*

Robert Stephenson's tubular bridge over the River Aire at Brotherton, opened in 1850, and designed on the same principle as his Britannia Tubular Bridge over the Menai Strait.

A side view of the Brotherton Bridge, on the spur line connecting Kottingley with the York & North Midland Railway at Burton Salmon, used by the first Great Northern Railway trains to reach York.

[*Both, British Railways*]

Above, opened in 1879, with the extension across the River Wear from Monkwearmouth – the new station at Sunderland. In later years the platforms were narrowed to give four platform faces. *Below*, the site of the original York terminus. In the background is the fine office block brought into use by the North Eastern Railway in 1906, and between is the original station building on Tanner Row.   [*Both, British Railways*

CHAPTER IV

The Newcastle & Carlisle Railway

By 1830 work had begun on the construction of another railway which was to prove of considerable importance. Before the end of the eighteenth century minds on both sides of the country had been directed towards the possibility of some form of communication between the East and the West Coasts across the narrowest part of England, between Newcastle and Carlisle. As far back as 1794 a canal had been proposed, and William Chapman prepared plans for one, 93½ miles in length, from a dock at Ouseburn bridge, Newcastle, by way of Hexham, Haltwhistle and Carlisle to Maryport, on the Cumberland coast. But the Pennines would be a formidable obstacle, and would make necessary many locks; in any event the estimated cost of over £355,000 put the proposition out of court.

For thirty years nothing happened, but after a ship canal had been opened in 1823 between the Solway Firth and Carlisle, the cross-country idea was revived. Now, however, William Chapman, who had prepared the plan and estimate for the former canal across the country, declared that a railway would be the more suitable means of communication. A public meeting in Newcastle on 21st August, 1824, endorsed his view and he was requested to make fresh estimates as to the comparative costs of a ship canal and a railway. Having done so, he reported that a canal of sufficiently ample dimensions to accommodate ships would cost £888,000, whereas a railway could be built for £252,500. To a county meeting convened at Newcastle on 26th March, 1825, Chapman's view proved conclusive, and it was decided to form the Newcastle-on-Tyne & Carlisle Railroad Company, with a capital of £300,000. A fortnight later the entire amount had been subscribed and the shares were at a premium.

Several years were to pass, however, before anything was done. Before a Bill was presented to Parliament a second survey was made jointly by Chapman and two other engineers, to plan an amended route which would cause as little interference as possible with landed property. This began at Newcastle Quay, crossed the ~~Tees~~ *Tyne* between Scotswood and Blaydon and continued on the south bank of the river to Hexham, following the course which has remained unchanged to this day through Bardon Mill and Haltwhistle to Greenhead. From here through Wetheral and Scotby to Carlisle, the amended plan was considerably to the south of Chapman's original route, but it improved the gradients, which now were of a maximum steepness of 1 in 264 westbound and 1 in 129 eastbound.

Certain interested parties employed George Stephenson to survey an alternative route out of Newcastle, on the north bank of the Tyne, but this, though it would have avoided the Scotswood bridge over the river, would have had gradients as steep as 1 in 36 and 1 in 48, which would have required working by stationary engines. At a later date Stephenson's route came prominently under review when Charles Bacon, one of the principal opponents of the scheme, claimed that the periodic floods to which Tyneside was subject might put anything from 10 to 20 miles of the proposed line on the south bank under water. George Stephenson agreed with this view; moreover, it was estimated that his route out to Hexham would save £47,640. Nevertheless the Bill for Chapman's route had a relatively easy passage through Parliament and received the Royal Assent on 22nd May, 1829. It authorised the raising as capital of £300,000 in shares and £100,000 by loan, to build 63 miles of railway.

Now the remarkable point is that not only was horse rather than steam traction contemplated as the motive power, but that the Act specifically forbade the use of steam locomotives. Clause 6 laid it down that 'No locomotive or movable steam engine shall be used on the said railways or tramroads for drawing waggons or other carriages, or for any other purpose whatsoever; and no steam engine shall be erected or used for any of the purposes aforesaid, within view of . . . ' here followed a list of prominent gentlemen's residences, including Naworth and Corby Castles . . . 'nor within a distance of one thousand yards to the east of Stella Hall, nor nearer, on the west, than the point where the line of the said railways or tramroads will be intersected by a certain common highway called the Water Lane'.

But for this clause, needless to say, the landowners who could not bear the sight of steam would have opposed the Bill. As with the Stockton & Darlington Railway, the Newcastle & Carlisle was intended to be open to public use on the payment of tolls similar to those of the S. & D.R.; passenger tolls were fixed at 6d. for 5 miles, 1s. for 10 miles and 5s. for the through journey. The first general meeting of shareholders, held on 16th October, 1829, saddled the enterprise with a board of no fewer than 30 directors, including the Earls of Carlisle and Durham and four members of Parliament.

In March, 1830, work began with the ceremonial laying of the first stone of the Wetheral viaduct, near the west end of the line. This was one of a number of notable engineering works, some of which were the biggest of their kind at that time. The Wetheral viaduct, with its five arches of 80ft span and length of 564ft, was to carry the line at a height of 95ft above the River Eden. Not far away was the viaduct at Corby, with seven 40ft arches, 480ft long and at a maximum height of 70ft. Both took nearly four years to build.

As to earthworks, the cutting through the Cowran Hills, near How Mill, nearly a mile long and for more than a quarter of that distance from 90 to 110ft deep, established a record for depth to that date. A tunnel was the original intention, but the sandy soil and many springs would have made this too difficult a task. To avoid slips, the sides of the cutting were kept to a batter of $1\frac{1}{2}$ to 1, as a result of which the cutting was 305ft wide at its deepest point and required the excavation of nearly 1,000,000 cubic yards of soil. The highest embankment was one of 70ft over the Hell Beck; as to tunnelling, two short tunnels only were needed, one 202 yards long near Haltwhistle, and the other, 170 yards long, near Corbridge.

For a time the work was held up because the financial resources were exhausted, but was resumed after the Company had managed to borrow £100,000 from the Exchequer Loan Commissioners. As the first section of the line, from Blaydon to Hexham, was nearing completion in 1834, the question of motive power was being seriously reconsidered. Steam traction was now becoming much more reliable than when horse traction had been decided on ten years earlier. With steam locomotives the speed would be higher, and far fewer crossing loops would be needed on the single-track sections. The prohibition of steam in the Company's Act had to be borne in mind, of course, but it ought by now to be possible to induce Parliament to rescind that particular clause.

So in anticipation that Parliament would do so, three steam locomotives were ordered, one each from Robert Stephenson & Co., R. & W. Hawthorn and Edward Bury. The decision was also reached by the directors that it would be impossible to mix steam and horse traction on a line of such length, and that steam locomotives should be used exclusively. A much heavier track was being laid than that of the Stockton & Darlington Railway, with malleable-iron rails weighing 42 lb per yard, in 15ft lengths, laid on substantial stone blocks to a gauge of 4ft 8in.

Before the end of 1834 some freight traffic was being worked between Blaydon and Stocksfield, and on 3rd March, 1835, there was a ceremonial opening for passenger traffic of the 16¾ miles from Blaydon to Hexham. attended by the Mayor of Newcastle. A company of 600 people was carried in two special trains, one headed by Robert Stephenson's *Rapid* and the other by Hawthorn's *Comet;* the passenger accommodation comprised three coaches, a number of wagons fitted with seats, and several carriages of local gentry mounted on trucks. Various delays, including the derailment of a wagon or two, caused the outward journey to take nearly 2½ hours, but the return trip was much more rapid. The following day a regular passenger service was begun with steam locomotives – completely ignoring Clause 6 of the Act! – twice daily in each direction, and with a connecting coach service between Blaydon and Newcastle. Freight was transhipped from steamer to train and *vice versa* at Blaydon Quay.

Now, however, one of the landowners along the route, Bacon Grey, who like his father, Charles Bacon, had opposed the use of steam, applied in the Court of Chancery for an injunction to prevent any further use of steam power. The result was that the train service had to cease at the end of March, but such was the storm of indignation aroused by Grey's antisocial move that he was obliged to give way; the trains resumed running early in May, 1835. Six weeks later, on 17th June, a second Newcastle & Carlisle Railway Act authorised the use of steam locomotives, though subject to the condition that they burned coke and not coal.

A terminus as far away from Newcastle as Blaydon, and on the opposite side of the Tyne, soon proved anything but convenient. The Act just mentioned also authorised an extension of the line along the south bank of the

Tyne from Blaydon to Gateshead, with a bridge across the Tyne from there
to the Spital in Newcastle. But this was subject to the Blaydon, Gateshead
& Hebburn Railway, which had obtained an Act in 1834, not having
within a year exercised their right to build westwards as far as Derwenthaugh, the point of confluence of the River Derwent with the Tyne.
Eventually the two companies agreed that the Newcastle & Carlisle should
build eastwards as far as Derwenthaugh and the Blaydon, Gateshead &
Hebburn the remainder, but although the latter began their section, later
complications with other companies caused them to decide on a change in
their plans.

By agreement, the Newcastle & Carlisle then assumed responsibility for
the whole, opening the 1¾-mile extension from Blaydon to Derwenthaugh
on 11th June, 1836, and the continuation from there to Redheugh (Gateshead) on 1st March, 1837. Meantime another section of the line had been
brought into use, the 7½-miles from Hexham to Haydon Bridge, on 28th
June, 1836; the 20 miles from Carlisle to the Blenkinsopp Colliery at
Greenhead followed eleven days later; and on 18th June, 1838, railway
communication between tidewater on the East and West Coasts was completed by the opening of the 11 miles between Haydon Bridge and Greenhead.

The Hexham to Haydon Bridge and Carlisle to Greenhead openings
were both celebrated suitably by processions over the line, an amusing
incident in the latter case being the breakage of a coupling on the train
carrying the Mayor and Corporation of Carlisle, whereby these celebrities
got left behind until their absence was discovered. But these celebrations
were of little moment in comparison with the vast display that commemorated the opening throughout from Gateshead to Carlisle. On 15th June,
1838, a special train carrying the directors had travelled the length of the
line, and 18th June was the day appointed for the formal opening, which
can have had few parallels in railway history.

The proceedings began with five trains leaving Carlisle in succession
from 6 a.m. onwards, and reaching Redheugh between 9.30 and 10 a.m.
The Mayor and Corporation of Carlisle here crossed the Tyne with the
directors to take breakfast in the Newcastle Assembly Rooms. The river
crossing unhappily was attended by the collapse of a gangway, which threw
a dozen or more guests, including some ladies in flimsy silk dresses, into
the water. Breakfast was protracted until a good hour after its advertised
time, and on the return of the party, now with the Mayor and Corporation
of Newcastle also, it was found that the Corporation of Gateshead, which
had arrived in good time, had secured its seats, but that the crowd had
invaded all the rest of the reserved places.

The returning party from Newcastle thus had a considerable hunt for
accommodation, and the *Gateshead Observer* of that week related that 'the
chief magistrates of Carlisle and Newcastle were obliged to look for refuge
in a pig-cart'. It is believed that a total of some 3,500 pasengers took part
in the procession of trains, which required the services of the entire locomotive stock of the Company, the *Comet* alone excepted – 14 loco-

motives in all. The *Rapid* preceded the procession as pilot; the remaining 13 locomotives were pulling between them a total of 130 coaches and wagons. The biggest trains were those of *Goliath* with 19 vehicles and *Atlas* with 17.

A good deal of time was spent at Blaydon while the engines took water, and not until 1.50 p.m. did the head of the procession get under way westwards once again. Nature now took a malevolent hand in the proceedings; what had been a foggy morning changed to persistent rain, soaking all those who had not the good fortune to be in covered vehicles. With over an hour spent at the various stops the journey from Blaydon to Carlisle in these wretched conditions took 3¾ hours, and it was not until six in the evening that the last of the trains reached the Canal Basin at Carlisle.

For the Newcastle contingent, however, this was by no means the end; they had got to get back to Tyneside. By 6.30 p.m. the first of the returning Tynesiders were besieging London Road Station, where the trains were being marshalled for the return journey, and needless to say the first-comers made for the covered coaches, getting in through the windows — portly females included – if the doors were locked. But the regulations demanded all kinds of attention to the engines, coaches, wagons and the line before the return journey could even be begun; the first train did not start back until just before 10 p.m.

The troubles were not yet over. A thunderstorm was now raging, and the discomfort of the passengers in the open wagons, especially the ladies in light summer attire, is better imagined than described. To make matters worse, at Milton, in the darkness, the engine *Carlisle* ran into the rear of the preceding train, throwing its tender and some coaches off the line; not until 1 a.m. was the line cleared and the journey resumed. The anxiety in Gateshead at the non-appearance of the cavalcade – as there was no telegraphic communication at this early date – was considerable. Not till 3 a.m. did the leading train put in an appearance, but it was 6 o'clock in the morning before the last of the trains arrived. It was a day which those who participated in it would not be likely to forget for a long time!

One section only of the Newcastle & Carlisle Railway now remained to be completed, and that was its means of access direct to Newcastle. The cost of bridging the Tyne from Redheugh, Gateshead, to the Spital at Newcastle proving prohibitive, there had been a reversion to Chapman's original plan of a bridge at Scotswood, and by the time of the formal opening from Blaydon to Carlisle this extension was well under way. Its main feature, of course, was the bridge, a skew structure with 11 spans of 60ft each, giving a headroom of 35ft above low water, built entirely of timber save for the masonry abutments. So the last 3¾ miles of the line were opened on 21st May, 1839, to a temporary terminus near the Shot Tower. Not until October of that year, however, was a regular passenger service brought into operation throughout between Newcastle and Carlisle.

For some time after the opening the trains carried first and second class passengers only, but later on some primitive third class accommodation was provided in the form of planks laid over open wagons; the coaches weighed from $2\frac{3}{4}$ tons to $3\frac{1}{2}$ tons, an average train load being from 26 to 30 tons. The fastest times between Newcastle and Carlisle were 3 to $3\frac{1}{4}$ hours. A feature of the working in which the Newcastle & Carlisle differed from other railways was that the trains took the right-hand track on the double sections, and thus passed one another on the left. From the earliest most of the locomotives were provided with steam whistles, but the outstanding achievement was that of the *Tyne*, a Hawthorn locomotive which acquired a steam organ with pipes, invented by the vicar of the Tyneside village of Ovingham, an innovation which mercifully never came into general use.

In 1837 the Newcastle & Carlisle Railway distinguished itself in another way. Its Milton station, later Brampton Junction, was in the charge of a stationmaster named Thomas Edmondson, who also had to issue the tickets. This was a laborious business, as it meant that both paper ticket and counterfoil had to have written in, by hand, the number, date, time of train departure and destination. Edmondson therefore himself printed a number of tickets for different destinations on cardboard, and arranged them in vertical tubes, with springs at the bottom which pushed each pile of tickets upwards as the top one was withdrawn. He still had to number and date them, but in August, 1837, he invented an ingenious dating press which, when the ticket was inserted and the upper and lower halves of the press were moved inwards by the knuckles, duly impressed the date. A year later machinery for printing railway tickets was brought into use generally, and station work and accounts were simplified enormously in consequence.

It only remains to add that, despite its unpropitious opening ceremony, the Newcastle & Carlisle Railway never failed, during its independent existence, to pay a dividend of from 4 to 6 per cent. Also, though threatened in 1848 with absorption by the York, Newcastle & Berwick Railway, and in later years by the Maryport & Carlisle Railway, as well as a possible lease by the Caledonian Railway, it succeeded in remaining independent until it became a part of the North Eastern Railway in 1862. Meantime, after agreement had been reached in 1845 with the then Newcastle & Berwick Railway for the building of a joint Central Station in Newcastle, as described in Chapter X, the Newcastle & Carlisle was extended in 1846 over a viaduct of 44 arches from its first Shot Tower terminus to a second temporary terminus on the site of the present Forth Goods Station, and finally into the imposing Newcastle Central Station in 1850.

CHAPTER V

From the Durham Mines to the Sea

WE are now entering on a very complex period of pre-North Eastern Railway history. Coal and the means of bringing it down to the sea were still the major factors in railway development; not until 1841 was the first section to be opened, from York to Darlington, of what today is the East Coast main line. All the new lines brought into use in these early days were therefore lateral, like those of the Stockton & Darlington and Newcastle & Carlisle Railways already described. It is estimated by W. W. Tomlinson in his book *The North Eastern Railway* that the ultimate N.E.R. system was a fusion of lines built by no fewer than 53 public companies and 21 private companies, *plus* 10 railways either built jointly with other railways or held under lease.

But railway development in North-Eastern England, and particularly in the County of Durham, was no easy matter. Many of the landowners were influential men who could bring considerable pressure to bear in Parliament against the approval of railway schemes, or cause expensive deviations of the routes originally planned. There was no small jealousy between the Tyne, Wear and Tees authorities as to which of the three rivers should acquire most of the coal shipping trade. Greed also manifested itself in the pernicious 'wayleave' system, whereby grasping landowners thought to enrich themselves quickly, not by working the coal under their land, but merely by exacting heavy charges for the passage of coal over it. Many railway schemes were affected adversely in these ways.

As we saw in Chapter IV, the Clarence Railway, of which the Act received the Royal Assent in May, 1828 (a few days after the second Stockton & Darlington Act, which authorised the building of a branch of the S. & D.R. to Middlesbrough), was born of the fear that valuable Stockton trade might be diverted to the new port on the south side of the Tees. We have now to give some attention to the Clarence Railway. It was promoted, as will be remembered, by Christopher Tennant, to be the successor to the original Tees & Weardale Railway proposal, which in 1825 had failed to secure parliamentary approval. The Act of 1828 sanctioned a line from Haverton Hill, on the north bank of the Tees, to a junction with the Stockton & Darlington Railway at Simpasture, 14 miles distant, with three branches bringing up to just under 27 miles the total route mileage. In general, the tolls to be charged were to be less than those of the Stockton & Darlington. The Company was authorised to raise £100,000 in shares and £60,000 by loan, and allowed six years to build the line.

Questions having arisen as to whether the best route had been chosen, a new survey was made, and three deviations were proposed, in part to avoid three inclined planes which would have needed to be worked by fixed engines, and also to reduce the size of the earthworks. Additional branches were planned also, in particular one to the City of Durham, and the remainder to serve other mines in the area. There was some idea of a branch up into Weardale as far as Wolsingham and Stanhope, but this was later abandoned. Most important, it was decided that Samphire Batts, later to be known as Port Clarence, would be a better site for the shipping staiths than Haverton Hill, as at the former loaded ships could lie in the Tees at low water.

At the last moment the Clarence Railway Company seems to have had cold feet about its projected junction with the Stockton & Darlington at Simpasture, but opposition by a local coal owner to any attempt to drop this branch resulted in the insertion in the Bill of a clause compelling the Company to proceed, as originally intended, with the section of line between Stillington Moor House and Simpasture. Opposition of precisely the opposite kind came from the Marquis of Londonderry, who was developing a new harbour at Seaham from which to ship coals from his various pits, and foresaw in the Durham branch of the Clarence Railway a future competitor. Needless to say, the Stockton & Darlington Railway offered strong opposition also.

Despite their objections, however, the second Clarence Railway Bill passed both Houses of Parliament and received the Royal Assent on 1st June, 1829. It authorised a main line $15\frac{1}{2}$ miles long from Samphire Batts to Simpasture, the 13-mile Durham branch, and shorter branches to Stockton and to the Deanery, Sherburn and Byers Green mines, making up a total of $45\frac{1}{4}$ miles. To cover the extra mileage the Company was authorised to raise, either by bonds or mortgage, an additional £100,000. Doubtless because of the objections of landowners, the Act forbade the use of locomotives over parts of both the Durham and the Byers Green branches. Eventually, a curtailment of the Durham branch was more than balanced by two other short branches, to Chilton and Merrington, bringing the total mileage up to $47\frac{3}{4}$ miles.

Work on the line was begun at a time when the prospects were far from bright. Coal prices on the Tyne and Wear had fallen to so low a level as to undercut those on the Tees, with the result that by 1829 shipments from the Tees had dropped to less than one-fifth of what they had been in 1828. Nevertheless construction of the Clarence Railway was pressed forward, at first of the main line to Simpasture, the Stockton branch and parts of the Durham and Sherburn branches.

Some very heavy earthworks were involved, such as Norton Toll Gate cutting, 5 miles from Port Clarence, 60ft deep; Whitton Cutting, 3 miles farther to the west, 42ft deep; and in particular Rudds Hill cutting, near the present station at Ferryhill, which was cut through solid rock to a depth of no less than 67ft. Crossing the Bishopton Beck valley needed an embankment 75ft high, and two others, at Stillington and over Billingham Beck, were 60 and 50ft high respectively. The lines had been well planned, with flatter gradients than those of the Stockton & Darlington and no need for any inclined planes.

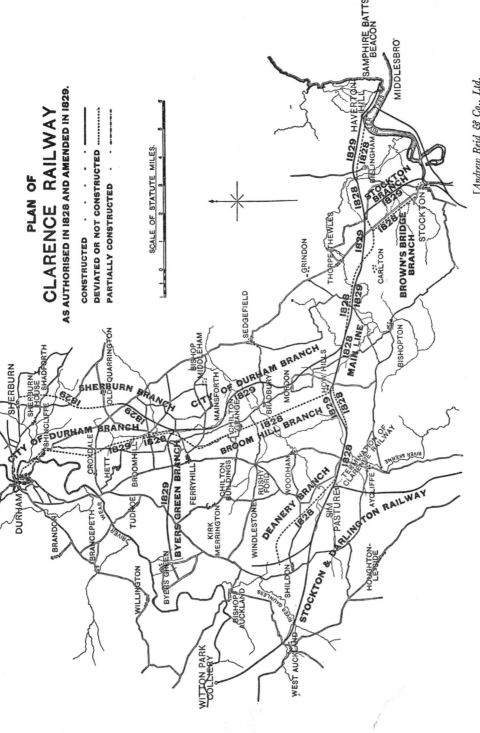

PLAN OF
CLARENCE RAILWAY
AS AUTHORISED IN 1828 AND AMENDED IN 1829.

CONSTRUCTED
DEVIATED OR NOT CONSTRUCTED
PARTIALLY CONSTRUCTED

SCALE OF STATUTE MILES.

[Andrew Reid & Co., Ltd.

Construction proceeded so rapidly that by August, 1833, the first coal was being worked down to Stockton, while by the beginning of 1834 a staith at Haverton Hill had come into use; the first deep-water staith at Port Clarence, reached by a substantial river-bank embankment, saw its first shipment a few months afterwards. Early in 1834 some 28 miles of line were open, though for much of the way in a far from finished condition. The reason for the haste was the loan of £100,000 from the Exchequer Loan Commissioners, on which interest was falling due. But there were many difficulties, and not the least the measures taken by the Stockton & Darlington Railway, without scruple, to make the transfer of coal from their line to the Clarence Railway at Simpasture an unprofitable business.

By July, 1834, the Clarence Company had to ask the Exchequer Loan Commissioners to take over the control of its affairs; and when the latter set about completion of the works, replacing temporary wooden bridges by permanent structures and doubling the line in anticipation of using locomotive engines, the Clarence Railway, which had to finance the work, found itself even more embarrassed financially. Its later history is so bound up with other developments in the County of Durham that for the time we must leave it in order to deal with other contemporary railway construction.

Near the end of 1831 three men, William Wallis of Westoe, Cuthbert Rippon of Stanhope, and William Harrison of Monkwearmouth, entered into a partnership for the purpose of making lime from the limestone at Stanhope with the aid of coal from the seams at Medomsley, north-east of Consett, of which Wallis had obtained a lease. For this purpose Stanhope and Medomsley required to be connected by railway. Harrison had a much more daring plan in mind, though this was kept secret for some time in order that it might not interfere with negotiations for the acquisition of other pits or influence the scale of the wayleaves that might be demanded; it was to continue the line north-eastwards to some point on the Tyne below Newcastle.

The preliminary survey of the Stanhope and Medomsley section was made by Harrison's son, T. E. Harrison, who was later to achieve note by becoming, first General Manager, and afterwards Chief Engineer, of the North Eastern Railway. While Rippon and Wallis soon withdrew from the partnership, William Harrison was joined by his brother, J. F. Harrison of London, and by Thomas Barnard of Deptford. The new partnership, having arranged terms with Rippon for a lease of his Stanhope limestone quarries, raised in London the necessary £150,000 to form the Stanhope & Tyne Railroad Company and began work in the summer of 1832.

As we have seen already in the case of the Stockton & Darlington and other of the earliest railways and wagonways in the north-east, inclined planes worked by stationary engines were no unusual feature in so hilly a county as Durham. But it would be impossible to have found in Britain any other railway with so extraordinary a gradient profile as the Stanhope & Tyne. Starting from Stanhope Lime Kilns, at an altitude of 796ft, the wagons were drawn up half a mile inclined mainly at 1 in 8 by a winding engine at Crawley, 1,123ft above the sea. For over a mile a second rope drew them up at 1 in 32 and then 1 in 13 to Weatherhill, 1,445ft above sea-level. Next followed an easy stretch, worked by horses, of ¾-mile to the summit at Parkhead, at 1474ft altitude, which in Great Britain (apart from the Snowdon Mountain Railway) was surpassed as a railway summit only by the 1,484ft of Druimuachdar, on the Highland main line.

From Parkhead the wagons were lowered by a tailrope down a 1 in 80 gradient for 1½ miles to Meeting Slacks, and from there down a steeper gradient at between 1 in 35 and 47 to the head of what was known as Nanny Mayor's Bank, a self-acting 1 in 14 double-track incline on which the descending loaded wagons pulled up the returning empty wagons. From the foot of this incline horses again took charge, pulling for 1¼ miles and then travelling in comfort in dandy-carts for 2 miles until Hownes Gill was reached. This is a cleft some 106ft deep and 800ft across, with its sides inclined almost precipitously at 1 in 2½ to 1 in 3.

A viaduct was first planned, but later it was decided to build two inclined planes, with a single 20 h.p. engine installed at the bottom of the ravine to lower the wagons down one side and haul them up the other. The inclination being so steep that some of the contents might have fallen out had the wagons travelled up and down in the normal way, cradles were provided on which the wagons could be carried in a horizontal position.

One wagon only could be dealt with at a time, and the crossing was a complicated business. Each wagon in turn, on reaching Hownes Gill, was run on to a turntable, turned to a transverse position, moved on to one of the cradles and lowered to the bottom. Across the floor of the Gill was a platform with turntables at all four corners – the inclines being double track – and the wagon, turned through a right-angle on the first turntable reached, was then run across the platform to the opposite side, turned again, mounted on another cradle, hauled to the top, and on the fourth and last turntable resumed its normal running position.

From Hownes Gill onwards the Stanhope & Tyne Railway had to negotiate an almost endless succession of inclined planes, most of them worked by stationary engines, but some self-acting, On the former the wagons were lowered or drawn up by lengthy tail-ropes, whereas the latter were operated on the funicular principle, the weight of the descending train, generally of loaded wagons, being used to pull up the ascending and mainly empty wagons. Some of these inclined planes were on gradients as relatively easy as 1 in 71 and even 1 in 102, which would have given little difficulty to later locomotive power, but were too steep for horse haulage; the self-acting inclines, however, were as sharply inclined as 1 in 17 to 1 in 25.

In all, the various inclines – up to and down from Carr House, the Annfield inclined planes, the self-acting Stanley, Twizell, Eden Hill and Stella Gill inclines, and the two long inclined planes near Vigo – added up to a total of 11 miles of inclined planes and 3 miles of self-acting inclines. The intervening stretches worked by horses totalled 10½ miles of main line and 4 miles of branches, while the last 9¾ miles of this 37¾-mile system, to the Tyne at South Shields, were level enough to be operated by steam locomotives.

On the Tyne at South Shields the Stanhope & Tyne had erected some coal drops of a more advanced design than any other in use up to that time. A vibrating frame, 54ft 6in long and pivoted at the bottom – which could swing outwards far enough to enable vessels to receive their loads when lying in no more than 13 to 16ft of water at low tide – was counterbalanced by a chain of heavy cast-iron links, which weighed 5 tons; a brake wheel, 16ft in diameter, controlled the operation. One of these coal drops, which cost about £500 each exclusive of foundations and the wooden gangway approach, could handle from 25 to 35 chaldron wagons per hour. The wall upon which they stood was intended to form part of a dock with eight shipping berths and big enough to hold 16 ships, but there was not sufficient finance available to carry out this part of the scheme.

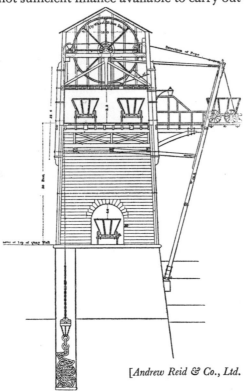

[Andrew Reid & Co., Ltd.

T. E. Harrison, del.   J. Lowry, sc.

STANHOPE & TYNE RAILWAY
COAL DROP

The opening of the Stanhope & Tyne Railway throughout to South Shields took place on 10th September, 1834, and on that day 100 wagons of coal from Medomsley were run down the line and shipped. At first the traffic over the line was relatively small, for the Company's own collieries as yet had not reached full production. But three pits owned by other companies, which until then had used other wagonways to the Tyne, diverted their traffic to the Stanhope & Tyne, and so, with the lime traffic from Stanhope, helped to make the operation profitable. Unlike the other railways already described, the Stanhope & Tyne was a purely private line, and had not therefore been built under an Act of Parliament.

In the same year, 1834, three other short railways in the same area received parliamentary sanction; they were the Blaydon, Gateshead & Hebburn, whose Act received the Royal Assent on 22nd May; the Durham Junction, 16th June; and the Durham & Sunderland, 13th August. As already described in Chapter IV, the Blaydon, Gateshead & Hebburn Railway had been promoted as an extension from Blaydon of the Newcastle

& Carlisle Railway – which at that time had not been completed farther east than Blaydon – along the south bank of the Tyne to Hebburn. The moving spirit behind it was John Clayton, the Town Clerk of Newcastle, who planned to link this railway up with other lines, the Stanhope & Tyne in particular, and to bring as much coal as possible down to the Tyne for shipment rather than its making its way to the Wear. Eventually most of the construction was carried out by the Newcastle & Carlisle, which in 1835 absorbed the Blaydon, Gateshead & Hebburn.

The Durham & Sunderland Railway was planned to begin to the south-east of the City of Durham at Shincliffe, and to run north-eastwards by way of Pittington, Moorsley and Hetton-le-Hole to Murton, where it would be joined by a branch from Haswell. It would then reach the coast at Ryhope and continue to the south side of the Wear at Sunderland. It was unique in that by a decision of the directors it was to be worked only by stationary engines; and for some time after the opening of its first section on 9th August, 1836, this was the method exclusively used. Some of the ropes required were of unparalleled length. From Fallowfield on the Haswell branch the wagons were lowered by a rope 3,000 yards long down to Murton Junction, dragging behind them a second rope no less than 6,000 yards (nearly 3½ miles) in length and without a single splice. This passed round a winding wheel of the 42 h.p. stationary engine at the bank-head, and was used, on the funicular railway principle, to haul up the incline the returning empties.

Next the wagons were lifted to Seaton Bank Head by a 52 h.p. stationary engine, from which they ran by gravity down a gradient of 1 in 60 to 43½, unwinding in their descent another rope, 4,650 yards long, for the ascending empty wagons. A third stationary engine, at Sunderland Moor, of 70 h.p., by an arrangement of ropes attended to the final stage of the journey between Ryhope and Sunderland, and was responsible for controlling the movement of both loaded and empty wagons over a total distance of 5½ miles. The weight and length of the ropes soon gave trouble, but there is no record of any change in the method of haulage over both the original section between Sunderland and Haswell, and the later opening from Murton to Shincliffe, completed in sections between 1837 and 1839.

At one stage, late in 1836, after a breakage had brought the Ryhope inclined plane to a stand, a remarkable experiment was made by fitting a wagon with a mast and sail; in a favourable wind a speed of 10 m.p.h. was attained. But nothing seems to have come of this trial. Passengers were first carried on the Durham & Sunderland Railway between Sunderland and Ryhope in October, 1836, and in the spring of the following year the service was extended to Haswell. The total length of the D. & S.R. was 16 miles.

The Durham Junction Railway, 7 miles long, was planned as a branch of the Stanhope & Tyne, to reach pits in the Rainton area, to the north of Pittington on the Durham & Sunderland. The intention of John Clayton, its promoter, was to continue from Rainton to an end-on junction at Haswell with the Hartlepool Railway, to which we shall come next, and so to provide a through route from Newcastle to Hartlepool, but this was never

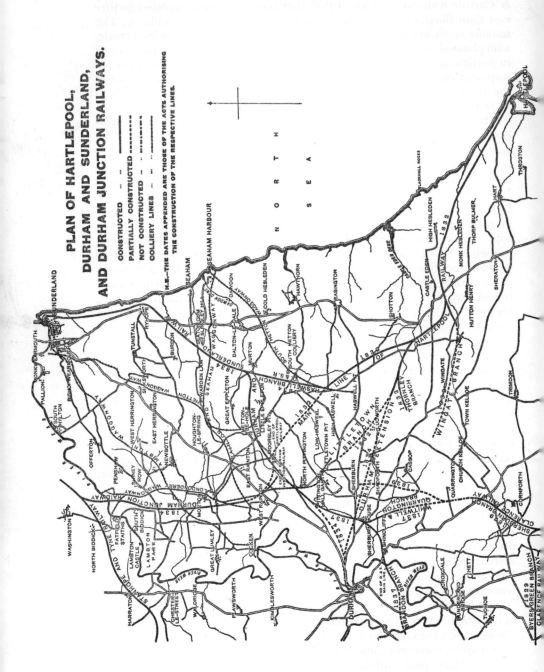

PLAN OF HARTLEPOOL,
DURHAM AND SUNDERLAND,
AND DURHAM JUNCTION RAILWAYS.

CONSTRUCTED
PARTIALLY CONSTRUCTED
NOT CONSTRUCTED
COLLIERY LINES

N.B.—THE DATES APPENDED ARE THOSE OF THE ACTS AUTHORISING
THE CONSTRUCTION OF THE RESPECTIVE LINES.

carried out. The Durham Junction was to earn distinction in another way, however, for later on it formed a link in the first main line from York to Newcastle. But this was not to happen until 1844, after the Durham Junction had been absorbed by the Newcastle & Darlington Junction Railway, as described in Chapter IX, when also the branch was opened from Belmont to Gilesgate in Durham City; until then the Durham Junction stopped short at Rainton Meadows.

The Durham Junction had one engineering feature of considerable note in its Victoria Bridge over the River Wear between Washington and Penshaw. This masonry structure, 811ft long, had one arch of no less than 160ft span, another of 144ft, and two of 100ft, with six small 20ft arches at the two ends. It was of sufficient importance to be exhibited on the opening day, in August, 1838, to members of the British Association, who also inspected the coal drops of the Stanhope & Tyne Railway at South Shields.

We have now to consider another railway which had been promoted some years earlier, midway between the Tyneside lines and the Clarence and Stockton & Darlington Railways. New collieries were springing rapidly into existence in Central Durham, and it began to be realised that neither the Tyne nor the Wear nor the Tees offered them the most direct access to the sea. A much nearer port would be Hartlepool, which had a harbour, although this had been allowed to get into a very dilapidated condition. Christopher Tennant, the moving spirit in the promotion of the Clarence Railway, had now moved from Stockton-on-Tees to Hartlepool, and became the principal backer of this new enterprise. A public meeting which he convened in Durham on 18th October, 1831, decided to seek the opinion of George Stephenson as to the best possible route, and of Sir John Rennie and Thomas Milton as to how Hartlepool Harbour might be improved.

Stephenson proposed that the line should begin in the Hetton area, and then proceed through Haswell, Easington, Castle Eden and Hesleden, with three short branches, to reach Hartlepool by a final stretch along the coast. At Hartlepool it was intended to convert the inner harbour into a dock and to construct another dock to the west of it, both of very large capacity, to transform the salt water lagoon known as the Slake into a tidal harbour, and to cut through the narrow peninsula to the west of the town in order to provide direct access from the sea.

In order to comply with the Standing Orders of Parliament, when the Bill was presented, because sufficient finance had not been raised in advance the original scheme had to be cut down; the railway was now planned as single instead of double track and the space to be excavated for the dock was limited to between 12 and 13 acres. Despite opposition, the Act for the Hartlepool Dock & Railway Company received the Royal Assent on 1st June, 1832. It authorised the construction of a main line 14 miles long, 9¼ miles of branches, and the acquisition of 65 acres of land for the docks.

The original intention of the Hartlepool Dock & Railway promoters was to begin their line at Moorsley Colliery, to the north-east of Durham City, as well as to tap the Haswell Colliery. It was to forestall Hartlepool that both the Durham Junction Railway and the Durham & Sunderland

Railway, already described, were promoted, the former in hopes that Haswell coal would still go down to the Tyne, and the latter, 9½ miles only from Sunderland as compared with 14 miles from Hartlepool, equally to make certain that some Haswell coal would be shipped on the Wear. By a second Act the Hartlepool Railway was authorised to make a 7-mile branch to Durham, and to use stationary rather than locomotive engines on the main line. The authorised capital was £279,000 (£209,000 in stock and £70,000 by loan).

The worst difficulties in carrying into effect the Hartlepool Dock & Railway Company's Acts were those encountered in building the harbour works. In order that shipment of coal might begin at the earliest possible date, it was decided to give the tidal harbour preference over the work on the docks, and the first ship actually anchored in the former in July, 1835, three years after construction had begun. The channel providing access from and to the sea at first was kept scoured by an extremely efficient series of sluices; there were six apertures 14ft 8in wide and 4ft 3in high, arranged in pairs and closed by cast-iron sluice gates moving in brass grooves, raised and lowered by double-handled cranes. Even at a distance of more than half-a-mile from the gates the entrance to the outer harbour could be deepened from 6 to 9in by the action of two consecutive tides.

Unfortunately, however, in October, 1835, some serious damage to the paving in front of two pairs of the gates rendered them useless, and the more limited action of the third pair, after a considerable amount of sand had accumulated in the inner harbour, had to be relied on until Pier and Port Commissioners had completed a stone jetty which altered the set of the ebb tide and improved matters.

Meantime the work on the railway itself had been in progress. As with other lines in the country, the disinclination to tunnel made necessary earthworks on a very considerable scale. In particular, 800,000 cu. yards of soil in all were removed from the great Crimdon cutting, which at the maximum was 70ft deep and up to 240ft wide at the top; the embankments at Hesleden Dene, Elderacres and Pespool were 85, 70 and 60ft high respectively; and for some 2 miles across Hart Warren an embankment over 30ft high had to be thrown up. The original intention to continue inland to the Moorsley and Littletown collieries was abandoned when no assurance could be obtained from the North Hetton Coal Company that their coal would be shipped at Hartlepool; the main line was, therefore, carried no farther than Haswell. Whereas the first coal was moved over the Hartlepool Railway from the Thornley pit branch as far as Castle Eden in January, 1835, it was not until 23rd November of that year that the first coal train was able to work from Haswell to Hartlepool, over the full 12¼ miles of the main line. By the end of the year, including branches, 14½ miles of line were in use, and 17½ acres of water in the harbour.

The aggregate length of railway that had now come into use in the North of England was 168 route miles, and 64 miles further were approaching completion. The total length authorised in this area was 302 miles, exactly equal to the combined length of the London & Birmingham,

The two opening bridges across the River Ouse at Selby. *Above*, the original bascule bridge of the Hull & Selby Railway, completed in 1840, seen as opened for river traffic, and *below*, the present swing-bridge on the East Coast main line, brought into use in 1891. The swing span of the latter can be seen in the background, at right angles to the track.

[*Both, British Railways*

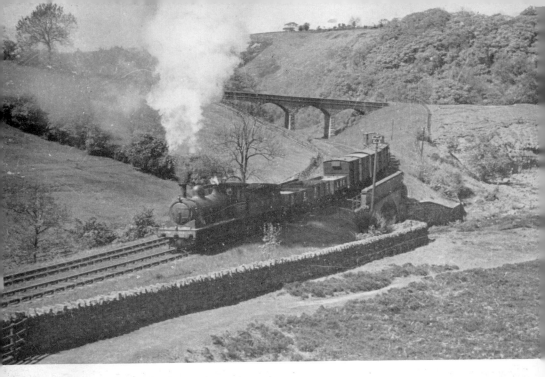

Above, a sylvan scene on the winding Whitby & Pickering line near Goathland, taken in later North Eastern Railway years. *Below*, the north portal of the Leeds & Thirsk (later Leeds Northern) Railway's Bramhope tunnel.

(*Both, British Railways*

Left, the exterior of Harrogate Station, but little changed in appearance since its opening in 1862.

Above, the 31-arch Crimple Viaduct, opened in 1848 as part of the approach from the south to Harrogate, seen in later years with the 'Queen of Scots' Pullman express.

Right, Lambley Viaduct on the Halt-whistle–Alston branch, opened in 1852.
[*All, British Railways*

Deepdale Viaduct, on the South Durham & Lancashire Union extension of the Stockton & Darlington Railway to Kirkby Stephen and Tebay, opened in 1861. *Left*, the massive wrought iron supporting trestles during building, of a maximum height of 161ft. *Below*, the completed viaduct in later North Eastern Railway days. It was 740ft. long.

Right, a viaduct of later years carried on circular masonry piers across the Gaunless valley.

[*All, British Railways*

London & Southampton, Liverpool & Manchester and Grand Junction Railways, the principal railways that had been sanctioned by Parliament up to that time in other parts of the country.

Before we leave the mining lines in the County of Durham, it is necessary to refer to one more, of slightly later date, of which the development was bound up with that of certain of the lines already described, and which in later years was to provide portions of certain important main lines in the county. This railway, the Brandling Junction, also was distinguished by bearing the name of its promoters rather than that of the towns or localities that it served. The Brandlings, John and Robert William, controlled a coal-mining area from the south-east to the west of the South Shields peninsula, and in May, 1835, they issued a prospectus for a railway from Gateshead to Monkwearmouth, across the River Wear from Sunderland, and with a branch from Brockley Whins to South Shields.

There were some complicated negotiations due to the fact that part of the proposed route would parallel that of the Blaydon, Gateshead & Hebburn Railway, but when, as described in Chapter IV, the Newcastle & Carlisle took over the uncompleted work on the former line, by agreement the N. & C. decided to proceed no farther east than Derwenthaugh (Gateshead). The Brandling Junction, on its part, undertook to connect up with the N. & C. line at Gateshead, to relay and work the original Tanfield wagonway (described in Chapter I), and to lay in a branch to Jarrow, which would make it possible to work the Marquis of Bute's coal from Tanfield Lea Colliery to Jarrow for shipment. The necessary Act received the Royal Assent on 7th June, 1836.

The first portion of the Brandling Junction Railway to be opened, on 15th January, 1839, was 1¼ miles in length, from Redheugh Quay up a rope-worked 1 in 23 incline to Greenesfield, from which it was carried on a stone viaduct through Gateshead. This section gave the Newcastle & Carlisle access for the first time to a deep-water quay. Between Gateshead and Monkwearmouth construction was relatively easy, and the line was opened for passenger and goods traffic to both Monkwearmouth and South Shields on 5th September, 1839. At Brockley Whins the Brandling Junction and the Stanhope-on-Tyne Railways crossed one another on the level, and on 9th March, 1840, a spur line was opened to connect the two. A Tyne Dock Company was formed to develop the shipping facilities at South Shields, but owing to financial difficulties the project lapsed, and it was a good many years before the Tyne Dock came into existence.

The Tanfield branch, a wayleave line, was put in order. Its steeper gradients, at 1 in 12 to 21, were rope-worked by stationary engines; a short length of Newcastle & Carlisle track gave access to it from the Brandling Junction line at Redheugh. On 11th November, 1840, a branch was opened to Tanfield Moor, 1½ miles long and with its 1 in 15 to 22 gradient worked by a stationary engine; this permitted the Brandling Junction to divert to its own line and shipping staiths coal which for some years past had been carried by the Stanhope & Tyne Railway down to South Shields. The further history of the Brandling Junction we shall come to at a later stage.

CHAPTER VI

From Leeds to Hull and Whitby to Pickering

WE must now pass to other railway schemes in North-East England, some of which had been conceived well before the lines already described, but which for various reasons were slow in getting under way. In every case they were concerned with providing access to the sea, though as compared with the lines that we have considered the transport of coal was not the primary consideration. Maritime trade, not only of a coastwise description but also to and from the Continent, was becoming of increasing importance, and it was the rivalry between ports, now awakened to a far greater degree than ever before by the prospect of improved land transport, that was causing the initiation of a stream of railway projects.

As far back as 1824, about the same time as the first surveys were being made for a railway between the North Sea and the Irish Sea from Newcastle to Carlisle, a scheme had been launched for another cross-country line, to form part of continuous railway communication between Leeds and Liverpool. On 29th December, 1824, at a public meeting in Leeds, the Leeds & Hull Railway Company was formed, with a capital of £500,000. Seven months earlier the Liverpool & Manchester Railway Company had come into being, and in January, 1825, another company, the Manchester & Leeds Railway Company, was promoted to form the centre link in this chain. But the public failed to subscribe as had been hoped to the Leeds & Hull scheme, and the canny Yorkshiremen concerned decided to hold their hand until it was seen whether or not the Liverpool & Manchester Railway would prove successful. The engineering experience gained in the construction of the latter also might prove useful to the Leeds & Hull Company.

Meantime, however, a new port was being established well up the Humber, at Goole, and in 1828, with the help of a new canal between Ferrybridge and Goole, Yorkshire woollens were beginning to pass in no small volume by steam packet between Goole and Hamburg, thus bypassing Hull. Something needed to be done quickly. It was, therefore, resolved for the time being to cut down the proposed Leeds & Hull Railway to a line between Leeds and Selby only, from which it would be possible to move freight in barges down the Ouse and Humber to Hull for shipment, and vice-versa. The Leeds & Selby Railway Company was formed on 20th March, 1829, and a fresh examination was made of George Stephenson's original plans, by an engineer named James Walker. The result was a new route, beginning at the Leeds end at Marsh Lane instead of Farbank, tunnelling through Richmond Hill to avoid the three inclined planes proposed by George Stephenson, and with no gradients steeper

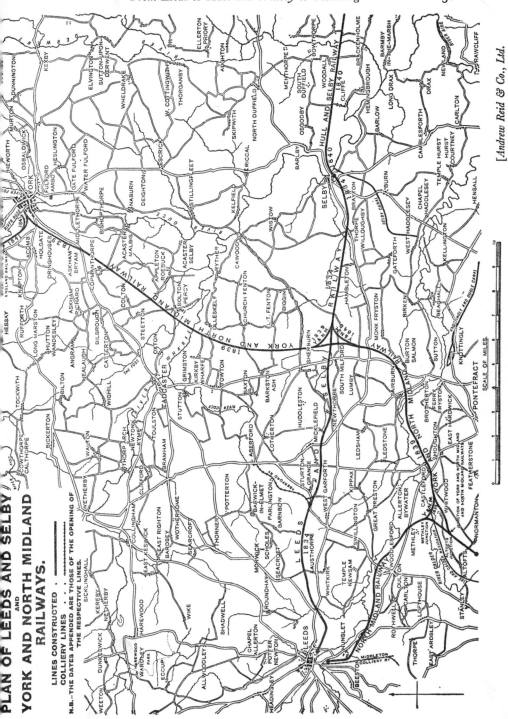

PLAN OF LEEDS AND SELBY
AND
YORK AND NORTH MIDLAND
RAILWAYS.

LINES CONSTRUCTED . . . . .
COLLIERY LINES . . . .

N.B.—THE DATES APPENDED ARE THOSE OF THE OPENING OF
THE RESPECTIVE LINES.

SCALE OF MILES

[Andrew Reid & Co., Ltd.

than 1 in 135, so that either horses or locomotives could be used for traction. The length was to be just under 20 miles.

A Bill was brought before the following session of Parliament. The most strenuous of the opposition came from the Aire & Calder Navigation, whose traffic to and from Goole might well be affected, but this and other objections failed to secure the defeat of the Bill, which was passed and received the Royal Assent on 29th May, 1830. Work on the route began in October of that year, and was carried out in very substantial fashion. The biggest engineering task was the tunnel under Richmond Hill, within ¼-mile of the Leeds terminus, which took from November, 1832, to June, 1833, to complete. It was for a double line, 700 yards long, 22ft wide at the springing of the arch, and with a maximum height of 17ft above rail. Three shafts were provided for ventilation purposes as well as for lighting. There were several cuttings through sandstone or limestone, the deepest of them, 43ft in depth, near Milford, and one of the embankments reached a maximum height of 54ft, at Halton, near what is now Cross Gates station.

By the autumn of 1834 one track had been completed, and after a party of the directors and their friends had been carried on 18th September from Leeds to Selby and back in a train of four open carriages, hauled by the locomotive *Nelson*, the line was opened formally four days later. The inaugural run was less auspicious than it might have been. A train of three yellow-painted first class coaches and six open seconds, drawn by *Nelson*, had been made up, and was packed with 156 passengers. A start had been arranged at 6.30 a.m., so that any passengers who so desired might be able to catch the morning steam packet from Selby to Hull. But none was destined to make the connection. For as soon as *Nelson* reached the beginning of the up gradient, the engine slipped to a standstill on the wet rails, and despite liberal applications of sand, it took 40 minutes to cover the first 2 miles. One second class coach was then dropped to lighten the load, but even so, the uphill progress was so snail-like that the spectators, of whom some 20,000 were massed alongside the line, were calling on the enginemen and police officers to get out and 'push her along'.

No fewer than 70 minutes were spent in climbing the 4½ miles to the summit at Brown Moor, but matters then improved; the next 4 miles took 14 minutes only, and on reaching the down grade beyond Garforth, *Nelson* managed to accelerate to a quite lively 20 m.p.h., so covering the last 13½ miles in 42 minutes and getting into Selby shortly before 9 a.m. On the return the time was cut from the more than two hours of the outward journey to 76 minutes, and *Nelson* brought his train into Leeds at 11.10 p.m.

On 22nd September, 1834, the regular train service began, twice a day in each direction, and with much more modest loads than that of the inaugural trip it was possible to lay down a schedule of 65 minutes each way. Passengers continuing from Selby to Hull could make use of the Selby Packet Company's ships, but these were uncertain to a degree, owing to the frequency with which they grounded on shoals in the Ouse and Humber.

W. W. Tomlinson has quoted in amusing fashion from a contemporary what happened on such occasions. 'Passengers were called upon to assist in keeping the vessel going to prevent her from lying quietly down on the mud. Whenever, in a coarse, gruff voice, the captain gave emphatic word of command, "Rowl her!", the crowd, like sheep at the bark of a dog, walked across the deck, treading on one another's heels and suffering much personal inconvenience. At the same time they hauled upon a rope, previously sent on shore and made fast to post or tree, till the vessel was disengaged from her soft bed and again afloat in a channel nearer the shore.' There, we read, they might lie for two hours or more, and so it is not surprising that the voyage over the 33 miles by water from Selby to Hull took 4½ to 5 hours, or even more if against an incoming tide or a strong head wind. However, the steamers were operated as far as possible with the tides, and it is on record that on one occasion at least in these early months the journey from Leeds to Hull was completed by rail and water in no more than 4½ hours all told.

By December, 1834, the second track had been laid, and the carriage of freight could begin. One immediate result was a reduction of the tolls over the Aire & Calder Navigation, and not before it was time, seeing that that company had been paying an annual dividend of some £70,000 on a capital of £26,700! During its first year, the Leeds & Selby Railway carried 100,913 passengers, or between eight and nine times the number that had travelled previously by coach between the two towns. For the period, the two terminals were quite pretentious. The Leeds train shed, with three roofed bays, was 197ft long, and housed four tracks, two for passenger trains and two for wagons; that at Selby was bigger, 240ft long and with six tracks (see plans on p. 55). At both ends of each station the tracks were connected by turntables with a transverse track for the release of locomotives or individual coaches or wagons after arrival.

The irregularity of the water transport between Selby and Hull was such, however, that the completion of the original Leeds & Hull scheme already had become an urgent necessity. So it was that in November, 1834, the Hull & Selby Railway Company, already formed, gave notice of its intention to apply for parliamentary powers. Two alternative routes had been surveyed, one *via* Cottingham and the other *via* Hessle, but as the former would have involved a tunnel through Waldby Hill, whereas the latter was through flat country almost throughout, the Hessle route was decided on.

The only earthwork of any note was a cutting some 40ft deep at Hessle; except for slight rises and falls over bridges there was no gradient steeper than 1 in 572; and 18 miles of the line were dead straight. As it was necessary to leave a clear passage when required for vessels passing up and down the Ouse at Selby, the river was crossed by a cast-iron bridge 191ft long, of which one span was designed on bascule principles. Two counterweighted flaps, each of 93 tons weight, could be raised or lowered in slightly less than a minute by hand-operated quadrants and racks, leaving a clear river opening of 45ft. An unusually substantial type of permanent way was laid, partly with 55 lb per yard flat-bottom rails on longitudinal sleepers, and partly with 63 lb rails on tranvserse sleepers; the rails also were not bolted direct to the sleepers, but were secured in chairs or saddles by oak keys.

1st July, 1840, saw the formal opening of the Hull & Selby Railway throughout the 30¾ miles of its length. At midday four trains in succession left Hull in torrential rain, and reached Selby shortly after 2 p.m. The return journey was begun at or after 4 p.m., now in brilliant sunshine, with the special trains travelling over the flat country at between 26 and 30 m.p.h., indeed, the first train completed the journey in no more than one minute over the even hour. At a dinner held in the new goods warehouse at Hull, one of the speakers was the renowned George Hudson, of whom there will be much to relate later.

Through railway communication had now become established between Leeds and Hull, but a development of far greater importance which had taken shape was the linking of this line with other railways now completed that for the first time made a through railway journey possible between York and London. But before we deal with the link in question – the York & North Midland Railway – it is necessary to devote a little attention to a historic line which had been opened meantime in North Yorkshire, the Whitby & Pickering.

Whitby was another North-East Coast port with ambitions. The only land access to Whitby up to the 1830s was over rough moorland tracks, and as far back as 1793 a canal between Whitby and Pickering had been mooted but found impracticable. By 1826 the idea of access by railway was being discussed, and Thomas Storey, an engineer called in to report, was recommending a line, 39½ miles in length, not to Pickering, but up the Esk valley and through Kildale and Stokesley to a junction with the Stockton & Darlington Railway near Yarm. The optimistic idea behind this plan was that some of the Durham coal might be worked down to Whitby for shipment. A survey was also made for a branch to Pickering.

But whereas Storey's first estimate of the cost of the scheme was a modest £120,000, a later revised estimate very nearly doubled this figure, to £226,000, and considerably weakened the faith of the promoters in their engineer. So, in 1832 George Stephenson was called in, and it did not take him long to advise against the Whitby & Stockton proposal. With a summit level of 602ft to be surmounted at Kildale, there was little hope of rail transport between Stockton and Whitby being able to compete with that by rail to Middlesbrough and water from there to Whitby. But he was in favour of the Whitby & Pickering project, which he considered could be carried out at an average cost of £2,000 per mile, and offered considerable possibilities in the carriage of coal, lime, whinstone, freestone, timber and agricultural produce.

By September a company had been formed to carry out Stephenson's plan; no opposition was offered in Parliament to the Bill, and this received the Royal Assent on 6th May, 1833. An extraordinary feature of the Act was that whereas one of its clauses permitted the use of steam locomotives over the line, a later clause expressly forbade them! This later clause remained effective during the whole of the independent history of the Whitby & Pickering Railway, for horses were still used until it had been

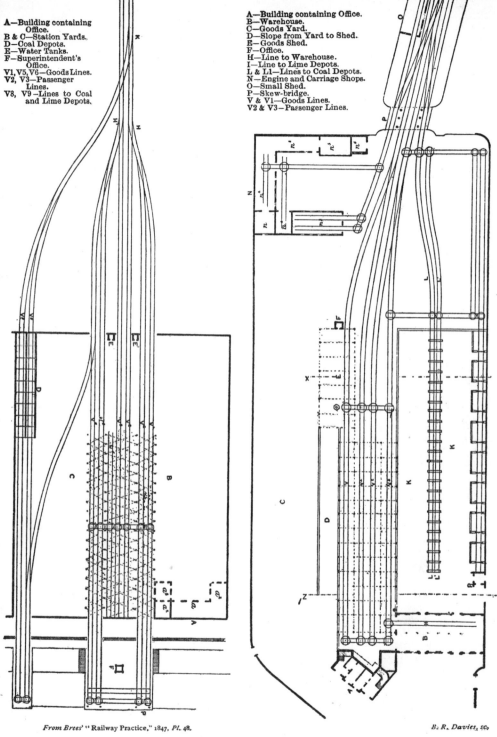

A—Building containing
    Office.
B & C—Station Yards.
D—Coal Depots.
E—Water Tanks.
F—Superintendent's
    Office.
V1, V5, V6—Goods Lines.
V2, V3—Passenger
    Lines.
V8, V9—Lines to Coal
    and Lime Depots.

A—Building containing Office.
B—Warehouse.
C—Goods Yard.
D—Slope from Yard to Shed.
E—Goods Shed.
F—Office.
H—Line to Warehouse.
I—Line to Lime Depots.
L & L1—Lines to Coal Depots.
N—Engine and Carriage Shops.
O—Small Shed.
P—Skew-bridge.
V & V1—Goods Lines.
V2 & V3—Passenger Lines.

From Brees' "Railway Practice," 1847. Pl. 48.

B. R. Davies, sc.

SELBY STATION PLAN.

LEEDS STATION PLAN.

LEEDS & SELBY RAILWAY TERMINALS

[*Andrew Reid & Co., Ltd.*

absorbed by the York & North Midland Railway in 1845, and had been physically connected at Pickering with that line in 1846.

The course of the River Esk winds considerably, and this complicated the location of the line. To avoid having to build two swingbridges at a point a mile from Whitby where the river was still navigable but made a long loop to the west, authority was obtained to divert the stream, which was successfully accomplished. At Ruswarp, however, a five-span timber bridge, 312ft long, was needed, and between Sleights and Grosmont, where the valley contracts and the river becomes more sinuous than ever, no fewer than eight bridges over the Esk had to be built.

At Grosmont the line turned southwards into the valley of the Murk Esk, passing through a short tunnel, 120 yards long. This valley was followed as far as Beck Hole, eight miles from Whitby. From here an inclined plane was needed, 1,500 yards long, to climb at 1 in 15 from 214ft altitude to a summit at the entrance to Newton Dale, 532ft above the sea. Next followed a descent, mostly at 1 in 71 and 1 in 125, to Newton Dale siding, and from there more steeply at 1 in 68–60–75–104 to Levisham, after which the 24-mile line dropped on easier grades to Pickering.

By 8th June, 1835, the railway had been completed as far as Grosmont, six miles from Whitby, and in the first year more than 12,000 passengers had been conveyed by coach over it, while some 10,000 tons of stone also had been worked by horses down to Whitby. Finally, on 26th May, 1836, three years after the passing of the Act, the line was formally opened through to Pickering. Fortunately the day was fine, and it was a festive occasion. On arrival at Beck Hole, the special train was divided into sections of three coaches apiece, which were hauled in turn up the incline, counterbalanced by descending coaches or wagons which passed the ascending vehicles at the midway loop, to the accompaniment of a brass band and the firing of guns. After the train had been reassembled at the summit, it was drawn by horses as far as the beginning of the 1 in 71, and then let loose to proceed by gravity, attaining a top speed of some 30 m.p.h.; over the easier gradients from Levisham onwards the service of horses was needed once again.

These became the regular methods of working, save that soon after opening it was decided for safety reasons to work the coaches up and down the incline singly. As it took an average of 4½ minutes to get each coach up or down, this gave waiting passengers at Beck Hole time to dash to a neighbouring inn to quench any real or fancied thirst; and so profitable did this refreshment business become that eventually the landlord erected a tent each summer alongside the railway to satisfy the cravings of those passengers who did not welcome the pedestrian exertion of hurrying to and from his inn. On the average, the journey between Whitby and Pickering took a little less than 2½ hours.

The incline continued in use until a serious accident occurred in 1864 due to the breakage of a rope, two passengers being killed. A more substantial rope was installed at once, but to avoid further risk and the delay to trains caused by the incline, a deviation was decided on by the North

Eastern Railway, which by now had absorbed the York & North Midland. This deviation, beginning just south of Grosmont, called for a gradient which for 2¾ miles right off is at 1 in 49. After it was opened on 1st July, 1865, the line from Grosmont to Beck Hole went out of use, save that in some summers in much later years the N.E.R. ran an autocar service between Whitby and Beck Hole for holidaymakers.

No more than £105,100 had been spent on the original Whitby & Pickering Railway, which was of very light construction. After its acquisition in 1845 by the York & North Midland, and following a visit to Whitby by George Hudson, it was decided, in preparation for locomotive haulage, to spend some money in improving it. One of the improvements was to double the line, until then single track, and at the same time to relay it with heavier rails. The timber bridge over the Esk at Grosmont was replaced by a stone structure and a new timber viaduct was substituted for the light structure at Ruswarp; five other bridges were rebuilt with iron girders. The original tunnel at Grosmont also was replaced by a new tunnel, 143 yards long, and with considerably more ample clearances than the previous structure, while the first stations at both Whitby and Pickering were rebuilt in stone. On 4th June, 1847, the first train drawn by a steam locomotive made its way into Whitby.

CHAPTER VII

The First Link with London — The York & North Midland Railway

In these early years there were two men who undoubtedly exerted a greater influence on the spread of railway communication in Great Britain than any others. One, needless to say, was George Stephenson, the engineer; the second, destined to wield immense power in the financial realm, was George Hudson. It was in a farming community that Hudson was born and brought up, and to some extent he had a peasant mentality. Beginning life among Methodists, in later years he joined the Church of England, and became a staunch Conservative, whereas most of the other railway promoters were of the Liberal persuasion.

Hudson's early business life was as a draper's assistant in York, but his ability was such that in course of time he himself became a linendraper on a big scale. In 1827, when 27 years of age, he inherited a legacy of £30,000 – no mean fortune in those days – and with such financial standing he was able in due course to found and to become Chairman of the York Banking Company. So influential did he become in York that three times in succession he was elected Lord Mayor of that city. He had no knowledge of railways, and at first had little interest in the railway projects of his time; but he had developed considerable ability in the financial realm, and he soon came to the realisation that the spread of railways offered a golden opportunity for making money. As events later were to prove, however, this astute man was not going to be over-scrupulous in the way in which he conducted his railway affairs.

On 30th December, 1833, a meeting had been convened under Hudson's inspiration at Tomlinson's Hotel in Low Petergate – later the Londesborough Arms – for forming a company to build a railway from York to Leeds. But while surveys and discussions were still proceeding as to the best route to follow, some vastly more important projects were coming into view. A well-known canal engineer named Nicholas Wilcox Cundy was promoting a 'Grand Northern Railway' to run from London to York by way of Cambridge, Peterborough, Grantham, Newark, Lincoln, Gainsborough and Selby, and its northern extremity might well be combined with the York & Leeds line. In October, 1834, Cundy travelled down to York and addressed a public meeting in the Guildhall to such effect that a resolution was passed in favour of his plan and a local committee formed to collaborate with the central committee in London.

Shortly afterwards another engineer, Joseph Gibbs, proposed a rival plan for a 'Great Northern Railway', to follow somewhat the same course, and he also made the journey to York to interview the local committee In 1836 his plan got as far as a Bill presented to Parliament, but this was thrown out. The York and London committees had therefore to reconsider Cundy's Grand Northern route, but decided to call in another opinion in the person of an engineer named James Walker. His survey favoured part of Cundy's route and part of that proposed by Gibbs; the result was a second Bill, presented to Parliament in 1836, for a 'Northern & Eastern Railway'. Parliamentary approval, however, was given only to the section from London to Cambridge – destined in later years to form a part of the Great Eastern Railway – so that for the time being York was still without any immediate prospect of having a railway link with London through the Eastern Counties. In any event there had been considerable doubt as to whether a railway which throughout its length would pass through almost entirely agricultural country could be expected to pay adequate interest on a capital expenditure estimated at £4,000,000.

But salvation was to come from another direction altogether. The London & Birmingham Railway was approaching completion; a railway called the Midland Counties was projected from a junction at Rugby with the London & Birmingham through Leicester to Derby; and a North Midland Railway Company was formed in 1835 to continue with a line from Derby through Chesterfield and Rotherham to Normanton and Leeds. The York party could now see that a line from York to a junction with the North Midland at or near Normanton not only would give them the desired through rail communication with London, but also, by connections with the Leeds & Selby Railway where the two lines would cross near Milford, would provide railway routes both to Leeds, on the west, and to Selby and Hull, on the east.

Thus it was that at a meeting at York on 13th October, 1835, the York & North Midland Railway was formed, with a capital of £200,000. Shareholders in the already formed York & Leeds Railway were permitted to transfer their holdings to the new company. George Stephenson, who earlier had come into contact with Hudson, was appointed Engineer of the Y. & N.M.R. The York & North Midland Bill got through Parliament without difficulty, and received the Royal Assent on the same day as that of the Hull & Selby – 21st June, 1836. A fortnight later the Great North of England Railway Act also received the Royal Assent, but we shall come to that line in the next chapter.

Construction of the initial stage of the York & North Midland was a fairly easy proposition. The line was almost dead level; the only bridge of any note was that over the River Wharfe between Bolton Percy and Church Fenton, 274ft long and with a central arch of 60ft span. When the line had been completed as far as the junction with the Leeds & Selby Railway at South Milford, an opening ceremony was planned for 29th May, 1839. At that time George Hudson, Chairman of the Company, was serving one of his terms as Lord Mayor of York, and the function was devised, so a contemporary journal wrote, 'with becoming public spirit'. The day, therefore, began in the Guildhall, with a breakfast 'of the most sumptuous descrip-

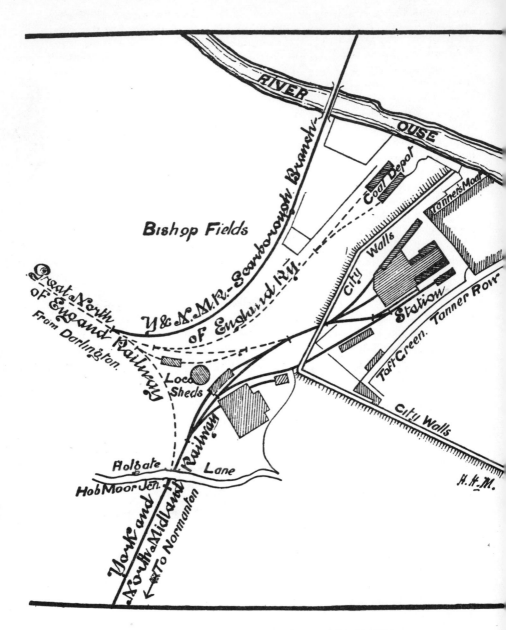

THE ORIGINAL STATION AT YORK

tion', to which were invited the directors of the newly-formed North Midland and Great North of England Railways, the members of the York Corporation and the magistrates, the York clergy and the local gentry.

After having been lavishly fed and doubtless wined also, the guests moved in procession from the Mansion House to the railway terminus, where a train had been assembled comprising five first, ten second and three third class coaches, with the Robert Stephenson locomotives *Lowther* and *York and Leeds* marshalled fore and aft respectively. In the train, the party was hurried to Milford in 36 minutes, at an average speed of just under 24 m.p.h. There was a stay at Milford from 1.42 to 2.23 p.m. and the return journey was completed without incident in 41 minutes. The climax of the day was a dinner, with George Hudson in the chair, and George Stephenson, recalling some of his early struggles in getting the first railways on their feet, as one of the after-dinner speakers; to conclude the rejoicings there was a ball. This must have been the most elaborate programme ever planned to celebrate the opening of no more than $14\frac{1}{4}$ miles of railway!

Almost a year passed before the opening, on 11th May, 1840, of the Sherburn to Burton Salmon section of the York & North Midland; the last $6\frac{3}{4}$ miles, from there to the junction with the North Midland at Altofts, $23\frac{1}{2}$ miles from York, was completed by the end of June. On this length a cutting up to 48ft deep had to be made through limestone at Fairburn and the River Aire had to be bridged just west of Burton Salmon, by a stone viaduct 305ft long with three skew arches of 65ft span. Meantime work had been going on apace with the far bigger railway projects to the south. The Midland Counties Railway from Rugby through Leicester to Derby was completed in time for opening on 1st July, 1840; and the North Midland – which with no fewer than 200 bridges and seven tunnels in its length of 73 miles had cost some £3,000,000 – from Derby as far as Rotherham on 11th May, and throughout to Leeds on the same day as the York & North Midland opened to Altofts Junction, 30th June, 1840.

This might indeed have been the occasion for a celebration on the grand scale, for York now for the first time had railway communication throughout to London, *via* Normanton, Chesterfield, Derby, Leicester and Rugby to Euston. But George Hudson and his fellow-directors this time were content to entrain on 30th June in a special train of four first class and one third class coaches, drawn appropriately by the locomotive *Hudson*, in which they travelled from York to Altofts Junction and from there continued over the North Midland to Oakenshaw, where formal opening took place of the line through from Derby to Leeds. From the following day, 1st July, 1840, it became possible to leave York daily at 7.30 in the morning and, including half-an-hour at Derby for refreshments, to be in London, 217 miles distant by this route, at 9.30 the same evening.

Where the York & North Midland Railway crossed the Leeds & Selby, a north-to-east connection had been laid in between Sherburn-in-Elmet and a point to the east of South Milford, at the site of the present Gascoigne Wood sidings. Here trains from York connected with Selby and Leeds trains, passengers requiring to change. On 27th July, however, a spur connection was opened at Methley between the York & North Midland and the North Midland Railways, permitting through running from York to Leeds, and though this added 4½ miles to the distance, some of the traffic was immediately diverted *via* Methley. The Leeds & Selby now became an easy prey to George Hudson, who without delay negotiated a 31-year lease of the Leeds & Selby by the York & Midland at an annual rental of £17,000, with the option of purchase at a later date. Thus it was that from 9th November, 1840, passenger trains ceased to work over the Leeds & Selby between Leeds and Milford Old Junction; those from Leeds to both York and Selby from then on travelled by the Methley spur. On 7th November, 1840, there was brought into use a new south-to-east spur line at Milford; at its convergence with the York & North Midland, between Sherburn and Burton Salmon, a new station called Milford Junction was built. Passengers from the south for Selby and Hull, who previously had had to change at Sherburn Junction, now did so at Milford Junction.

If Hudson had thought to deal as easily with the Hull & Selby directors as he had with those of the Leeds & Selby Railway, he soon found that he had a more thorny proposition to handle. The Hull & Selby had refused to support the Leeds & Selby in the negotiations which had preceded the lease of the latter to the York & North Midland and certainly was in no mood to be leased itself. The H. & S. also had refused already a proposition from the Y. & N.M. for joint operation of its line. In an attempt to coerce the Hull & Selby, Hudson and some friends purchased the steam tugs which previously had pursued their uncertain course up and down the Ouse and the Humber between Selby and Hull, but which by agreement had been abandoned by the Leeds & Selby Company as soon as the Hull & Selby was opened, and transferred to these tugs all the through freight traffic for Hull which was not in need of urgent delivery.

But the absorption of the Hull & Selby Railway was not to be deferred for very long. On 1st March, 1841, the Manchester & Leeds Railway, six years later to become a part of the Lancashire & Yorkshire Railway, had opened a line through Wakefield to a junction with the North Midland at Normanton. Shortly afterwards the M. & L., with its eye on the North Sea, projected an extension from Wakefield through Pontefract to Goole, with a connection to the proposed London & York Railway, if the latter followed the route first proposed, which would enable the M. & L. trains to reach Selby and so continue over the Hull & Selby line to Hull. The friendly relations between the Manchester & Leeds and the Hull & Selby culminated in an alliance between the two companies which took effect from 1st January, 1844.

This was more than George Hudson could tolerate, and fortunately for him two prominent shareholders in the Hull & Selby Railway were not enamoured of the alliance with the Manchester & Leeds. And when it came to a proposed amalgamation, early in 1845, of the Manchester & Leeds, Hull & Selby, Wakefield, Pontefract & Goole and Leeds & West Riding Junction Railways, a committee of dissatisfied shareholders in the Hull & Selby waited on Hudson at York to find out on what terms he would be prepared to take a permanent lease of their line. These were 10 per cent annually on the original capital with the option of purchase at the rate of £100 for each £50 share. At two meetings of the Leeds & Selby shareholders their directors were defeated, and with a slight adjustment of the terms – an increase from £100 to £112 10s., for example, as the price for L. & S. £50 shares – the Hudson offer was accepted. On 1st July, 1845, the transaction was consummated, and the Leeds & Selby became a part of the York & North Midland system and at the same time of the growing Hudson empire. It should be emphasised, however, that this was a lease and not an amalgamation.

Meantime a great deal else had been happening, much of which will be described in later chapters, for the period known as the 'Railway Mania' was approaching, and railways were being projected in all directions. On 10th May, 1844, the North Midland, Midland Counties, and Birmingham & Derby Railways had amalgamated to form the Midland Railway, one of the biggest railway systems in the country at that date, with Hudson as Chairman. The York & North Midland, with himself also as Chairman, had obtained Acts in May and June, 1844, to build a line from York to Scarborough which would throw off, at Malton, a branch to Pickering; there it would link up with the Whitby & Pickering Railway, which by the same powers would be acquired by the Y. & N.M.

The construction of the York and Scarborough line achieved a record for speed, for the 42-mile main line and the 6½-mile Pickering branch were completed in less than a year, and at the low cost of less than £6,000 per mile. Its most expensive engineering work was the bridge over the River Ouse by which the line started out of York; this was erected in no more than 3½ months. Cast-iron piles were driven into the river bed to support the central pier, without recourse to any coffer-dam, and this carried the outer ends of the two 75ft cast-iron girder spans. At Huttons Ambo the River Derwent was crossed by a 400ft timber viaduct, and a five-span brick viaduct spanned the Washbeck Valley at Scarborough. Here a handsome station was built, with a glazed roof 348ft long and 88ft wide spanning the tracks, fronted by a stone building with a colonnade. The York arrangements were awkward from the operating point of view, as, to avoid a level crossing over the coal branch of the Great North of England, the York & North Midland trains had to draw out of the terminus over the latter's line, and then reverse on to the Ouse bridge.

The York and Scarborough line and the Pickering branch were opened with ceremony on 7th July, 1845. Similar junketings took place as those which had commemorated the opening of the first section of the York & North Midland Railway six years before. Following a breakfast at York and a procession, the locomotives *Hudson* and *Lion* tackled a massive train of no fewer than 35 coaches, crowded with passengers who had been given free passes from all parts of the Hudson domain, and ran it to Scarborough and back; a luncheon at Scarborough and a dinner at York completed the day's festivities. The free travel operated for five days on end, before the new lines settled down to normal working.

CHAPTER VIII

The Great North of England Railway

IT is remarkable that up to the year 1835 all the railways which had been promoted in the County of Durham and in North Yorkshire had been of an east-west description, and chiefly in order to carry coal from the mines down to the seaports for shipment. Not until the York & North Midland Railway had been formed in October, 1835, as described in Chapter VII, had there emerged the first idea of a trunk railway communication from London to North-East England. This would stop short at York, however, and it is not surprising that active minds in the County of Durham should now concentrate on the extension of this trunk route to Newcastle and beyond.

In this project Joseph Pease of the Stockton & Darlington Railway was the moving spirit. The North Midland Railway directors had ideas of extending their line northwards from Leeds to Newcastle, but Pease and his friends were determined that the route should lie through York. Characteristically, they looked towards such a line as giving 'a cheap and expeditious transit for coals into the heart of the North Riding and to the city of York itself', and for that reason they thought that those interested in the Stockton & Darlington should be the first to subscribe to the new undertaking. Also they considered that such a line would be managed much better by local men with intimate knowledge of the commerce and agriculture of the district than by the London committee of the North Midland which was planning to extend in a northerly direction from Leeds.

A Central Provisional Committee of the Stockton & Darlington and York & North Midland Companies was, therefore, formed a fortnight after the formation of the York & North Midland, to promote a line from York to Newcastle, including a branch to Leeds – the latter to forestall the North Midland Company – with a nominal capital of £1,000,000. As it was anticipated that construction through the hilly country between Darlington and Newcastle would be more difficult than that across the Great Plain of York south of Darlington, it was decided that the survey north of Darlington should be made first; it was thought that if parliamentary powers could be obtained for the Darlington–Newcastle section in 1836, and for the Darlington–York section in 1837, it would be possible to complete both sections by roughly the same date.

In a speech by Joseph Pease at Newcastle in November, 1835, it was revealed that George Stephenson already had planned a route, and this was the one eventually favoured. It began at a junction with the Blaydon, Gateshead & Hebburn Railway near Redheugh Quay, Gateshead, and then

Above, Belah Viaduct, biggest of all the massive structures on the extension of the Stockton & Darlington Railway to Tebay. Its maximum height was 196ft, and its length 1,040ft. A train of empty mineral wagons is being worked across in N.E.R. days. *Below*, extreme winter conditions between Barnard Castle and Kirkby Stephen; Barras station buried in snow.
[*J. W. Armstrong and British Railways*

Stockton & Darlington stations which have remained with but little change over the years. *Above*, Darlington North Road, and *below*, Barnard Castle in North Eastern Railway days.

[*H. C. Casserley and British Railways*

Left, Parkhead, on the Waskerley – Stanhope branch, 1,474ft above the sea and the highest point on the North Eastern Railway.

[*H. C. Casserley*

Above, is seen the Hownes Gill viaduct which replaced the former inclined planes on both sides of the gorge, as completed in 1858 and, *below*, when under construction. It was on the line from Crook to Consett.

[*British Railways*

Two masterpieces of design by Robert Stephenson, both opened in 1850. *Above*, the Royal Border Bridge at Berwick, with its twenty-eight arches on piers which at their maximum are 126ft above the bed of the River Tweed. *Below*, the High Level Bridge across the Tyne at Newcastle, with six spans of 125ft each.   [*Both, British Railways*

ran south up the Team Valley past Chester-le-Street and Old Durham to Shincliffe. From there it would have paralleled the City of Durham branch of the Clarence Railway through the Thrislington Gap, then continuing southward, where the latter turned east, past Aycliffe to a junction with the Stockton & Darlington Railway, 1½ miles of the latter's track being used past Darlington to Croft.

South of Darlington the line would have had a direct course to a point near Thirsk, where it would have forked, the western arm continuing through Boroughbridge, Knaresborough and Tadcaster to Leeds, and the eastern to a junction with the York & North Midland but passing some three miles to the west of York, at Hob Moor, from which a branch would have been constructed into the city. This plan did not commend itself to the York & North Midland Railway, which urged a deviation *via* Skelton into York, with a bridge over the River Ouse which could be used also by the lines projected by the Y. & N.M. to Scarborough and Whitby.

Eventually the Central Provisional Committee, though laying it down as a principle that a railway of national importance should not be diverted from its course to serve merely local interests, realised that the city of York in later years might become a railway centre of considerable importance, and so agreed to the deviation. It is astonishing to recall that Joseph Pease was farsighted enough to foresee the coming of a day when freight would need to be transported at 30 m.p.h. and passengers would demand to be carried at 60 m.p.h., and that for this reason he recommended that the Great North of England Railway should purchase sufficient land to lay down four parallel tracks. Many years were to elapse, however, before a four-track main line became necessary.

Now north of Darlington the new main line obviously was going to cross several of the existing railways from the Durham mines to the coast, and chief among them the Stockton & Darlington, the Clarence and the Stanhope & Tyne. The first of the three was sharing actively in the promotion of the new scheme; traffic over the third was unlikely to be affected; but it was a different matter with the Clarence Railway. Why could not their Durham branch form a part of the new main line rather than the Croft branch of the Stockton & Darlington? Stockton-on-Tees, always jealous of Darlington, also became thoroughly roused, especially as other railway projects in the county at that time, for new branches of the Clarence Railway (particularly the 12-mile Durham & South-West Junction Railway to connect the Auckland and Coundon mines with the Chilton branch of the Clarence) were being threatened by the Great North of England.

Indeed, Christopher Tennant and the Stockton party accused Joseph Pease and the Stockton & Darlington of 'trying to get possession of the county', while the Stockton & Darlington on their part alleged that the Clarence Railway was making a 'sinister' attempt to get Parliament to sanction a branch line destined to harm the Great North of England by filching some of its traffic. The Clarence Company also claimed that a deviation of the Great North of England in such a way as to use the existing

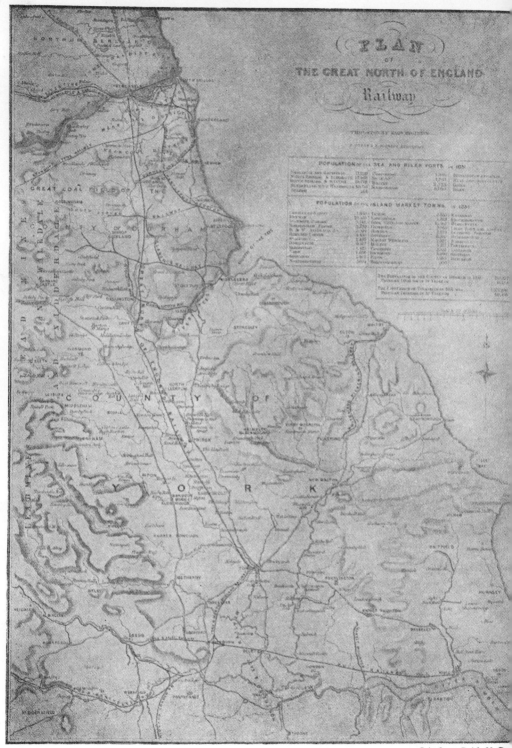

[*Andrew Reid & Co.*

THE GREAT NORTH OF ENGLAND RAILWAY

Clarence line between Mainsforth and Blackgate and to continue from there across the Wear near Finchale Abbey would save some £300,000 in constructional costs.

But three eminent engineers called in to give an independent opinion decided against the Clarence proposal and reported that no better route could be devised than that originally laid down by George Stephenson. Eventually the Durham & South-West Junction Railway Bill, the passing of which might have bettered the unfortunate financial position of the Clarence Railway at that time as well as being of benefit to the Hartlepool Railway, was passed by the House of Commons but was thrown out by the Lords.

Pease and his friends now proceeded with their Bill, and without losing any time about it. For they heard that surveys were being made, with influential backing, for a line up the West Coast from England to Scotland, and they calculated that the prospects were remote that Parliament would sanction both East Coast and West Coast routes at the same time. From this it is clear that the promoters of the Great North of England were looking much further ahead than merely connecting York with Newcastle; their ultimate aim was a through route from London to Edinburgh. They had the satisfaction of receiving the Royal Assent to their first Act, covering 34½ miles of line from Newcastle to Darlington, on 4th July, 1836. The authorised capital was £1,150,000, sufficient, in the promoters' estimate, to cover the whole line from Newcastle to York. Almost exactly a year later the second Act received the Royal Assent, for the 43 miles of line from Croft southwards to York, but for reasons just given the additional capital authorised did not need to exceed £180,000.

There was now a rush by various existing lines in the County of Durham to plan a link-up with the Great North of England Railway. These included the Durham & Sunderland, Durham Junction, West Durham – a revival of the former Durham South-West Junction – and a new South Durham Railway, The West Durham project was for a continuation of the Durham & South-West Junction Chilton branch to St Helen's Auckland, with a branch to Bishop Auckland and another to join the Hagger Leases branch of the Stockton & Darlington. The project of the South Durham, or Weardale Junction Railway, was to continue the Byers Green branch of the Clarence Railway to Frosterley in Weardale.

Next, a party in Hartlepool, not content to see coal traffic diverted by the Clarence Railway from their harbour to Port Clarence, evolved a scheme under the grandiose title 'Great North of England, Clarence & Hartlepool Junction Railway', which was simply to be the Wingate branch of the Hartlepool Dock & Railway extended for 8½ miles past Ferryhill to join the Byers Green branch of the Clarence Railway, plus two branches linking the extension with the Great North of England main line. This latter company duly obtained its Act on 3rd July, 1837.

Stockton-on-Tees did not intend to be left out in the cold, however, and Christopher Tennant and his friends at the same time were planning a Clarence & Hartlepool Union Railway, 8 miles long, with a 1¼-mile branch to Seaton Carew, which would make it possible for coal coming down the Clarence Railway to be shipped from Stockton as well as from Hartlepool. At the time the Stockton & Darlington Railway was preparing its counter-measures, in particular a Bishop Auckland & Weardale Railway, which was to run for 16¼ miles from the foot of Black Boy bank at Shildon to Frosterley in Weardale, there to tap the stone traffic, and to have two branches, one of 3¼ miles to Crook and the other for 1½ miles to Bishopley. The route chosen would have involved a tunnel ¾-mile long under the high ground north of Shildon, to cut out the Black Boy incline. But because of opposition it was decided not to proceed at that time with the section from Witton to Frosterley and the Bishopley branch. Some of these projects were abandoned because of shortage of money; but powers were obtained in 1837 for the last-mentioned scheme in its truncated form (under the title of Bishop Auckland & Weardale Railway), and also by the Durham & Sunderland Railway to carry out its deviation plan and make its branches; finally, the Durham Junction Railway was authorised to build a branch to Houghton-le-Spring.

Although the Great North of England directors had deliberately obtained the Act for their Darlington to Newcastle line a year before that for the Croft-York section, in the intervening year practically no work was done on the former, and by 1837 work was so well forward on the York & North Midland line that it was decided for the time being to concentrate all possible energy on the section from Darlington to York, in the hope of being able to link up with the Y. & N.M. directly the latter was opened. So, although contracts had been let for some of the works on the Northern section, the first sod of the new lines that was cut, on 25th November, 1837, was at Croft, south of Darlington. In the event, however, the Great North of England was well behind time; the York & North Midland, as we have seen, was opened throughout its length on 30th June, 1840, but it was not until 4th January, 1841, that the G.N.E. was able to begin freight traffic between Darlington and York, while passenger trains did not start to run until 30th March of that year.

Yet the Great North of England engineering work had been of a relatively simple description. Of earthworks there were few, the only ones of any size being the cutting between Croft and Dalton (later known as Eryholme) and the embankment past Northallerton. The only bridges of any note were the four-span masonry bridge, 471ft long – at that time one of the biggest skew bridges in the country – across the Tees at Croft, and a three-span masonry bridge across the Ouse at Nether Poppleton, just north of York. The choice of the latter site had been opposed by the York & North Midland, for its location was such as to deprive them of the opportunity of using the same bridge for their extension from York to Scarborough.

The Great North of England joined the York & North Midland just outside the city wall, near what is the south-east corner of the present York station. Inside the wall a fine station was built jointly by the two companies, at a cost of £47,000, the Y. & N.M. paying slightly the larger share because their offices were located in the station building. This structure, faced with polished stone, fronted Tanner Row, and led to a train shed 300ft long and 100ft wide. Despite its size, this at first was provided with two platforms only, one for arrivals and one for departures.

Access to it by rail was through a handsome pointed archway, still in existence, pierced through the city wall, by permission of the York Corporation, who had to be paid £500 for the privilege. The Great North of England also laid a freight line outside the wall to a quay on the River Ouse, from which a second arch, through the Bar Wall, gave access to a coal depot and goods wharf near the North Postern. For the time being a temporary station at Bank Top, Darlington, had to serve as the northern terminus. In a report presented to the Great North of England directors by Robert Stephenson it was stated that, over a course which was as nearly as possible level, the railway had been laid on 'straight lines to an extent unparalleled in this country'.

The first trains to pass over the new railway were two carrying coal, made up of no fewer than 99 and 101 wagons respectively, on 4th January, 1841. Four Stockton & Darlington locomotives – the *Pilot, Witton Castle, Magnet* and *Tory* – two to each train, succeeded in covering the 44 miles at an average speed of 15 m.p.h. deducting a wait of two hours at Thirsk while the debris of a fallen overline arch was being cleared away. This, incidentally, was not the only casualty of its kind, and after several more bridges had collapsed, the engineer, Thomas Storey, resigned. His successor was Robert Stephenson, and it was under the latter's supervision that the railway was completed.

This was in time for the formal opening for passenger traffic, which, as stated previously, took place on 30th March, 1841. On the opening day two trains were worked from Darlington to York, one of seven coaches and the other of sixteen. For the occasion the Manchester & Leeds Railway had loaned a species of observation car called the *Gondola*, about 18ft long; the sides were of plate glass with silk curtains and the furniture comprised mahogany sofas upholstered with plush. At each end the car had an open observation platform. The locomotive builders, R. & W. Hawthorn, had supplied the locomotives; *Wensleydale* ran ahead as a pilot, and the trains were drawn by *Ouse* and *Leeds*.

There was no great haste, as the journey, including stops, lasted nearly three hours, but on the return a special train carrying Joseph Pease, who had reached York too late to join either of the inaugural trains, made the run at an average speed of 26 m.p.h. He was in time to join the other celebrants at a dinner party held in the Kings Head Hotel at Darlington. By this time a total of 425 route miles had been opened for traffic by 15 different railways in North-Eastern England, all eventually to become a part of the North Eastern Railway.

Reference was made a little earlier to the plan in 1836 of Christopher Tennant and his Stockton friends to connect that town by rail with the Hartlepool Dock & Railway, and beginning in May, 1839, apparently without any parliamentary sanction, this line had been carried to completion by 9th Feburary, 1841. It built its own station on the east side of the Norton Road at Stockton, but used the metals of the Clarence Railway as far as Billingham; here it diverged to travel for 8 miles through Greatham and Seaton Carew to Hartlepool, and ended at the south-east corner of the Tide Harbour Wall. One quite substantial work along its length was a 700-yard viaduct of 92 arches resting on timber piles, across the marshes at Greatham.

With the help of this line a passenger could now travel by a Stockton & Darlington Railway train from Darlington to the S. & D. station at Stockton and from there by omnibus to the Stockton & Hartlepool station; the latter railway and the Durham & Sunderland then carried the passenger on to Sunderland, with a change of train at Haswell (because the Hartlepool Railway would not permit any through running); next came resort to another omnibus, across the River Wear to Monkwearmouth, to join the Brandling Junction Railway train for Redheugh, from which a final omnibus excursion was needed across the Tyne into Newcastle. After the opening of the first section of the Great North of England Railway a hardy traveller could leave York at 6 a.m., Darlington at 8.45 a.m., Stockton at 9.30 a.m., Hartlepool at 10.30 a.m., Sunderland at 1 p.m., and finally, changing at 2.30 p.m. into a Newcastle & Carlisle train at Redheugh, could arrive, completely exhausted, in Carlisle by 5.30 p.m.!

By contrast, the G.N.E. main line in 1845 was the *venue* of some important speed trials conducted as part of an enquiry by a Royal Commission set up in that year to decide the relative merits of the standard 4ft 8½in railway gauge and the 7ft broad gauge of the Great Western Railway. The narrow gauge advocates were represented by a Stephenson long-boiler 4-2-0 locomotive known as 'A', which on the last day of 1845 ran a 50-ton train from York to Darlington at an average of 48 m.p.h.; later it worked 80 tons over the same course at 43¼ m.p.h., and with 40 tons attained a maximum of 60 m.p.h. On the second day No. 54 of the York & North Midland Railway, which also was tested, had a less happy experience, as she left the track at speed and turned right over.

The Great Western contestants, which were tried out between Paddington and Didcot, proved considerably superior to their rivals, notwithstanding the less sporting methods of the narrow gauge protagonists, such as charging their locomotive's boiler with water that was nearly boiling, flying starts and various other devices. Of these the most sinister was the substitution at Paddington, under the cover of night, of sand for grease in some of the axleboxes of the Great Western test train. Even so, the issue could hardly be in doubt seeing that by that date 2,013 miles of standard gauge track had been laid as compared with 223 miles only of the broad gauge. The Royal Commission, therefore, while commending the Great Western locomotive performance, reported to Parliament in 1846 that it would be advisable not to sanction any further 7ft gauge projects in Britain.

CHAPTER IX

The Newcastle & Darlington Junction Railway

IN building the southern portion of its authorised main line, from York to Darlington, the Great North of England Railway had used up the whole of its authorised capital, with practically nothing done on the northern section, and no money left to carry on northwards. But by now the need for a direct line between Darlington and Newcastle was becoming so urgent that another company, the Northern Union Railway, had been promoted in 1839, and had given notice in February, 1840, of its intention to seek parliamentary powers to carry out this work.

Some complicated negotiations followed, in which George Hudson and Joseph Pease were both much to the fore, in coming to a decision as to the most suitable route. In particular, the Stockton & Darlington and the Clarence Railways, which were almost continuously at loggerheads, were both anxious that parts of their lines should be used for the purpose. By 1841 the matter was becoming doubly urgent, for Parliament had appointed a Commission to report on future railway communication between England and Scotland, and the Commissioners were inclined to favour the West Coast rather than the East Coast route, which, as mentioned in Chapter VIII, for some time past had been causing concern in the York camp.

A meeting was, therefore, convened at Newcastle on 30th April, 1841, with George Hudson in the chair, and deputations present from all the railways between Rugby and the Tyne, eight in number, that were concerned in the establishment of an East Coast route to Scotland. At this meeting it was decided to prepare without delay for a direct railway from Darlington to Newcastle, using existing lines as far as possible in order to reduce to a minimum the new construction needed. Robert Stephenson was engaged to survey and select the best possible route.

His proposal was to follow from Darlington the original Great North of England course authorised by Parliament as far as Brafferton, near Aycliffe, diverging slightly to the west of it for part of the distance, but at Preston-le-Skerne to bear well away to the east; later, the line would parallel the Sherburn branch of the Clarence Railway and finally join this at Mainsforth, the present Ferryhill. From Thrislington new construction would be resumed northwards to join the Durham Junction Railway at Rainton, to the north-east of Durham City, and Durham Junction metals would then be followed to the junction of that railway with the Stanhope & Tyne near Washington. The final stage would be to where the Stanhope & Tyne crossed the Brandling Junction line on the level at Brockley Whins, and here a new south-to-west curve would be laid in to give a direct run to Gateshead. This route from Darlington to Gateshead would be $7\frac{1}{2}$ miles longer than that which the Great North of England had been authorised by Parliament in 1836 to build, but it would cut the new construction down from $34\frac{1}{2}$ to $25\frac{1}{2}$ miles.

One railway, however, was considerably dissatisfied with these plans; it was the Stockton & Darlington. Why was it, Joseph Pease and his friends asked, that the existing railways whose lines were to be used were all to the north and east of the County of Durham – the rival Clarence Railway in particular – whereas no attention was being paid to possibilities in the south of the county? The Stockton & Darlington ran parallel to the proposed route for some distance out of Darlington, and 5 miles of it, as far as Simpasture, might well be used with an addition of no more than $1\frac{1}{2}$ miles to the length of the Newcastle & Darlington Junction Railway. Moreover, the Great North of England Railway, an essential link in the future south-to-north main line, had been built largely under Stockton & Darlington auspices and with the fruit of S. & D.R. engineering experience, and this company therefore felt that it was entitled to some say in the future development of what in the first place had been a Great North of England plan.

A public meeting at York in November, 1841, of the Newcastle & Darlington Junction Railway Company, however, rejected the Stockton & Darlington proposal, and though Joseph Pease continued by every means in his power to get part of his line incorporated in the scheme, he was up against a tougher character in the person of Hudson. Indeed, it is clear that already Hudson had made up his mind to get rid, if he could, of the Pease influence on railway development in North-Eastern England, even to the extent of the extreme measures that he took four years later, as described in Chapter XI, to obtain exclusive control of the Great North of England. Meantime he advanced as his reason why no part of the Stockton & Darlington Railway should be included in the Newcastle & Darlington Junction main line that so important a trunk route ought to be as independent as possible, though in the view of projected use of Clarence, Durham Junction, Stanhope & Tyne and Brandling Junction tracks this was a somewhat unconvincing argument.

It should be interpolated here that during these years the Stockton & Darlington Railway had been carrying out some very important developments. It had advanced the major proportion of the £120,000 spent at Middlesbrough in the building of a dock with a water area of 9 acres, and an entrance lock offering a depth of water of 15ft at neap tides and 19ft at spring tides, capable of accommodating up to 150 of the relatively small ships of the period. A branch of the S. & D.R. fanned out to form ten double-track sidings leading to a raised platform adjacent to the quay, on which 1,200 wagons could stand simultaneously. Along the quay were ten coal drops which could handle up to 105 tons of coal an hour between the wagons and the ships.

At the other extremity of its line the Stockton & Darlington had begun work on its Bishop Auckland & Weardale Railway extension, which Parlia-

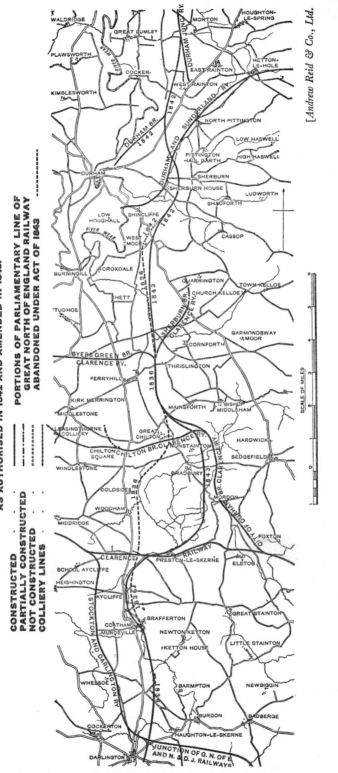

PLAN OF NEWCASTLE AND DARLINGTON JUNCTION RAILWAY,
AS AUTHORISED IN 1842 AND AMENDED IN 1843.

CONSTRUCTED
PARTIALLY CONSTRUCTED
NOT CONSTRUCTED
COLLIERY LINES

PORTIONS OF PARLIAMENTARY LINE OF
GREAT NORTH OF ENGLAND RAILWAY
ABANDONED UNDER ACT OF 1843

[Andrew Reid & Co., Ltd.

ment had authorised in 1837, including the costly double line Shildon Tunnel, 1,225 yards long, which was financed by a separate company. Completed in January, 1842, after nearly three years' work, this gave the S. & D.R. direct access to the Coundon Collieries, and also for passenger trains to a temporary terminus at South Church, or St Andrew Auckland.

From here, in May, 1842, a four-horse omnibus began to ply to and from Rainton, connecting there with the Durham Junction Railway trains to Gateshead *via* Brockley Whins. The through journey occupied 3¼ hours, and cost its patrons 8s. first and 6s. second class. In order to attract passengers reaching Darlington from the south away from the alternative route to Gateshead by the coast, already mentioned, the Stockton & Darlington management stationed a man daily at Darlington Bank Top station, so W. W. Tomlinson relates, to urge on them the superiority of the South Church and Rainton route.

When in the summer of 1842 the Newcastle & Darlington Junction Railway Bill came before Parliament, it was opposed by various groups, including, needless to say, the Stockton & Darlington Railway. Other opponents included the Dean and Chapter of Durham, who, regrettable to relate, were among the most grasping of all the landowners with whom the various railways in the County of Durham had to deal. Several of the lines from the Durham mines to the sea, described in Chapter V, had had to pay exorbitant sums to this ecclesiastical body for wayleaves over the latter's land, and now came a fresh example of rapacity. In 1836 the Dean and Chapter had sold some land to the Great North of England Company, when the latter was about to begin work on the route originally authorised, for £9,000, but when the original scheme was abandoned without the land having been touched, they bought it back for £1,300. Now, when the same 50 acres of land were required by the Newcastle & Darlington Junction Company, the Dean and Chapter demanded a price of £12,000, and this notwithstanding the fact that the land was required in part for the very branch of the railway to Durham City which this body had stipulated should be included in the scheme! Not surprisingly, the matter went to law; the railway company had offered £2,400 for the land, and eventually had to pay £3,500 instead of £12,000. Nevertheless the Dean and Chapter in the end had made a net total of £11,200 on the sale, which was pretty good going.

The opposing parties failed to influence either the House of Commons or the House of Lords, however, and the Newcastle & Darlington Bill went through, receiving the Royal Assent on 18th June, 1842. The Company was authorised to raise a share capital of £500,000, and a further £166,000 by loan. From Darlington to Shincliffe the Act laid it down that the original Great North of England route must be followed, without the later deviations; otherwise the line was as proposed, save for the stipulation that a branch must be laid to serve the City of Durham. However, in a second Act, of 16th April, 1843, the Company was authorised to include the deviations between Darlington and Shincliffe that had been proposed by Robert Stephenson. This Act covered other important developments also to which we shall come in a moment.

Even at this late stage Joseph Pease and the Stockton & Darlington party were reluctant to let go. Soon after the N. & D.J.R. Act became law, they approached the latter Company with an ingenious proposal that the Newcastle & Darlington should have the free use of 5 miles of Stockton & Darlington track, all maintenance charges included, on the basis that from 5 years after the passing of the Act the N. & D.J. should pay the S. & D. 6 per cent interest on half the amount estimated to have been saved by not building a corresponding 5 miles of new line, and after that the normal N. & D.J. dividend on the same sum. But this proposition was no more acceptable than any which had preceded it, and early in 1843, seven years after Joseph Pease and his friends had obtained the original Great North of England Act for the Darlington–Newcastle section, work on the Newcastle & Darlington Junction Railway began.

There might have been complications at this time due to the financial condition of certain of the railways which were to form a part of the new line. The Durham Junction Railway was working at a loss, and would not be able to find the £12,000 needed to lay a more substantial track over that part of its line to be used by the Newcastle & Darlington trains.

In even worse case was the Stanhope & Tyne Railway, which owned more than half the shares in the Durham Junction; with its whole succession of rope-worked inclined planes operation had proved so costly that the line was now practically bankrupt. Lime making at Stanhope had been abandoned and the section of line between there and Carrhouse was no longer in use, while other traffic had been lost. But in 1841 various financial interests had come to the rescue; the Company had been re-organised under a new Act obtained on 23rd May, 1842, as the Pontop & South Shields Railway; the quarries at Stanhope had been sold to the newly-established Derwent Iron Company at Consett; and substantial new traffic had helped to set the Pontop & South Shields Railway on its feet once again.

As to the Durham Junction, the problem was solved by an offer from George Hudson that the Newcastle & Darlington Junction should purchase the D.J.R. outright. The latter, of which Robert Stephenson was the Chairman, asked a price of £100,000, but Hudson refused to pay more than £88,500, the original cost of the line, and as usual he got his way. The second Newcastle & Darlington Junction Railway Act, that of 16th April, 1843 already mentioned, sanctioned the acquisition, and the final agreement between the two companies for the transfer was reached on 14th September of the same year. Certain companies which had acted as guarantors to the Durham Junction agreed to the cancellation of their rights to lease the line had they desired to do so.

There now remained the Brandling Junction Railway, which the Newcastle & Darlington trains would require to use from Brockley Whins into Gateshead. The financial state of the Stanhope & Tyne before its reorganisation as the Pontop & South Shields had prompted an investigation into Brandling Junction affairs also, with damaging results. It was revealed that the 6 per cent dividends which the directors had been handing out had been drawn from capital rather than from net revenue, and at this revelation Brandling Junction shares promptly fell to half their previous value. In this case also reorganisation at the management level, and additional sources of traffic, helped to give the railway a new lease of life. In particular, the Brandling Junction took over from the Pontop & South Shields all the passenger and freight working between Brockley Whins and South Shields, and a new 1¼-mile spur between Harelaw and Tanfield Moor, giving access to the ironworks at Consett, brought in further traffic. But the Brandling Junction was not destined to remain independent for much longer.

Construction of the Newcastle & Darlington Railway proceeded with exceptional speed; indeed, its first section, the 2½ miles from Rainton to Belmont, with the 2½-mile City of Durham branch, was opened on 15th April, 1844, only fifteen months after the beginning of the work. Although some of the earthworks were heavy, particularly the 8oft deep cutting at Ferryhill, and averaged 70,000 cubic yards per route mile, the cost of the line worked out at no more than £15,000 per mile. Three high viaducts were constructed entirely in timber, the biggest of them, that over the Sherburn Valley, being 66oft long and with a maximum height of 7oft.

The second Newcastle & Darlington Act had authorised the building of an independent terminus at Gateshead, and for this an excellent site was obtained in Greenesfield, overlooking the Tyne; the handsome station building, designed architecturally on Ionic lines, fronted the train shed, 352ft long and 88ft wide, which housed two passenger platforms. A vastly more important development also authorised by the second Act was the building of a high level bridge across the Tyne from Gateshead into Newcastle, but this problem was to be tackled later, as described in Chapter X.

The first train to carry the directors through from York to Gateshead made the journey on 24th May, 1844, but the date fixed for the public opening of the Newcastle & Darlington Junction Railway was 18th June of that year. At long last through railway communication had been established between London and Newcastle, and what this meant was demonstrated in no uncertain fashion on the opening day. For a special train which had started from Euston terminus in London at 5.3 a.m., and travelled via Rugby, Leicester, Derby, Chesterfield, Normanton, York and Darlington, made its way into the Gateshead terminus at 2.24 p.m.; deducting stoppages totalling 70 minutes the actual running time for the distance of 303 miles had been 8 hours 11 minutes, which meant an average speed throughout of 37 m.p.h. No doubt it was a very light train, for its passengers numbered nine only.

To accommodate the many North of England guests taking part in the opening celebrations, three trains of six coaches apiece, drawn by the locomotives *Nathaniel Ogle*, *Brandling* and *Mountain*, and preceded by *Edinburgh* as pilot, were run from Gateshead to Darlington, there to meet a special train which had brought from York George Hudson and a large party of directors and other celebrities. At Darlington a massive train of 39 first

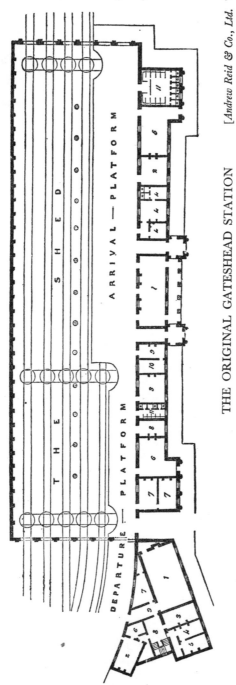

[*Andrew Reid & Co., Ltd.*

THE ORIGINAL GATESHEAD STATION

class carriages – including the Manchester & Leeds Railway's handsome observation coach *Gondola* described in Chapter VIII – was made up for the return journey, and was triple-headed by the locomotives *Wear*, *Glasgow* and *Edinburgh*. A stop was made at Sherburn Viaduct to enable the company to view this notable engineering work, and after some delay in back-shunting the train over the north-to-west curve at Brockley Whins – the new south-to-west spur not yet being ready – Gateshead was reached at 4.30 p.m.

The customary dinner followed, and in many ways was a notable occasion. In reply to a congratulatory address from a member of the Gateshead Corporation, Hudson stressed the fact that never before in British history had a distance of over 300 miles been covered in so short a time as that of the special from London that day. John Bright expatiated on the far-reaching consequences, both economic and social, that would follow the building of railways. And George Stephenson himself kept the company spellbound as he described how thirty years earlier he had built his first Killingworth engine.

One of those present, who five months previously had been appointed Manager of the Junction lines, was James Allport, destined to become famous in later years as General Manager of the Midland Railway and to receive a knighthood. Another was Henry Tennant, a future General Manager and Vice-Chairman of the North Eastern Railway. Regular passenger service over the Newcastle & Darlington Junction Railway began on the following day, 22nd February, 1844, with Great North of England locomotives used throughout between Gateshead and York. The first publicly advertised time between Gateshead and London, including $2\frac{3}{4}$ hours spent at intermediate stops, was $12\frac{1}{2}$ hours.

It was not for long that Hudson was prepared to let his trains work over independent lines, and a month after the opening of the Newcastle & Darlington Junction Railway he gave notice to the Brandling Junction directors that he intended to buy their line outright. The latter's prospects had improved to such an extent, as a result of additional traffic, and in particular the use of their lines by N. & D.J.R. trains, that they were not prepared to agree at anything less than a prohibitive price. But they had under-estimated their George Hudson, who at the next Newcastle & Darlington half-yearly meeting announced that he was having surveys made for an independent line, 13 miles long, from Washington on the Pontop & South Shields line direct to Gateshead, which would both shorten the N. & D.J.R. journey by 3 miles and also obviate any use of Brandling Junction tracks.

Within eight days of this announcement the Brandling Junction directors were approaching Hudson to sell out, and on his terms. Actually he bought the Brandling line in his own name, but on 16th August, 1844, the smaller company was transferred to the Newcastle & Darlington, and on 1st September the latter took possession, closing the former Brandling Junction terminus at Oakwellgate, Gateshead, and concentrating all the traffic at their new Greenesfield station. On 19th August, 1844, the new

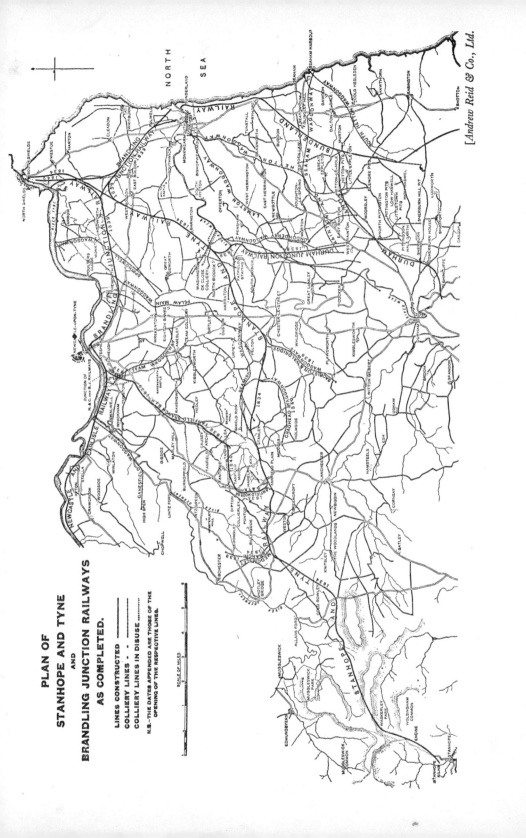

PLAN OF
STANHOPE AND TYNE
AND
BRANDLING JUNCTION RAILWAYS
AS COMPLETED.

LINES CONSTRUCTED ————
COLLIERY LINES - - - -
COLLIERY LINES IN DISUSE ·········

N.B.—THE DATES APPENDED ARE THOSE OF THE
OPENING OF THE RESPECTIVE LINES.

SCALE OF MILES

[Andrew Reid & Co., Ltd.

south-to-west curve at Brockley Whins, which had been built jointly by the Newcastle & Darlington and Pontop & South Shields Railways, was brought into use. Up to that time it had been necessary for trains from the south to proceed over the level crossing with the Brandling Junction line towards South Shields, and then to back round the north-to-west spur into Brockley Whins station, from which the engines had to work tender first into Gateshead. But this delay, which had lasted for two months, was now at an end, and a proportionate quickening of the journey was possible.

The Brandling Junction acquisition left only the Pontop & South Shields and Clarence Railways as independent concerns providing parts of the route followed by Newcastle & Darlington Junction Railway trains. By 1845, however, Hudson had succeeded in arranging to purchase the Pontop & South Shields for the N. & D.J.R., less the latter's colliery properties, which were otherwise disposed of, though possession was not taken until 1st January, 1847. For the time being the Clarence Railway still retained its independence, and the Great North of England continued to separate the Hudson-controlled lines north of Darlington from his growing empire south of York.

Newcastle Central Station, of which the central portion was opened in 1850. *Above,* the two main through platforms, with carriage roads between. *Below,* the frontage on Neville Street, which remains but little altered. [*Both, British Railways*

Notable viaducts on the Whitby, Redcar & Middlesbrough Union Railway. *Above*, Kilton Viaduct, between Skinningrove and Loftus, in later years replaced by a solid embankment because of subsidence trouble due to iron ore mining *Below*, the 152ft-high Staithes Viaduct, 700ft. in length. [*Both, British Railways*

Typical scenery on the coast line between Saltburn, Whitby and Scarborough. *Above*, Sandsend Viaduct, with a local train headed by a Class 'D' 4-6-2 (rebuilt from 4-4-4) tank. *Below*, a coast train climbing the dreaded 1 in 39 of Ravenscar bank.

[*E. R. Wethersett, British Railways*

Darlington Bank Top Station. *Above*, the approach from the south; the station, looped off the main line, can be seen to the right of the signalbox, with the clock tower behind. *Below*, interior, showing south end of the up platform and bay platforms to the left.

[Both, British Railways

CHAPTER X

From Newcastle to Berwick and the
High Level Bridge

WE have now to transfer our attention from the south to the north side of the River Tyne. The next serious step in the development of the East Coast Route to Scotland had been preceded by some years by the opening in 1839 of the first public railway in Northumberland, from Newcastle to North Shields. The idea had originated as far back as 1830 in North Shields but as usual in these early days had met with strong opposition.

Newcastle, it was claimed, might lose some of its maritime importance by cargoes landing at and being shipped from North Shields and the number of men employed on the river would be reduced; proprietors of coaches and river packets would lose money by the diversion of their trade, as also landowners deriving revenue from wayleaves; North Shields shop-keepers would lose trade because of their townspeople going into Newcastle instead to shop; and it was even argued by Tynemouth lodging-house owners that no Newcastle residents would spend summer holidays in their town if they could take the train to Tynemouth, have a bathe, and be back by breakfast time!

Despite strong arguments as to the excellent prospects of such a line, however, two rival parties failed to agree as to the best route, and the same thing seemed likely to happen again when the project was revived in 1833. But eventually the rival schemes were submitted to an independent arbitrator, who reported in favour of a route beginning at Shield Field, Newcastle, crossing the Ouseburn Valley with a viaduct, and continuing through Old Walker and Wallsend to Saville Street, North Shields. In the final scheme, adopted on 7th October, 1835, the 1,600-yard tunnel first proposed under Byker Hill was to be avoided by a deviation and the branch from Percy Main to a proposed new dock at Coble Dene was to run instead to the steam ferry terminal at North Shields; while in 1836, instead of a branch to Tynemouth, it was decided that the main line should be continued to that town.

The Duke of Northumberland tried to have introduced into the Bill a clause which would bar the railway from carrying coal without the consent of adjoining landowners – in order to prevent diversion of coal traffic from any existing wagonways – but eventually it was agreed that a toll of ¾d. per ton of coal per mile should be levied on the railway as landowners' compensation. With this inclusion the Bill for the Newcastle & North Shields Railway passed both Houses of Parliament and received the Royal Assent on 21st June, 1836.

Two viaducts of exceptional note for the period had to be built, across the Ouseburn Valley and Willington Dene respectively. The Ouseburn Viaduct, 918ft long, had three arches of 116ft span and two of 114ft, flanked by smaller masonry arches, and at its maximum was 108ft above the valley. Willington Dene Viaduct, though 1,048ft long, was not quite so high, being 82ft above ground at the deepest part of the valley; it had one 128ft arch, four of 120ft and two of 115ft, seven arches in all. The design was similar to the Wiebeking system of laminated timber arches, resting on masonry piers, that had been applied successfully in building the Pont d'Ivry across the Seine in Paris; each arch was built up from three parallel ribs, every rib comprising fourteen layers of 22in by 3½in planks pinned together by bolts and wooden trenails, and with the ribs tied by transverse bolts and diagonal braces. A pair of stout timber diagonals extended from the crown of each arch to the upper part of the adjacent piers, and radiating struts helped both to provide strength and also to maintain the correct distance between the arch and the bridge floor above. The whole had a most graceful appearance, and it is not surprising that these viaducts attracted considerable attention from both engineers and the public.

A short tunnel had to be traversed immediately after leaving the terminus at Newcastle, and it was proposed to provide this with gates at both ends and to use it at night as a carriage shed. The biggest earthwork on the line was the Pandon Dene embankment, with a maximum height of 80ft. No fewer than nine wagonways between adjacent coal-mines and the Tyne had to be crossed in the first 3½ miles, which explains the concern of their owners as to possible loss of part of their revenue by transfer of coal carriage to the railway. At the time of completion a temporary terminus had to be used in Newcastle, at one corner of Carliol Square; a permanent station had been planned in Pilgrim Street, but later this scheme was abandoned in favour of the Central Station, described later in this chapter.

18th June, 1839, was fixed for the opening ceremony and as with the official opening of the Newcastle & Carlisle Railway precisely one year to the day earlier, the proprietors were most unkindly treated by the weather. Two trains had been assembled, partly of covered and partly of open stock, and the Hawthorn locomotives *Wellington* and *Hotspur* made morning and afternoon trips along the line respectively. It had been arranged to entertain some 700 ladies and gentlemen in a large marquee in the grounds of Tynemouth House, and there the party assembled between 4 and 5 o'clock in the afternoon.

An hour later there broke one of the most violent thunderstorms in living memory, with a deluge of rain which soon began to penetrate all the crevices in the canvas. The ladies were shepherded for shelter into the house, but the proceedings continued in the partially flooded marquee, toast list and all, until at about 6.30 p.m. the two trains set off for Newcastle with as many of the drenched company as they could carry. A second journey had to be made to collect the remainder. Regular passenger service began on the following day. The Tynemouth extension, however, was not ready for traffic until 29th March, 1847.

Meantime various minds had been concentrating on the far greater enterprise of railway communication between Newcastle and Edinburgh, eventually to form a link in the East Coast chain. A company was being formed in Scotland in 1836 for a railway over the 29 miles from Edinburgh to Dunbar, and this plan was prompting consideration by various parties in Newcastle of a line from the south to link up with it. At a meeting in Berwick in July, 1836, a resolution was passed in favour of making a 'Grand Eastern Union Railway' to follow somewhat the same course as the present East Coast main line from Newcastle, passing within short distances of Morpeth, Warkworth and Alnwick to Tweedmouth, crossing the Tweed by a high level bridge to Berwick, and then continuing through Reston and Grantshouse to Dunbar.

A rival proposal, strongly favoured by the Newcastle & Carlisle Railway, was to use that line as far as Hexham and then to proceed up the North Tyne Valley and over Carter Fell – a route which George Stephenson described as 'totally impracticable'. But the rivals were not to be deterred by this opinion; instead they broadened their plan by including branches to Kelso, Selkirk, Hawick, and even Glasgow, though to some extent modifying their original route at the same time.

Nothing appears to have been done until 1844, however, when the need for this main line was becoming more and more urgent. The Lancaster & Carlisle Railway had obtained its Act on 6th June of this year, and the fierce struggle between the protagonists of two rival routes between Carlisle and Glasgow was approaching the settlement which was to permit the incorporation of the Caledonian Railway in the following year. The completion of the West Coast Route to Scotland, and a very direct route at that, was foreshadowed at an early date, whereas the hoped-for East Coast Route still had a gap of some 125 miles between Newcastle and Edinburgh, not to mention its circuitous nature south of York and dependence on the rival route for access to London over London & Birmingham metals from Rugby.

George Hudson now bestirred himself. The Scottish Edinburgh–Dunbar plans at this date had extended to a 'Great North British Railway', promoted in 1843, for a line from Edinburgh through to Berwick, to whose capital Hudson arranged for the York & North Midland Railway to contribute £50,000. By now the Newcastle & Berwick Railway Company had been formed, and Hudson came to an agreement in November, 1844, with the Newcastle & North Shields Railway for the amalgamation of the latter with the Newcastle & Berwick, the N. & N.S. continuing to operate independently for the time being.

Trouble was being experienced by the Newcastle & Berwick promoters due to the opposition of Lord Howick, whose property was likely to be interfered with by the route for the railway which George Stephenson recommended. Lord Howick now decided to back a rival 'Northumberland Railway' scheme, with a different line which would avoid his property. Hudson, against Stephenson's advice, offered to vary the Newcastle & Berwick route, even at the cost of steeper gradients and increased cost, to avoid Lord Howick's land, but Howick was now committed to the rival line.

Fortunately for Hudson and his party, however, the Northumberland Railway was proposing to use the atmospheric system of traction that was being installed on the London & Croydon Railway, and the House of Lords Committee decided that the reliability of this method of traction had not been proved sufficiently to warrant its use on a railway of such length as that now proposed. Lord Howick's party therefore withdrew their opposition, and on 31st July, 1845, the Newcastle & Berwick Railway obtained the Royal Assent to its Act.

But even when the Newcastle & Berwick line had been completed, and the main trunk line had reached Gateshead from the south, there would still remain the vast problem of bridging the Tyne gorge between Gateshead and Newcastle. The question had first been examined as far back as 1836. Before their bridge had been built higher up the river at Scotswood, the Newcastle & Carlisle Railway had wanted to join with the Brandling Junction and the Great North of England in building a low level bridge at Redheugh, with an inclined plane on the north side of the river to get the trains up into Newcastle.

The engineer Thomas Storey, however, proposed a high level bridge, 74ft in level above high water, which though far more costly would do away with inclined plane working on both sides of the river, and this the Great North of England and the Brandling Junction both favoured, as also did George Stephenson. On the north side of the river a line was proposed to connect with the Newcastle & North Shields Railway. It should be added that a company had already been formed, with capital of £125,000, to build a high level suspension bridge between Gateshead and Newcastle for road traffic.

During the next seven years neither plan had progressed any further. The Newcastle & Darlington Railway, which had replaced what was to have been the northern section of the Great North of England, was approaching completion into Gateshead, and plans for the Newcastle & Berwick were well under way. The construction of a high level railway bridge had therefore now become a matter of the first importance. George Stephenson having expressed the opinion that the best site for the bridge would be between Greenesfield, Gateshead, and Castle Garth, on the Newcastle side, a company was formed to build it; George Hudson and George Stephenson were both appointed to join the management committee and Robert Stephenson to act as consulting engineer.

In the end, however, it was the Newcastle & Darlington Junction Railway which in its second Act, of 16th April, 1843, obtained parliamentary sanction both to build its Greenesfield station at Gateshead and also the long-wanted high level bridge across the Tyne. Also the Newcastle & Darlington and Newcastle & Berwick Railways decided to build the bridge at their own expense, so that it should be under their own exclusive control, rather than that it should be financed and built by a separate company.

The 1836 company formed to build a road suspension bridge apparently had got no further with its plans, and at the end of 1844 George Hudson therefore approached the Town Improvement Committee of Newcastle to lay his plans before them, proposing that a double-decked bridge should be built to accommodate both the rail and the road traffic. The result was a unanimous decision by the Newcastle Corporation to support the Newcastle & Berwick Railway Bill, which was not to receive parliamentary approval until the following year. From the high level bridge the railway would be carried on a viaduct into a large Central Station south of Neville Street, which would be shared with the Newcastle & Carlisle Railway. Another line would be constructed to connect with the Newcastle & North Shields Railway at Pilgrim Street, and this exit also would form the first section of the Newcastle & Berwick Railway.

Construction of the Newcastle & Berwick line proceeded with fair rapidity. The first section, of 14½ miles from a junction with the Newcastle & North Shields Railway at Heaton to Morpeth, was opened on 1st March, 1847; the second portion, of 19¾ miles from Tweedmouth southwards to Chathill, followed suit on 29th March; while the remaining gap was closed with the opening, on 1st July, 1847, of the line between Morpeth and Chathill. Viaducts were required over the Blyth, Wansbeck, Coquet and Aln rivers, and the trains worked for a time over temporary wooden structures until the permanent masonry bridges were ready. For the time being also the trains had to use the Newcastle & North Shields terminus at Carliol Square until the new Central Station was ready; between here and Gateshead passengers were carried across the Tyne by omnibus.

Just as the Tyne gorge still formed a gap between the Newcastle & Darlington and Newcastle & Berwick Railways, so at the north end of the latter line there was the wide gap of the Tweed Valley. The North British Railway had opened its line from Edinburgh to Berwick by 18th June, 1846, more than a year before the Newcastle & Berwick had come into operation throughout its length, but as yet 'Berwick' in the latter title was a terminus of the Northumberland line that existed only on paper. Not until 15th May, 1847, was the foundation stone laid of the Royal Border Bridge between Tweedmouth and Berwick, and nearly three years elapsed before the keystone of the last arch was built in.

Robert Stephenson was the engineer, and it is a tribute to the ability with which he carried out his work that today, well over a century since the viaduct was opened for traffic, after no more than a normal amount of maintenance it is carrying trains of a weight and speed undreamed of in his time. This magnificent structure, the largest of its kind that had been built up to that date, had 28 semi-circular arches of 61ft 6in span, carried on piers which gave the bridge a maximum height, from the river bed to the parapets, of 126ft. The overall length was 2,160ft and the total cost was £120,000. Freight traffic began to work over the viaduct on 20th July, 1850, but the formal opening did not take place until 29th August of the same year, when Queen Victoria, who was travelling up to Scotland on that day from Castle Howard on the York & Scarborough line, performed the ceremony. It was this distinguished lady who granted the railway permission to call its new viaduct the 'Royal' Border Bridge.

But Queen Victoria had already opened an even greater structure – the High Level Bridge across the Tyne, which had cost more than twice the Border Bridge. Robert Stephenson had been responsible for a unique design, that also still exists with but little variation from its original form. Between approach viaducts of masonry arches on both sides of the river he had built up five masonry piers, which between them and the approaches supported six spans of 125ft each; the total length of bridge and approaches was 1,337ft, and from high water mark to rail level there was a total height of 112ft, far greater than the 74ft proposed by Thomas Storey in 1836. Transverse arches lightened the weight of masonry on the supporting piers.

The main arches were in pairs of cast-iron construction, linked together by wrought-iron ties to counteract lateral thrust. A series of square iron pillars, hollow in cross-section, stood on the arches across their width to carry the weight of longitudinal girders, which in their turn carried the cross-bearers supporting the upper bridge floor on which the trains ran. From below the arches ran similar pillars carrying by suspension the public roadway, which was 22ft 7½in below the railway level. In all, exclusive of the cost of land, the High Level Bridge cost £243,000. Trains first begun to cross it on 15th August, 1849, but the formal opening by Queen Victoria, already mentioned, took place on a journey which she was making southwards from Scotland on 28th September of the same year.

Finally there was the Central Station at Newcastle, financed jointly by what at its opening had become the York, Newcastle & Berwick Railway – an amalgamation to be describe in Chapter XI – and the Newcastle & Carlisle Railway, which entered it at the west end. It was one of the finest stations in Great Britain at the time of its construction. Its architect, John Dobson, had planned a colonnade of classic design which would have extended the whole length of the 594ft frontage to Neville Street, with a massive portico in the centre, but eventually the design was modified, partly for reasons of economy, and partly because it had been decided to transfer the office staff of the York, Newcastle & Berwick Railway from York to a more central location in the station building at Newcastle.

Even so, the Doric frontage eventually adopted was very impressive. The arched station roof was in three bays each 60ft wide, and from end to end was on the graceful curve which still remains. The station was opened by Queen Victoria on the same day as the Royal Border Bridge at Berwick, 29th August, 1850. On the day following, York, Newcastle & Berwick trains began to use the station, which for them was terminal, as trains from both York and Berwick entered from the east, and those running through required to reverse. Newcastle & Carlisle Railway trains, on the other hand, entered from the west, though their line of access was not ready until 1st January, 1851.

It should be added that the spur line from Washington direct to Pelaw, just east of Gateshead, with which George Hudson had threatened the former Brandling Junction Railway directors, had been opened in the same year, 1850, cutting out the previous circuit of York, Newcastle & Berwick Railway trains *via* Brockley Whins. In this way the approach to Newcastle from the south had been still further improved.

CHAPTER XI

The Rise and Fall of George Hudson

At long last a through East Coast main line had now come into operation between York, Newcastle, Berwick and Edinburgh, but the continuation southwards over what was to be its final course as yet was far from complete. By April, 1850, Great Northern Railway trains had certainly begun to run into York, but over a route *via* Boston, Lincoln, Gainsborough, Retford, Doncaster, Knottingley and Church Fenton, that was even more circuitous than the one from Euston *via* the Midland and York & North Midland Railways that had been in use up to that time. By far the most notable happening of the 1840s, however, had been the meteoric rise to fame of George Hudson, the 'Railway Mania', and the downfall of the one who had been its foremost instigator.

Now that railway transport had proved its almost immeasurable advantages over horse traction, a fever of railway promotion and speculation had set in. By November, 1845, *The Times* estimated that some 620 railway schemes were on foot, the cost of which, if carried out, would amount to over £563,000,000. In the years 1844, 1845 and 1846 the Royal Assent was given to 438 Bills authorising the construction of 8,470 miles of railway, at a total estimated expenditure of £180,138,901. The rush of investors to get rich quickly was almost unbelievable. All classes of the community fought one another to grab shares – from titled people at one extreme to mill operatives and even parsons at the other. Lord Clanricarde told the House of Lords of a broker's clerk, son of a charwoman and earning no more than twelve shillings a week, who by some means or other had his name down for shares on the London & York Railway to a total of £52,000! Such was the extent of gambling in shares that 100,000 might change hands at Leeds in a single day.

Many of the vast network of lines projected offered a competitive menace to railways already established. In the first volume of his *British Railway History* C. Hamilton Ellis has described the subterfuges adopted by some of the railway promoters to keep their plans secret. Any railway thus threatened might refuse the promoters of a rival scheme, on their way to London to deposit their plans, permission to use its trains. One group, we are told, actually encased its plans in a coffin, which, after being carried to London by the very railway which had declined to convey the backers of the scheme, was conducted reverently from the railway terminus to the Board of Trade in a hearse attended by numerous 'mourners'! Opponents of new schemes did not hesitate to use violence, including the stealing of horses and the wrecking of coaches.

Now in order to be able to wield a greater influence in Parliament

George Hudson, already as we have seen three times Lord Mayor of York and Chairman of the York Banking Company, succeeded in 1845 in getting himself elected as Conservative Member of Parliament for Sunderland. Other railway magnates of this time had done the same thing; Daniel Gooch of the Great Western Railway, for example, had become Member of Parliament for the Cricklade Division of Wiltshire and Joseph Locke of the Grand Junction and other lines was elected to represent Honiton. But history reveals that the railway interests of these men took a far higher priority than any concern for their constituents. As for Hudson and Sunderland, however, it may be said that Monkwearmouth, the Sunderland terminus on the other side of the River Wear, did at least obtain a fine station building in celebration of his election.

By the middle 1840s Hudson had risen to the highest pinnacle of his fame. Sidney Smith, an eminent preacher at that time, dubbed him the 'Railway King'. He was the idol of the public; in the highest circles in London he was *persona grata*; he was even in favour, it is said, with Albert, the Prince Consort. He had little difficulty in swaying hard-headed business men or parliamentary committees. In two days alone he induced various companies to promote a total of forty railway Bills involving an expenditure of £10,000,000, which with the value of money today might have been three or four times that sum. It was said of Hudson by an observer that 'he walked quietly through Parliament with sixteen railway Bills under his arm'. But he had his enemies, needless to say, and in 1845 the empire that he had established was beginning to be threatened from various directions.

Hudson by now was Chairman of the influential Midland Railway, formed in the previous year by amalgamation of the Midland Counties, Birmingham & Derby Junction and North Midland Railways; also of the York & North Midland and Newcastle & Darlington Junction Railways and the newly-formed Newcastle & Berwick Railway. In the south he had just been appointed Chairman of the Eastern Counties Railway, and was busily engaged in promoting extensions of the latter. But this empire had its gaps. As yet Joseph Pease was still in control of the Great North of England Railway, from York to Darlington, separating the York & North Midland from the Newcastle & Darlington, and the Clarence Railway, used for some distance by the latter's trains, was not yet in Hudson's hands.

By far the biggest threat to Hudson was that offered by the Great Northern Railway, which after a two-year battle against the fiercest opposition, led by Hudson and also Carr Glyn and Captain Mark Huish of the London & Birmingham Railway, obtained the Royal Assent to its Act on 26th June, 1846. While a direct main line from London to York by way of Peterborough, Grantham and Doncaster was a logical constituent of an east coast route from London to Scotland, it would, of course, divert the whole of the through traffic to the north-east from Hudson's Midland and York & North Midland Railways. There was also the possibility that at a later date the Great Northern Railway, on reaching York, might attempt to get possession of the still independent Great North of England as an extension of its main line towards Edinburgh; indeed, by 1845 over-tures had already been made from London to the G.N.E. as to whether a lease of the latter's line would be favourably entertained.

Such a happening Hudson was determined at all costs to prevent. He therefore approached the Great North of England directors with a pro-posal which he himself described as 'the hardest bargain he ever drove', and which the G.N.E. Board would have been foolish indeed to reject. It was that the Newcastle & Darlington Junction, York & North Midland and Midland Railways jointly should be granted a lease of the Great North of England by guaranteeing a return of 10 per cent on the latter's £100 and £40 shares from 1st July, 1845; 10 per cent on the £30 shares from 1st July, 1847; and 10 per cent on some £15 shares to be issued later from 1st July, 1850. The leasing railways would be at liberty to buy the Great North of England at any time, and after 1st July, 1850, could be compelled to do so by the latter, at two-and-a-half times the nominal value of each share, as, for example, £250 for each £100 share.

For the Great North of England shareholders this was indeed an amazing bargain. No doubt Joseph Pease and his Quaker friends did their utmost to prevent the line from coming under Hudson's control, but probably the offer was too tempting to be resisted by the majority of the shareholders, which accounts for its acceptance. Hudson himself realised that it was uneconomic, but as we have seen already in Chapter IX he was determined to free the York to Newcastle main line from all Stockton & Darlington influence, and to his railway empire the Great North of England was of such strategic importance that the course he was taking, despite the poor financial state of the G.N.E. Company, was unavoidable.

What it meant to Great North of England capital may be measured from the fact that whereas in July, 1843, G.N.E. shares stood at 37 discount and a year later at par, by July, 1845, when the agreement was reached, the £100 shares were being quoted at £144 each. So, from 1st July, 1845, the Newcastle & Darlington Junction Railway took over the working of the Great North of England. A year later the Newcastle & Darlington Junction alone – independently of the York & North Midland and Midland Railways – exercised the right to purchase the Great North of England, and on 27th July, 1846, obtained the Royal Assent to an Act authorising a change of name of the two lines to the York & Newcastle Railway. A year later still, on 9th August, 1847, a further Act sanctioned the amalgamation of the York & Newcastle and Newcastle & Berwick Railways as the York, Newcastle & Berwick Railway Company, the entire main line from York to the Scottish Border now coming under a single control.

In 1848 a threat came from Scotland in the opening of negotiations between the Caledonian and Newcastle & Carlisle Railways for the former to lease the latter's line; immediately Hudson stepped in with a better offer, of 6 per cent per annum for three years and 7 per cent in per-petuity from then onwards, which the Newcastle & Carlisle Railway directors accepted. So, by an agreement dated 5th July, 1848, the York,

Newcastle & Berwick took control of the Newcastle & Carlisle from 1st August of that year, though this was not an amalgamation.

Another lease authorised by the 27th July, 1846, Act was of the Hartlepool Dock & Railway Company, of which the York & Newcastle formally took possession on 12th August, together with its impressively named Great North of England, Clarence & Hartlepool Junction Railway branch (to Ferryhill); amalgamation of both with the York, Newcastle & Berwick took place under an Act dated 22nd July, 1848. The Durham & Sunderland Railway and the Wearmouth Dock had also been acquired, and passed into York & Newcastle Railway hands on 1st January, 1847. Thus the Hudson empire was expanding with great rapidity; but right across the centre of it there still stretched the completely independent Stockton & Darlington and Clarence Railways.

It will be remembered that the original plans for the Great North of England Railway included a branch from Pilmoor to Boroughbridge, Knaresborough and Harrogate. When the people of Leeds realised that the G.N.E. had made no suggestion of extending from Harrogate into their city, they were up in arms. No doubt the engineering difficulty that the extremely hilly intervening country would offer was in part an explanation, but be that as it may, Leeds citizens decided to promote a railway of their own, to give Leeds a direct outlet to the north. So in 1844 they prepared a Bill for a line from Leeds to Thirsk, with branches to Harrogate and Knaresborough. This was immediately countered by the Great North of England, which obtained the agreement of its shareholders to seek powers for the extension of its proposed Pilmoor–Harrogate branch to Leeds by way of Spofforth. But by the summer of 1845, when the Bills came before Parliament, Hudson at last had taken control of the Great North of England, and on his instructions their Bill was withdrawn, the Leeds party thus having the field to themselves. As a result, their Act received the Royal Assent on 21st July, 1845.

The ambitions of the Leeds & Thirsk Railway directors, however, extended considerably farther than Thirsk. Within a few months of cutting the first sod of the new line, they were preparing plans to extend their line by branching from Melmerby, just short of Thirsk, through Northallerton and Stockton to Billingham-on-Tees. Needless to say, this plan met with vigorous opposition from Hudson, who was determined as far as was possible to isolate Leeds. Having abandoned the Great North of England Pilmoor–Leeds plan he could no longer oppose the Leeds–Thirsk line, but he proposed that its traffic should be carried over what had now become the York & Newcastle from Thirsk through Darlington to Thrislington (Ferryhill) and from there over the metals of the Hartlepool Dock & Railway, which he had just leased.

Eventually, however, he had to agree to a compromise on a very much more limited scale, whereby the Leeds & Thirsk undertook to use the York & Newcastle tracks between Thirsk and Northallerton only, a distance of less than 8 miles, but insisted on building $20\frac{1}{2}$ miles of its own new line from Northallerton to Billingham, with three short connecting lines to the

Stockton & Darlington and Clarence Railways. The Royal Assent to the Leeds & Thirsk Act was given on 16th July, 1846, and it gave powers also to the company to acquire the Stockton & Hartlepool Railway.

Having got the bit between their teeth, so to speak, the Leeds &Thirsk board decided to attempt a further invasion of Hudson territory. This was to promote a line from Egglescliffe – the modern Eaglescliffe, just south of Stockton-on-Tees – to Stillington, there to join the Clarence Railway, and then a second line from Ferryhill through Durham to Newcastle. Hudson immediately announced, at the half-yearly meeting of the York & Newcastle Railway in July, 1846, that his company intended to seek parliamentary powers to build a new direct line through the Team Valley from Durham to Gateshead, thereby giving the Y. & N. trains a considerably more direct route into Newcastle.

His next move was an attempt to buy up the Clarence Railway, but after he had offered in succession amounts of £315,000 and £350,000, the Leeds & Thirsk directors completely outbid him with an offer of £450,000, which the Clarence Railway directors accepted. The parliamentary authorisation to the Leeds & Thirsk to purchase the Stockton & Hartlepool Railway also was followed up with an offer to the latter of £240,000. In the end, as we shall see later, the parliamentary powers were never used, and neither of the offers came to anything. But the rosy dream of the Leeds & Thirsk to reach Newcastle faded when its Bill for this extension, though backed by the Town Councils of Newcastle, Gateshead and Durham, was thrown out by Parliament in June, 1847.

Early in 1848 the first section of the Leeds & Thirsk Railway, from Ripon to Thirsk Town, with a connecting spur at Thirsk to what had now become the York, Newcastle & Berwick Railway, had come into use. Later in the same year further stretches had been opened, in succession from Wormald Green to Ripon and then from Wormald Green to Weeton. On the second of these, opened on 13th September, was Starbeck, which served the town of Harrogate, on high ground a mile to the west of this station. But Harrogate itself had already been reached by one of Hudson's lines, for on 20th July, 1848, a branch of the York & North Midland had been completed from Church Fenton through Wetherby to a station near the Brunswick Hotel in what was known as Low Harrogate. There was nothing particularly 'low' about its altitude, however, which could be attained only by means of an immense brick viaduct across the Crimple Valley, 110ft high at its maximum, with 31 arches each of 50ft span.

For similar reasons of engineering difficulty, the formal opening of the remaining section of the original Leeds & Thirsk Railway, between Weeton and Leeds, did not take place until 9th July, 1894. By far its biggest engineering work was Bramhope Tunnel, through the high ridge to the north of Leeds that forms the eastern prolongation of the famous Ilkley Moor. Approaching from the Leeds side by a $4\frac{1}{2}$-mile climb at 1 in 100, the line was carried down an even steeper 1 in 94 incline through the 3,761 yards (over 2 miles) of the tunnel – still today the eighth longest in Great Britain – to the valley of the Wharfe at Arthington.

Bramhope Tunnel, 25ft 6in wide and 25ft high, designed for a double track, was driven through shale and sandstone. Water gave serious difficulties in carrying out the work; during the boring the engineer estimated that over 1,563 million gallons were pumped out, and ever since water has proved troublesome in the tunnel maintenance. Five years after the opening, on 19th September, 1854, there was a serious accident from this cause. A section of the tunnel fell in, and the mass of fallen masonry and rubbish was run into by a south-bound train. The five rear coaches became detached by the shock and ran backwards down the 1 in 94, but the guard, though injured, managed to bring them to rest in Arthington station. Unfortunately, they were followed by a sixth coach, which ran at speed into the stationary five, a number of passengers being injured, though none was killed. The line was closed completely while tunnel repairs were in progress, and was not reopened for passenger traffic until 1st January, 1855.

Viaducts were needed to bridge the Aire in Leeds and the Wharfe between Arthington and Weeton, the former with 23 arches of 48ft span, and the latter with 21 of 60ft each. There were also some considerable earthworks, one of the cuttings being 126ft deep. For some time after its opening, the Leeds & Thirsk Railway contributed a useful amount of through traffic to the York, Newcastle & Berwick at Thirsk; construction from Northallerton onwards did not get under way until a later date. Meantime there had been happenings of the greatest importance south of York, to which we must now give our attention.

In Chapter VII mention was made of the promotion of the Wakefield, Pontefract & Goole Railway, as an extension to the North Sea port of the Manchester & Leeds Railway, and as a link at Selby with the Hull & Selby Railway – a move which prompted George Hudson in 1845 to obtain a lease of the Hull & Selby by the York & North Midland Railway. The Wakefield, Pontefract & Goole would also establish a link with the Great Northern Railway, which by the summer of 1846, as we have seen, had obtained its Act; the former would reach Selby by laying in a spur connection where it crossed the proposed Great Northern line between Heck and Templehirst. To protect his railway network, Hudson in 1844 therefore projected lines in all directions, in connection with the York & North Midland and Midland Railways, first from Milford Junction on the Y. & N.M. for 18½ miles to Doncaster, to join a line from Swinton to Lincoln and from there to Ely (to join the Eastern Counties Railway, of which he had now become the Chairman), and also from Lincoln to Nottingham and Syston to Peterborough.

But in 1847 there was a very significant happening. The Great Northern Railway was making its way northwards, and was about to continue from Doncaster to Askern, there to make an end-on junction with a branch which the Wakefield, Pontefract & Goole was pushing south-eastwards from Knottingley. In 1847, tucked away in an Act which authorised various York & North Midland Railway extensions, Hudson obtained powers to make a short branch from Burton Salmon, on the Y. & N.M., to a junction with the Wakefield, Pontefract & Goole at Knottingley. Its ostensible purpose was to give the Y. & N.M. access to the lime country round Knottingley, and also to provide a new passenger service for Knottingley inhabitants to and from Leeds and Hull. But there is little doubt that Hudson was looking a great deal farther than this.

This farseeing man realised that once the Great Northern Railway was complete, by the course originally proposed, it would afford a considerably shorter route from London to York and beyond than the existing route by way of the Midland and York & North Midland, *via* Leicester, Derby, Chesterfield and Normanton. Though the traffic to and from London would be lost to the Midland, and to a large part of the York & North Midland, when the G.N.R. was complete, some at least of it could be salved for the latter if it could be brought on to York & North Midland metals at Knottingley instead of proceeding direct from Doncaster to York *via* Selby. Denison of the Great Northern Railway equally had come to the conclusion that more than 25 miles of new construction could be saved by the use of Wakefield, Pontefract & Goole metals from Askern to Knottingley and those of the York & North Midland thence to York, if he could swallow his pride sufficiently to approach his arch-enemy Hudson for the necessary agreement.

So this momentous meeting took place near the end of 1848. Hudson himself had to make a crucial decision. He could have had a few illusions as to what the reaction of Midland and London & Birmingham shareholders would be if he agreed to Denison's proposal, but equally he was acute enough to realise, as we have seen already, that the direct route from King's Cross must eventually form an essential part of the East Coast Route to Scotland. So an agreement was reached between the two men. On condition that the G.N.R. abandoned its intention to build an independent line from Askern to York, the York & North Midland would grant the necessary running powers at a price of £1,000 annually for the use of York Station and the payment of 60 per cent of the G.N.R. earnings on all its traffic passing between Knottingley and York, after deduction of the Government duty – terms that were eased considerably for the Great Northern after Hudson's downfall.

The short link between Knottingley and Burton Salmon involved one engineering feat of note. It was the lengthy single span over the River Aire at Brotherton, designed by Robert Stephenson on the same lines as his Britannia Tubular Bridge over the Menai Strait, which was opened in the same year. For a year from April, 1850, when the spur was opened, the trains ran over a temporary wooden structure. On 8th August, 1850, the first through train of the Great Northern Railway from London, which had started from a temporary terminus at Maiden Lane, used the metals of the York & North Midland Railway to reach York.

But there was no ceremonial introduction of the new service, neither was there any George Hudson waiting at York to greet the arrival of the first train by the new route. For Hudson, after his meteoric rise to power and brief reign as the 'Railway King', had now to learn by bitter experience that it is not possible both to run with the hare and to hunt with the hounds. As soon as the agreement between himself and Denison became known, the directors and shareholders of the London & North Western Railway (as the London & Birmingham had now become) and the Midland Railway were up in arms against Hudson for his 'perfidy' in having sold out to the enemy. Euston Square, the headquarters of the L.N.W.R., immediately took action. It was to form what became known as the 'Euston Square Confederacy', comprising the two companies mentioned and the Manchester, Sheffield & Lincolnshire, which by 1847 had completed a through route from Manchester to Grimsby *via* Sheffield. Whatever was arranged by the Midland Railway was over Hudson's head as Chairman, and the plan was this.

All traffic from London and the Midlands to the north-east was to be diverted from the York & North Midland and worked instead *via* Leeds and from there over the Leeds & Thirsk Railway to Thirsk, where it would be handed over to the York, Newcastle & Berwick Railway. Traffic for Hull, instead of proceeding *via* Normanton, Milford Junction and Selby, would be transferred to the Manchester, Sheffield & Lincolnshire for conveyance to Grimsby, from which port it would be ferried across the Humber to its destination. An approach was even made to the York, Newcastle & Berwick directors to join the 'Confederacy', but as the latter in this way would stand to lose traffic over its own line between York and Thirsk, the proposal was hardly attractive. On the contrary, the York, Newcastle & Berwick disapproved to such an extent of the new alliance entered into by the Leeds & Thirsk as to devise, in common with the York & North Midland, every possible means of keeping the traffic flowing *via* York, including that between Leeds and the north.

Without departing from the rates laid down by law, by certain ingenious methods the Y.N. & B. and Y. & N.M. together made it cheaper to send coal from Darlington to Leeds over the 76 miles of their route than over the 61 miles *via* Thirsk and the Leeds & Thirsk line. The same applied to merchandise. Cattle from the north to the Leeds & Thirsk line had to be unloaded at the Y.N. & B. Thirsk Junction, and driven or carted from there by road to Thirsk Town station of the L. & T.R. Every effort was taken at Darlington to discourage Leeds passengers from using the Leeds & Thirsk route, and if they were hardy enough to insist on doing so, they were made to change trains at Thirsk, and often to wait in Spartan conditions for their Leeds train. Not surprisingly, this led the Leeds & Thirsk Railway to take steps to proceed with the building of the remaining section of the line originally proposed, from Melmerby to Billingham, which would render them independent altogether of the York, Newcastle & Berwick Railway; but to this we shall come in Chapter XII.

And what of George Hudson? Up to 1848 he had ruled the boards of the various railways of which he was Chairman with undisputed authority. Although some of his actions might have been regarded as of dubious propriety, his success in negotiating agreement after agreement, and in general on the most favourable terms to his companies, made his co-directors prepared to accept his decisions without question. Equally he had no difficulty in swaying the shareholders at any company meeting; if anything had gone wrong and he were criticised he would adopt an air of injured innocence and would succeed in convincing them that the fault had been anyone's but his. Such devotion to him was hardly surprising when a railway such as the York & North Midland was paying 10 per cent dividend on its ordinary shares and the York, Newcastle & Berwick 9 per cent. But it was this uncanny prosperity that in course of time began to arouse doubts in some minds; and when in the half-year ending 31st December, 1848, the dividends of both companies dropped suddenly to 6 per cent, some shareholders came to the conclusion that it was time to take a closer look at the accounts. Hudson's action in admitting the Great Northern Railway to York was by no means the only one that at last spurred his opponents to a determined attempt to discredit him.

The first attack came at the half-yearly meeting of the York, Newcastle & Berwick shareholders on 20th February, 1849. One of the shareholders was a London stockbroker, and he had noticed that in the acquisition of the Great North of England Railway the price paid for certain of the shares had been extremely high. It turned out that these shares had been bought originally by Hudson, who had made a handsome profit for himself by disposing of them at a price considerably above that at which they were being quoted at the time on the London Stock Exchange. What Hudson had done was not illegal, but it certainly was highly improper for the chairman of a company to have acted in this way, and his action raised doubts on all sides as to his financial methods.

Committees of investigation were now set up by both the York, Newcastle & Berwick and York & North Midland shareholders, in May, 1849, with authority to examine all the railways' books and documents; in the same month Hudson resigned his chairmanship of both companies. The upshot was the discovery of all kinds of irregularities, none of them strictly illegal, but many were in the nature of sharp practice and all of them most undesirable for a man in his position. For example, he had bought some 10,000 tons of rails at £6 10s. per ton – certainly with his own money and at his own risk – but he had sold the rails to certain of the railways of which he was chairman at £12 per ton. When some of his companies were being floated, at the time of the 'Railway Mania' – when everyone was keen to obtain railway shares – surplus shares which had been placed 'at the disposal of the directors' were distributed among Hudson's friends or, more often, were appropriated by himself. Accounts of his companies had been manipulated in such a way that, by charging to capital items which properly should have been charged against revenue, the high dividends were actually being paid out of capital.

Nevertheless, the services that Hudson had rendered to his various companies had been immense. In many ways he had risked his own ample private means in speculative enterprises for the benefit of these companies as, for example, in buying the Londesborough Estate to protect the interest of the York & North Midland Railway at a critical time. By his judgment

Above, the King Edward Bridge, Newcastle, opened by King Edward VII in July, 1906. The two centre spans are of 300ft each. *Below*, Naburn swing-bridge across the River Ouse on the East Coast main line, 4 miles south of York.   [*Both, British Railways*

Above, the graceful central curved roof span of York Station, covering the two main through platforms. At the time of its opening in 1872 York was Britain's biggest station. *Below*, a part of Leeds New Station, opened in 1869.   [*Both, British Railways*

Left, prototype of a famous class, Fletcher's No. 901 as originally built.

Right, No. 908 of the '901' class, modified by Fletcher's successors into the form in which these engines ran for many years.

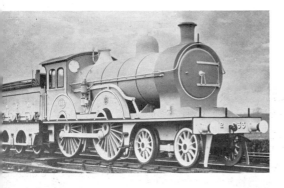

Left, Wilson Worsdell's handsome rebuild into a 4-4-0 of Fletcher 2-4-0 No. 933.

Right, No. 1809, one of the ungainly 'Whitby Bogies' built by Fletcher in 1864-1865 for the severe gradients and sharp curves of the Whitby & Pickering line.   [*All, Locomotive Publishing Co.*

Left, one of Fletcher's numerous 'BTP' (bogie tank passenger) 0-4-4 class, No. 1000.

Right, No. 62 of Class 'BTP' as modified by William Worsdell. These engines were extensively used in later N.E.R. years on push-and-pull train workings.

Left, No. 180 of the unpopular Class '38' 4-4-0s built in 1884 after McDonnell had succeeded Fletcher.

Right, No. 1463, one of the 2-4-0s built under the direction of the General Manager Henry Tennant, from 1885 onwards, after McDonnell's retirement.

[*All, Locomotive Publishing Co.*

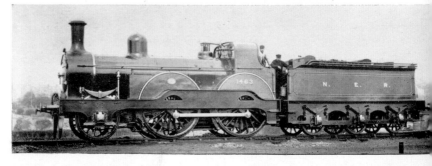

and foresight, aided by some particularly able legal advisers in York, he must have saved the York & North Midland, Newcastle & Darlington Junction and Newcastle & Berwick shareholders large sums of money. Although he was not adverse to massive bribery of landowners, he managed to acquire the land for the three railways just mentioned at an average of £2,400 per mile, whereas the Hull & Selby, Leeds & Thirsk and Great North of England had paid from £3,600 to £3,800 a mile for theirs. He invested personally some £10,000 in the Whitby Building Company, with the intention of bringing additional traffic on to the Whitby & Pickering line.

But the revelations of committees of investigation set up by the York, Newcastle & Berwick and York & North Midland shareholders were extremely damaging. For years past the accounts of both companies had been manipulated in such a way as 'to make things pleasant'. As soon as these malpractices had come to light, shares in the two railways dropped in value with a rush; the dividends of 10 and 9 per cent, which had fallen to 6 per cent in the second half-year of 1848, vanished altogether in the first half-year of 1849. These substantial losses made the shareholders very bitter, and actions were brought against Hudson to recover from him the profits he had realised on certain of his transactions in railway shares and also the premiums on the shares which he had appropriated. The fact that in 1849 and 1850 he paid out a total of over £212,000 to meet these claims is some measure of the wealth that he had acquired.

As already shown, however, there is much that could be said in his defence. To quote W. W. Tomlinson in his book *The North Eastern Railway*, 'Naturally Mr Hudson, who was labouring from morning to night on behalf of the Companies with which he was connected – planning, organising, negotiating, and beating down opposition with an energy almost unparalleled – felt himself entitled to a large share of the benefits accruing from his efforts. The value of his services it would be difficult to exaggerate. No professional man would have undertaken many of the duties which Mr Hudson performed without a very large remuneration.' Of the financial benefits derived by various other companies from Hudson's negotiations Tomlinson goes on to give ample evidence.

Even Gladstone had declared of Hudson, 'It is a great mistake to look back upon him as a speculator. He was a man of great discernment, possessing a great deal of courage and rich enterprise – a very bold, and not at all an unwise, projector'. But, alas, with power there had come the descent to the shadier transactions that had brought about his downfall. By the end of 1849 he had resigned all his chairmanships, including those of the Midland and Great Eastern Railways as well as those of the railways in North-Eastern England, and he had vanished from the railway scene. At the same time the inflated railway 'bubble' had been pricked, and the serious consequences of the 'Railway Mania' had now to be faced.

CHAPTER XII

The Railway Mania Aftermath

DURING the momentous period covered in Chapter XI there had been numerous other railway developments in North-Eastern England which now need attention. The 'Railway Mania' produced a vast number of projects for railways in all directions, many of them promoted by competing interests and therefore directly competitive. Mountainous country appeared to offer no obstacle at all. It is astonishing indeed, when we remember the care that was taken in deciding the route of the London & Birmingham Railway to ensure no gradient steeper than 1 in 330, apart from the rope-worked Camden Bank out of Euston, or Brunel's main line out of Paddington, practically level all the way to Bristol save for two short 1 in 100 gradients between Wootton Bassett and Bath, that some of the main routes contemplated through mountainous country in these wild schemes of the 1840s should even have been dreamed of.

There was, first, the York & Carlisle Junction Railway, in which the Great North of England offered to take up £250,000 of the share capital; this was to start at Northallerton and run *via* Catterick Bridge to Barnard Castle, where it would be joined by a branch from Bishop Auckland. From there the route would be roughly that of the South Durham & Lancashire Union Railway of later years, to Kirkby Stephen, branching into lines to Tebay and also to Clifton, both on the Lancaster & Carlisle line. Competing with this was the Northumberland & Lancashire Union project, starting at Gateshead and using the Team Valley to reach Durham, from which it would run to Bishop Auckland and Barnard Castle and follow the same course as the York & Carlisle Junction to Tebay and Clifton. To these two a formidable rival was the Yorkshire & Glasgow Union Railway, which would begin at Thirsk, proceed to Leyburn and up Wensleydale to Hawes; thence it would turn north and follow the route of the later Midland Railway to continue to Appleby and Clifton.

Running across these three routes were two proposed from the heart of Lancashire to the north-east. One, the Northern Counties Union Railway, was a later promotion to take over the York & Glasgow project, with a connecting branch from Bishop Auckland to Barnard Castle. The second, the Liverpool, Manchester & Newcastle Railway, was to run from Preston through Clitheroe to Settle and Hawes, also following between Hellifield and Garsdale the course of the later Midland Railway; this line would then have made its way down Wensleydale through Hawes and Askrigg to Richmond, where it would link up with the branch from Dalton (later Eryholme) to Richmond which the Great North of England was then building and opened for traffic on 10th September, 1846.

The latter project had the support of Hudson, but not so the rival Lancashire & North Yorkshire Railway, which was to branch from the Leeds & Bradford Railway at a point near Skipton, and to proceed from there right over the Pennines through Kettlewell to Middleham, and across lower Wensleydale to Scorton on the Richmond branch – a line which would have had the most fearsome gradients. There were other wildcat schemes too numerous to mention, and wildest of all, perhaps, the £5,000,000 'Newcastle & London Coal Railway', which was to be used solely for 'the conveyance of coals and goods at a moderate and regular speed'.

Few of the most ambitious of these schemes reached the stage of a Bill in Parliament, though years later certain parts of the proposed routes did actually come into existence. But many of the lines of moderate length obtained their Acts, and in part at least were constructed during this period; in some cases, however, the financial crash that followed the 'Railway Mania' resulted in postponement of the building of sections of the lines proposed, and when finally it was desired to complete these schemes, the powers had lapsed and fresh Acts had to be obtained.

First of all, the York & North Midland Railway in 1845 and 1846 obtained Acts for a network of lines in East Yorkshire, to a total of 107 miles. Two of these were lines converging on Bridlington, one from Hull in the south through Beverley and Driffield, and the other from Seamer (on the Y. & N.M. York–Scarborough branch) in the north through Filey. Then two further lines were to cross one another, scissors fashion, at Market Weighton, one from York to Beverley and the other from Selby to Driffield. The former would thus give a direct route from York to Hull, and the latter from the south, *via* Selby, to Bridlington and Scarborough.

Most of the construction was fairly easy, and in consequence speedy; the lines from Seamer as far south as Filey and from Hull to Bridlington were opened on successive days, 5th and 6th October, 1846, respectively. But it was not until 18th October, 1847, that the steeply graded section of $13\frac{3}{4}$ miles between Filey and Bridlington was ready for the trains, with its 5-mile climb at 1 in 92 from Bridlington past Flamborough and Bempton to the 345ft summit at Speeton. Again, both the railways converging on Market Weighton reached that town quickly, that from York being opened on 3rd October, 1847, and the almost dead straight line from Selby on 1st August, 1848, but many years were to elapse before the continuations to Beverley and Driffield respectively were brought into use.

In both cases fresh Acts had to be obtained. The North Eastern Railway had come into existence before an Act was obtained for the Market Weighton–Beverley line, and not until 1st May, 1865, did it become possible to travel from York to Hull by this route. Then twenty more years passed before an independent company with the imposing title of 'Scarborough, Bridlington & West Riding Junction Railway' was promoted to make a line in a south-westerly direction from Driffield through Market Weighton to join the new Hull & Barnsley Railway at Howden. This project the North Eastern Railway naturally opposed, but finally the

S.B. & W.R.J.R. agreed to cut its project down to the modest 9 miles across the Wolds from Driffield to Market Weighton and opened the railway for traffic in 1890. Though worked by the N.E.R., it is remarkable that this line remained independent until 1914.

Yet another independent railway in this area, backed by Hudson, was the Malton & Driffield Junction, which obtained its Act in June, 1846. This line also had to thread the Wold country with some very heavy gradients, particularly the 5¼ miles from the Malton direction, steepening from 1 in 100 to between 1 in 73 and 64 up to the 416ft summit at Wharram. On the opposite slope the necessity to bore a tunnel nearly a mile long at Burdale both increased the cost of construction and delayed the opening, which did not take place formally until 19th May, 1853, the public opening following a fortnight later. The remaining branch on the east side of the Great North of England main line was opened on the same day; authorised in 1846, it was from a junction about 7 miles south of Thirsk, between Pilmoor and Raskelf, to Malton, on the York & North Midland Scarborough branch.

We have now to transfer attention to the west side of the G.N.E. main line, where also railway extension had been in progress. As we recalled in Chapter XI, the original plans of George Stephenson for the Great North of England included a branch from Thirsk to Boroughbridge, Knaresborough and Leeds, but this was not covered by the 1837 Act. The comprehensive York & Newcastle Railway Act of 1846, however, included a 5¾-mile branch from Pilmoor to Boroughbridge, which was opened by the York, Newcastle & Berwick Company on 17th June, 1847; another 28 years were to pass before Boroughbridge became linked by rail with Knaresborough and beyond.

Meantime Knaresborough had been reached from another direction. In 1845 a company with the resounding title of 'East & West Yorkshire Junction Railway' had obtained an Act to build a railway 15¼ miles long from York to Knaresborough, with the use of York station as its eastern terminal. By March, 1848, this had been brought into use as far as the eastern side of Knaresborough, but once again the collapse of a bridge – this time the high viaduct acrosss the Nidd gorge – had delayed completion. When on 1st October, 1851, opening took place throughout, it was to an end-on junction with the Leeds Northern Railway (as the Leeds & Thirsk had now become), which four months earlier had opened a short branch from Starbeck to Knaresborough. From now on, York had a new through line to the outskirts of Harrogate.

In the few years of its independent existence, the East & West Yorkshire Junction Railway experienced several vicissitudes. It was first leased to the York, Newcastle & Berwick; then a Leeds firm named E. B. Wilson & Company took over the working; finally, although the Leeds & Thirsk had gone to the trouble of obtaining an Act to lease it, in 1851 the York & North Midland incorporated it by amalgamation.

It was in 1849 that the Leeds & Thirsk Railway changed its name to the Leeds Northern. Doubtless for want of the necessary finance to carry out its original plans for extension northwards, its railhead was still at Thirsk, so that it remained dependent on the York, Newcastle & Berwick to carry its traffic from there onwards. Much was happening in Durham during this decade, however.

In the west of the county the Bishop Auckland & Weardale Railway had been completed from South Church, or St Andrew Auckland, through Bishop Auckland to Crook by the latter part of 1843, and had been leased to the Stockton and Darlington. The Derwent Iron Company at Consett, which was just getting under way and had bought from the Stanhope & Tyne Railway the upper portion of their line, from Carr House southwards, and the quarries at Stanhope (as well as the short connecting line between Harelaw and Tanfield Moor), was now interested in obtaining direct railway communication with the southern part of the county. The Derwent Company, therefore, proposed a new railway from Waskerley Park, on the Stanhope & Tyne, down to join the S. & D.R. Weardale branch at Crook; so the Wear & Derwent Junction Railway came into being. This and the Weardale Extension Railway, 10 miles long from what later became Wear Valley Junction to Frosterley, completing the original Bishop Auckland & Weardale scheme, were both opened on 16th May, 1845.

Following the example of the bigger lines, the smaller companies were all now tending to come together, both for mutual protection and for more economical working. First of all, as we have just seen, the Stockton & Darlington Railway leased the Bishop Auckland & Weardale in 1843. Then the Derwent Iron Company sold its newly-acquired Carr House to Stanhope line to the Stockton & Darlington, which took possession on 1st January, 1845, shortly before the opening of the Wear & Derwent Junction. By 1846 a much wider scheme of amalgamation was being proposed; it was that the Wear Valley Company should purchase the Bishop Auckland & Weardale, the Wear & Derwent, the Weardale Extension and the Shildon Tunnel, and that the whole of this group should be leased to the Stockton & Darlington. This lease became effective, under statutory authority, on 1st October, 1847, the S. & D. binding itself to pay 6 per cent per annum on the total share capital. But payment of interest on this scale was destined to land the Stockton & Darlington in difficulties, as we shall see presently.

Meantime, the Clarence Railway also had been falling on hard times, and to follow what was happening, we must go back a little in history. Chapter VIII related how in 1837 a small railway with a big title, the 'Great North of England, Clarence & Hartlepool Junction Railway', promoted by a group in Hartlepool in competition with the Clarence Railway and its Stockton-on-Tees backers, obtained an Act for a line through Wingate and Trimdon to make a junction with the original Great North of England (later the Newcastle & Darlington Junction) Railway at Thrislington, near the present Ferryhill. By the middle of July, 1839, this was nearly complete when its promoters suddenly realised that they had not obtained powers in their Act to cross the Sherburn branch of the Clarence

Railway, as they would need to do about a mile north of what is now Ferryhill to reach Byers Green and so tap part of the West Durham coalfield in the interests of Hartlepool.

Needless to say, the Clarence Company showed no inclination to help their rivals; on the contrary, if a level crossing were to be laid in, they would be in a position to charge any tolls they liked for the passage of their rival's coal trains over their property. Driven into a corner, the Great North of England, Clarence & Hartlepool Junction had to apply for a new Act to authorise the substitution of an overbridge for a level crossing, and duly obtained it in 1843, but on letting the contract in December of that year discovered that the fighting resources of their opponents were by no means at an end. For the Clarence Company refused to allow the bridge-builders to trespass on any part of their land, and stationed watchers on the site day and night to ensure that there should be no such trespass; they even built high walls on their property to impede the work as much as possible. The Stockton & Hartlepool Railway, whose interests also were threatened, backed the Clarence Railway in its obstructive tactics.

In the end the bridge was built, but it was not until the autumn of 1846 that the diminutive Great North of England, Clarence & Hartlepool Junction Railway, authorised in 1837, was actually completed. Immediately afterwards, on 12th October, 1846, the G.N.E.C. & H.J.R. was taken over, with the Hartlepool Dock & Railway, by the York & Newcastle Railway (as the Newcastle & Darlington Junction had now become), by virtue of an agreement to lease and eventually to purchase that had been made with George Hudson in the previous year. Hudson's aim, at this point just before his downfall, had been to obtain control over all the ports on the Durham coast; he had succeeded in the case of the Tyne, Sunderland and Hartlepool, but not in that of Port Clarence and Middlesbrough.

As previously stated, the Clarence Railway in the middle 1840s was in difficulties. Early in 1842 the West Durham Railway, which brought most of the traffic on to the Clarence line at Chilton Junction, was unable to meet its expenses, and for several weeks closed down completely; the principal creditors were the Exchequer Loan Commissioners, who stepped in and took possession of the property. The shareholders rallied round, however, and by energetic financial measures succeeded in converting the debt into capital, so preventing the sale of the railway. Now the Stockton & Hartlepool Railway, which was in effect an extension of the Clarence Railway, intervened and by friendly agreement between the two companies took on a lease of the latter for 21 years from 22nd September, 1844. It was at this stage, as already related in Chapter XI, that Hudson in 1846 made his two offers to purchase the Clarence Railway, first of £315,000 and then of £350,000, but only to be outbid by the Leeds & Thirsk Railway's offer of £450,000. For lack of the necessary finance, however, we saw in Chapter XI that the powers of the Leeds & Thirsk to absorb the Clarence Railway were not exercised, and therefore lapsed; for the same reason the building of the former's independent line from Melmerby to

Billingham-on-Tees, to link the two systems together, was delayed for some years.

The next railway to cast covetous eyes on the Clarence property was the Stockton & Darlington, especially as the latter's coal traffic from the West Durham area was now being menaced by the Auckland branch of the York, Newcastle & Berwick Railway. Some of the leading Clarence Railway shareholders, also, were becoming dissatisfied with the way in which their leaseholders, the Stockton & Hartlepool Company, were tending to divert coal for shipment from Port Clarence to Hartlepool, and were secretly conducting *pourparlers* with Joseph Pease, of the Stockton & Darlington, as to the possible amalgamation of the two lines. But the poor condition of the Clarence properties, as reported upon by the S. & D. engineers, delayed a decision by the Stockton & Darlington Railway for so long that the Stockton & Hartlepool, under the direction of a financier named Ralph Ward Jackson, took action. It was that the latter company should assume all the Clarence Company's obligations, pay a dividend of £2 10s. per annum on the ordinary shares for five years, and have the option of purchase at the end of that period. Amalgamation was also arranged with the Hartlepool West Harbour and Dock Companies, which took effect from 1st July, 1851, and a powerful new group was thus formed.

Not until 1852 did the northern extension of the Leeds & Thirsk Railway, now the Leeds Northern, reach Stockton-on-Tees. It branched from the Thirsk line at Wath (the station later known as Melmerby), 3 miles north of Ripon, and from there ran in a north-north-easterly direction through Northallerton, Yarm and Egglescliffe. One of the engineering problems involved was the burrowing at a considerable skew under the main line of the York, Newcastle & Berwick Railway at Northallerton, which had to be done without any interference with the latter's train service.

The major engineering work, however, was at Yarm, where the line had to make a diagonal crossing of the wide valley of the Tees, and partly above the town itself. The substantial masonry viaduct had two 67ft arches across the river, and forty other arches of 40ft span in its total length of 760 yards. At Egglescliffe the Leeds Northern joined the Stockton & Darlington, and from here a deviation of the latter was carried out to enable the two lines to run parallel for some 2 miles until the S. & D.R. bore away to the east at Mount Pleasant – a four-track section which continues as such to the present day. The opening of the 29-mile Leeds Northern extension was celebrated on 15th May, 1852, by the running of a special train for shareholders and their friends from Leeds through to Stockton, with a procession from Stockton station to the new Town Hall.

We now come back to the Stockton & Darlington Railway, which also by the end of the 1840s was in considerable financial difficulties. We have seen already how the S. & D. Company had obtained leases in 1847 of a number of previously independent lines in West Durham; and to these had been added the Middlesbrough & Redcar Railway, authorised by Act of Parliament on 21st July, 1845, and opened on 4th June, 1846 – a short line destined later to be of great importance to the Stockton & Darlington and its successors.

The possibilities of this group of lines had not been lost on George Hudson, who in 1848 had succeeded in inducing the S. & D. directors to present a Bill to Parliament for the amalgamation of their railway with the York, Newcastle & Berwick. But in the following year had come Hudson's crash and the crisis in York, Newcastle & Berwick finances which put this project out of court. By 1850 the position had been reached, therefore, that the Stockton & Darlington had leased so many other railways, in each case on the basis of a guaranteed annual dividend on their share capital – and, moreover, a quite generous dividend – that the whole of the S. & D. revenue was likely to be mortgaged to meet these commitments.

It was at this crisis in Stockton & Darlington affairs that something happened which was to be of cardinal importance, not only to the railway, but to Tees-side and, indeed, to North-Eastern England in general. It was the discovery, on 8th June, 1850, at Eston, just east of Middlesbrough, of the main seam of Cleveland iron ore, which was to bring an era of vast prosperity to the entire district.

CHAPTER XIII

The North Eastern Railway is Born

In the last chapter we saw how the shaky financial conditions after the downfall of Hudson tended to bring the smaller railways together into groups, either by leases or amalgamations, and during the early 1850s the same process continued on a far larger scale. Railways were beginning to realise that unbridled competition could be very uneconomic, if not ruinous, and that friendly relations, or better still, complete fusion, would be by far the sounder policy for all concerned.

The most comprehensive of all these amalgamations was now to take place. It followed the penetration of York, Newcastle & Berwick territory by the Leeds Northern Railway, which in 1852 had reached Stockton-on-Tees and linked up with the Stockton & Darlington, Stockton & Hartlepool and Clarence Railways. Certain recent happenings had made this link-up a more serious matter for the York, Newcastle & Berwick. For in the same year not only had there been completed some considerable extensions to the West Hartlepool docks – including a new merchandise dock of 14 acres, a new graving dock 320ft long, and an increase in the harbour area from 13 to 44 acres – but also, by Act of Parliament dated 30th June, 1852, the Harbour Company had amalgamated with the Stockton & Hartlepool Railway, to which the Clarence Railway was leased, under the title of West Hartlepool Harbour & Railway Company. This fusion suited the Leeds Northern directors perfectly, and they set out to establish the closest relations possible with the new company.

A rate war broke out immediately between the Leeds Northern and the York, Newcastle & Berwick Companies. To such an extent was it carried that in July, 1852, the Y.N. & B. was carrying passengers over the 238 miles from Leeds to Newcastle and back for two shillings! The Leeds Northern, having vowed that its charges should never be higher than those of its rival, was doing the same. Obviously it was impossible for such a state of affairs to continue, and the first steps to end it were taken by T. E. Harrison, who had now become General Manager as well as Engineer of the York, Newcastle & Berwick. Some means must be found, he realised, to bring the two railways together, and this could not be done without including the York & North Midland also in any arrangement that might be made, as otherwise the last-mentioned railway might be at a considerable disadvantage.

Already Harrison had gained experience by the amalgamation of the Great North of England, Newcastle & Darlington Junction and Newcastle & Berwick Companies to form the York, Newcastle & Berwick, and knew what difficulties he would have to face. Needless to say, he had to get the agreement of his own directors to what he proposed, and at first they were all dead against him. But the evidence that he was able to produce as to the benefits which had accrued from the previous amalgamation convinced them, one by one, and also the boards of the other two companies concerned. Negotiations were entrusted to a committee of three very level-headed men – T. E. Harrison representing the York, Newcastle & Berwick, Alexander Clunes Sherriff the York & North Midland, and Henry Tennant – in later years to become General Manager of the North Eastern Railway – the Leeds Northern.

The financial terms of the amalgamation, which would have to be agreed by the shareholders of the three companies, were the most difficult problem. It was finally agreed that the basis should be the amount of traffic currently carried by each company. For dividend purposes, the capital of the three companies would remain separate, the Y.N. & B. shares being designated 'Berwick Capital Stock', the Y. & N.M. 'York Capital Stock', and the Leeds Northern 'Leeds Capital Stock'. The revenue from traffic would be pooled, and the net revenue after deduction of working expenses would be divided between the three companies on an agreed percentage basis. In view of the somewhat fictitious traffic figures resulting from the utterly uneconomic competition between the Leeds Northern and York, Newcastle & Berwick Railways up to that time, fixing the percentages was no easy matter; and matters were complicated further by the agreements between the Leeds Northern and the Stockton & Hartlepool and West Hartlepool Harbour Railway Companies.

Eventually the three boards reached agreement, however, on 2nd November, 1852, as to the desirability of a permanent union – that is, of amalgamation. At two of the shareholders' meetings to which the proposals were submitted – the York, Newcastle & Berwick and the York & North Midland – the shareholders were won over, but at the Leeds Northern meeting it was a different matter. The proprietors of the latter company regarded 7 per cent of the net receipts, rising later to $9\frac{1}{2}$ per cent, as a completely inadequate share for their company, and demanded more.

Another difficulty arose from the way in which the Leeds Northern directors proposed to distribute their share of the profits. To ensure what they described as 'an equitable adjustment of interests' they suggested that the preference dividends should be reduced from 6 and 5 per cent to 5 and 4 per cent respectively, which would leave enough over to provide for a payment of $2\frac{1}{2}$ per cent on the ordinary shares; if there remained any surplus it would be divided proportionately between the two classes. To compensate the preference shareholders for what they were to lose, it was then proposed that they should have their arrears of dividend paid in the form of additional 4 per cent preference stock.

But the preference shareholders refused to agree to any such arrangement, and insisted on their legal right to be paid in full before the ordinary shareholders received anything. No progress could be made with the amalgamation plan until this matter was settled, and in consequence the original Bill was withdrawn. Meantime, in order that the benefits of the *rapprochement* might be enjoyed without further delay, the three companies agreed to joint operation of their traffic, T. E. Harrison being appointed General Manager, and A. C. Sherriff Traffic Manager.

Certain happenings at that period, however, impressed on the directorates of the two wealthier companies that the desirability of the amalgamation was becoming urgent. One was the menace of three new railway schemes which might put the Leeds Northern Railway in a considerably stronger position. A branch was proposed of the Stockton & Hartlepool Railway from Greatham to the Haswell mining area of East Durham; a second proposed branch was from the Clarence Railway at Coxhoe through Sherburn, Pittington and Houghton-le-Spring to Sunderland; and the third and more imposing proposal was a 'Direct North Railway' to connect the Great Northern Railway at Doncaster with the North British Railway at Galashiels, using a section of the Leeds Northern as part of the route. All three might make substantial inroads on York, Newcastle & Berwick traffic.

But the best argument that Harrison could bring to bear on the York, Newcastle & Berwick and York & North Midland boards was that, just as the Great North of England, Newcastle & Darlington Junction and Newcastle & Berwick amalgamation had resulted in considerably more profitable operation, so the first year's joint operation of the York, Newcastle & Berwick, York & North Midland and Leeds Northern traffic was having exactly the same effect. For this reason the Leeds Northern could be offered better terms. These were 8 instead of 7 per cent of the net receipts in the first year, 9 per cent in the second year, and 10 instead of 9½ per cent in the third and subsequent years. The amended offer was accepted; the Leeds Northern preference shareholders gained their point; and the plans could now go ahead.

So impressed had the public been with the benefits of the joint working of the three railways – more and faster trains, better rolling stock, advantageous through rates for freight and minerals, and so on – that the new Bill went through Parliament practically without opposition. So, with the Royal Assent of 31st July, 1854, there came into existence the North Eastern Railway Company. By the terms of the Act it was the York, Newcastle & Berwick Railway which assumed the title of North Eastern Railway, the undertakings of the York & North Midland and Leeds Northern Railways being vested in that of the larger company. Included in the amalgamation was the small Malton & Driffield Junction Railway. The Hull & Selby Railway, which the York & North Midland had leased but never acquired, continued under lease to the N.E.R., a special clause being included in the Act for the protection of its shareholders.

The North Eastern Railway now could claim the distinction of being the largest single railway undertaking in the country, with 703 route miles of line and a further 17 miles under construction; in addition, it owned 44 acres of dock space and 26 miles of waterway. The total capital of the original 20 companies which had come together by stages amounted to some £23,000,000. It possessed a through main line from Normanton to

York, Darlington, Newcastle and Berwick, and subsidiary main lines from Leeds to Harrogate, Northallerton, and Stockton-on-Tees, and from Leeds to Selby and Hull (the Selby–Hull section, as we have just seen, still under lease).

In East Yorkshire there were the lines from York to Malton and Scarborough, with the Malton–Whitby, Malton–Pilmoor and Malton–Driffield branches; and the lines from York and Selby to Market Weighton. West of the principal main line there were the branches from Church Fenton to Harrogate and from York to Knaresborough and Starbeck; short branches from Pilmoor to Boroughbridge, Northallerton to Bedale and Dalton to Richmond; a number of lines in the coal-mining area of Durham, particularly from Ferryhill to Hartlepool, Penshaw to Sunderland, and the former Pontop & South Shields and Tanfield lines. North of Newcastle there were the North Shields line, short branches to Warkworth and Alnwick, and the longer branch from Tweedmouth to Coldstream and Kelso.

But right across the centre of this North Eastern territory there stretched the independent Stockton and Darlington, Stockton & Hartlepool and Clarence Railways, tapping the whole of the West Durham coalfield and carrying the coal across the N.E.R. main line down to Hartlepool and Middlesbrough for shipment. Farther north the important Newcastle & Carlisle Railway also retained its independence.

One of the N.E.R. branches just mentioned has not been referred to in previous chapters, from Tweedmouth to Kelso. This was of particular note in that a line from Spittal, opposite Berwick on the south bank of the Tweed, to Kelso had been authorised by Parliament as far back as May, 1811, ten years before the Stockton & Darlington Railway obtained its Act. But no start was made, and after an ineffective attempt 25 years later to revive the scheme, it was dropped. Not until the late 1840s did the Newcastle & Berwick Railway take action and obtain powers for a line up the Tweed valley from Tweedmouth. The first 20 miles of this, through Coldstream to Sprouston, was opened for traffic on 27th July, 1849, and two years later a 1-mile extension of this branch brought it into Kelso, to an end-on junction with the St Boswell's–Kelso branch of the North British Railway.

At the time of the amalgamation, work was proceeding on an important extension of the York, Newcastle & Berwick Railway, designed to link the former Durham & Sunderland Railway with Bishop Auckland and the West Durham coalfield. Originally planned in 1846, this was one of the projects held up after the Hudson crash, and it was not until 1853 that the York, Newcastle & Berwick Railway was able to let the contract for its construction. By now it was becoming realised that rope-worked inclines on railways designed to carry heavy traffic were a considerable handicap, and that they were to be avoided if possible. For this reason, the Durham–Bishop Auckland line, crossing a series of valleys in a transverse direction, involved some heavy engineering work. Three stone viaducts had to be built; one of nine arches over the River Wear at Brasside was no less than

130ft high at its maximum; a second over the same river at Newton Gap, of eleven arches, had a maximum height of 100ft; while the third was an eleven-arch viaduct over the western part of Durham City. There were also two wooden viaducts of great size, over the Browney and Dearness streams, not to mention a cutting up to 80ft deep at Neville's Cross. In these conditions construction was not rapid; indeed, it was not until 1st April, 1857, that the first passenger train was able to run over the length of the new line.

A railway thus ran through the centre of the City of Durham, eventually to form part of the East Coast main line, though 11 years were to pass before this came about. Meantime the course of the original North Eastern main line continued almost due north from what is now Tursdale Junction through Shincliffe, Sherburn (well to the east of Durham City), Leamside and Penshaw to Washington, where the trains turned north-westward by Hudson's spur to reach the former Brandling Junction line at Pelaw, just short of Gateshead, from which they crossed the Tyne into Newcastle.

The direct Team valley line from Tursdale Junction through Croxdale to join the Bishop Auckland branch at Relly Mill, using the latter over Durham Viaduct to Newton Hall Junction, and from there diverging to take a direct course through Chester-le-Street to Gateshead, was not to come into operation until 1868; while the King Edward Bridge across the Tyne, which would eliminate reversal of the East Coast trains in Newcastle Central Station by permitting through running, would not see completion until 1906.

The last remaining section of the present East Coast main line which had still to be built was that from Shaftholme Junction, north of Doncaster, through Selby to York, and this was not destined to be opened until 1871. Until then Great Northern trains from London to York must continue to use Lancashire & Yorkshire Railway metals from Askern to Knottingley before the spur line from there to Burton Salmon, laid in by the former York & North Midland Railway, brought them on to North Eastern Railway territory. Notwithstanding these temporary diversions, however, a direct East Coast Route had now come into operation over the metals of the Great Northern, North Eastern and North British Railways from King's Cross Station in London to the Waverley Station in Edinburgh.

From the time when the Great Northern Railway trains had first run into York, in 1850, the companies concerned in moving passengers and freight between England and Scotland – the London & North Western, Midland, York & North Midland, Great Northern, York, Newcastle & Berwick, North British, Lancaster & Carlisle and Caledonian Railways – had negotiated an agreement as to the most economical and equitable way of dividing up the traffic. So there came into force in 1850 what was known as the 'Octuple Treaty' – because eight railways were concerned in making it – or, to give its more official title, the English and Scotch Traffic Agreement. This now definitely defined the line from Euston *via* Birmingham, Crewe, Preston and Carlisle as the 'West Coast Route', but for the time being two lines shared the designation 'East Coast Route' – the original

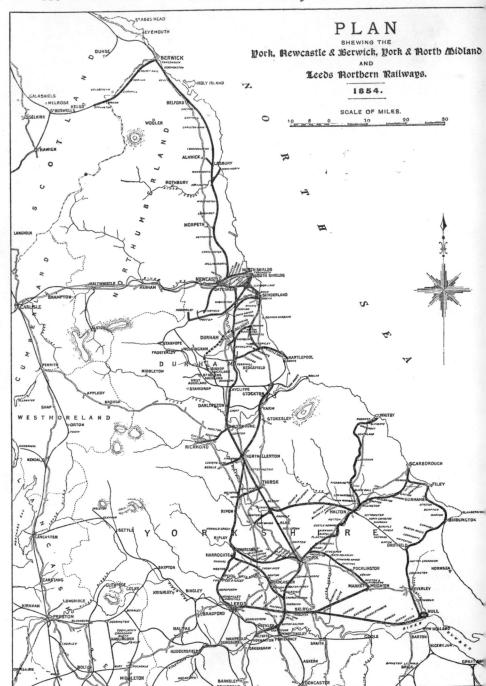

PLAN

SHEWING THE

York, Newcastle & Berwick, York & North Midland

AND

Leeds Northern Railways.

1854.

SCALE OF MILES.

[Andrew Reid & Co., Ltd.

route from Euston *via* Rugby, Leicester, Derby, Chesterfield and Norman-ton to York, or the Great Northern from Maiden Lane (until King's Cross was opened), *via* Peterborough, Grantham, Doncaster and Knottingley. From York, of course, both the latter combined to follow the York, Newcastle & Berwick to Berwick and the North British on to Edinburgh.

Mark Huish and the 'Euston Square Confederacy', to which we have referred already in Chapter XI, now set out to divert all the traffic they could from the Great Northern; fortunately for the latter, however, the agreement related only to Anglo-Scottish traffic and had no force south of York, where the Great Northern had a free hand to undercut its rivals in both time and rates and fares, and certainly did so. Moreover, in 1855 the original 'Octuple Treaty' ceased to operate, and a new agreement, now with the North Eastern Railway replacing the York & North Midland and York, Newcastle & Berwick Companies, was negotiated on terms consider-ably more favourable to the East Coast partners. From now on the main line to Edinburgh from King's Cross terminus, which had been opened in October, 1852, was recognised as the only 'East Coast Route' to Scotland.

An event shortly after the incorporation of the North Eastern Railway which considerably strengthened the company's position in the North of England was the opening for traffic, on 3rd March, 1859, of the great Tyne Dock, between Jarrow and South Shields, which had been under con-struction for four years. It comprised a 50-acre main basin, with 24ft 6in depth of water at a normal spring tide, a 9½-acre tidal basin, a main entrance 80ft wide, and a lock 300ft long by 100ft wide. Inside the dock were four jetties, two for loading coal which would afford considerable relief to the overworked Brandling and Pontop drops, and the other two for unloading incoming vessels. Between 400 and 500 of the ships of the period could be accommodated in the new Tyne Dock at one time, and both the Stockton & Darlington and Hartlepool Railways saw in this installation a a formidable future competitor.

It is surprising to relate that even as late as 1854, the year of incorpora-tion of the North Eastern Railway and all but 30 years after the opening of the Stockton & Darlington Railway, horse traction was still quite exten-sively in use on the railways of North-Eastern England, both for passengers and for coal haulage. In his book *The North Eastern Railway*, W. W. Tom-linson quotes a diverting extract from a September, 1854, issue of the *Stockton & Darlington Times* describing the excitements of a coach journey on the Hagger Leases branch of the Stockton & Darlington Railway. When the driver of one of the horse-drawn 4-wheel coaches was approach-ing a passing-loop, he would dismount, race ahead of the coach to move the switch, the horse not slackening its pace, and would remount as the coach passed him. No reins were used; the driver controlled his horse by shouting at the top of his voice

Inexperienced passengers who were told to keep a look-out for the 'Lambs' anticipated no risk from such inoffensive animals, but their minds were soon to be disabused. For the 'Lambs' proved to be trains of up to 18 or 20 wagons, running by gravity down the incline to Brusselton Bankfoot, mainly loaded with coal, but possibly including some passengers at the rear, and also two or three 'dandies' with their horses riding in them in comfort and with every appearance of enjoyment. A limited amount of hand signalling by men at vantage points at the pit-mouths above the valley served as a warning to drivers of passenger coaches mounting the gradient that 'Lambs' were on the way down, and these drivers then needed to lose no time in getting into the nearest loop in order to let the 'Lambs' sweep by.

Among other regular horse-drawn coaches, one, belonging to the West Hartlepool Railway, was still plying in 1854 between Billingham and Port Clarence. Another, a railway carriage with four compartments, ran on Sundays between Stockton and Middlesbrough until 1864. The West Hartlepool Railway also used to run a market train from Byers Green to Stockton, horse-drawn between Ferryhill and Byers Green. In the reverse direction, down the 1 in 173 and 1 in 103 from Spennymoor towards Ferryhill, the horse, after starting the train down the grade, joined the passengers by jumping in behind into its dandy-cart!

Passenger travel down some of the inclines had some distinct elements of risk. Tomlinson also describes a journey between Crook and Cold Rowley on a train of mineral wagons to which two passenger coaches were attached. Up the initial Sunnyside incline the train was rope-hauled, and then was worked as far as Waskerley Park Junction (the convergence of the line from Stanhope, the later Burnhill, 1,154ft above sea-level) by a locomotive. Now came the descent of Nanny Mayor's Bank, this time with the passenger coaches running loose behind the wagons, and controlled by their own hand-brakes only. In the reverse direction the whole of the lengthy Sunnyside incline was descended by passengers in the same way. There were no signals between Crook and Cold Rowley and no men stationed at the points; over the locomotive-worked sections the fireman had to get off the locomotive when necessary to move the loop points. No van was provided for the guard, who might have to perch insecurely on a buffer if the passenger coaches were full.

It may be added, in regard to signalling, that three of the main constituents of the North Eastern Railway – the York & Newcastle, York & North Midland and Newcastle & Berwick – had installed the electric telegraph in 1846 and 1847, and the Leeds Northern had followed suit in 1852 and the Newcastle & Carlisle in 1852 and 1853. The first semaphore signals were being introduced from 1852 onwards. But signalling is dealt with in Chapter XXVIII.

No. 340, a two-cylinder compound 2-4-0 of William Worsdell's design, built in 1880, subject of Worsdell's first experiment with piston-valves.

No. 779, one of William Worsdell's successful 'F' class and his first 4-4-0 design, also a two-cylinder compound.

Another two-cylinder compound Worsdell design was the 'J' class 4-2-2, with 7ft 7in driving wheels, of which No. 1517 is shown.

[*All, Locomotive Publishing Co.*]

4-4-0 development in the Wilson Worsdell era. No. 1638 of Class 'M' (1892) with outside steam chests. [*Locomotive Publishing Co.*

Above, No. 1621, which in the 1895 'Race to Aberdeen' covered the 124½ miles from Newcastle to Edinburgh in 113 min. It is shown as fitted later with superheater and now as exhibited in York Railway Museum.
[*Locomotive Publishing Co.*

Left, No. 1928 of Class 'Q'.
[*H. Gordon Tidey*

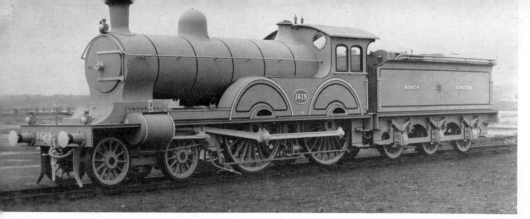

N.E.R. No. 1619, the only British locomotive which has worked with both two-cylinder and three-cylinder compound propulsion. Originally of Wilson Worsdell's Class 'M', No. 1619 was rebuilt in 1898 to the designs of W. M. Smith as a three-cylinder compound. [*British Railways*

The most successful 4-4-0 class in North Eastern history, a representative of Class 'R', introduced in 1899.

The most powerful of the North Eastern 4-4-0s were the 'R1' class engines, built in 1908, with 5ft 6in diameter boilers. [*Both, Locomotive Publishing Co.*

0-6-0 development on the North Eastern Railway. *Above*, a Fletcher 0-6-0 of the '708' class.
[*Locomotive Publishing Co.*

Right, one of the numerous Wilson Worsdell 'P' class.
[*W. J. Reynolds*

The final stage – a Class 'P3' 0-6-0 with 5ft 6in diameter boiler.
[*Locomotive Publishing Co.*

CHAPTER XIV

Cleveland Iron Ore

WHEN we left the Stockton & Darlington Railway in Chapter XII, it was with that company in a difficult financial position owing to the number of smaller railways which it had leased, on guaranteed terms that would be likely to absorb the whole of its net revenue. But the location of the main seam of Cleveland iron ore at Eston in the summer of 1850 was destined to change the whole position. A firm named Bolckow & Vaughan, which in 1846 had built some blast-furnaces at Witton Park, west of Bishop Auckland, was responsible for the discovery, and promptly laid in a private branch line from its Eston mine down to the recently opened Middlesbrough & Redcar Railway, which was leased to the Stockton & Darlington. A heavy traffic in ironstone now began to flow between Eston and Witton Park, much to the advantage of the S. & D.R.

But this was only the beginning. As soon as the extent of the Cleveland iron ore bed began to be realised, new railways were promoted in various directions. By 1851 the Derwent Iron Company of Consett had opened up an iron ore mine at Upleatham, near Saltburn, and had built a connecting line to the Middlesbrough & Redcar Railway; this was of even greater benefit to the Stockton & Darlington, for it meant a haul of no less than 54 miles for the ironstone, and was worth at least £10,000 a year to the railway. Dividends rose in a very short time from 4 to 10 per cent, and so far from Stockton & Darlington shareholders entering upon a lean time, they were now regarded on all hands as among the most fortunate of railway proprietors.

In view of this success, it is surprising that when the hard-headed Joseph Pease of the S. & D.R. and his son Sir Joseph Pease put up a scheme for a railway from Middlesbrough to Guisborough, with two branches into the Cleveland Hills, to tap further iron ore resources, they could find few backers, and even when they got their Act of Parliament on 17th June, 1852, it was a question if they would be able to raise the capital of £96,000. However, the Peases had sufficient faith in the future of the railway to guarantee dividends rising in stages from 4 per cent in the first year to 6 per cent in the fifth year and after, and the money was then forthcoming. Work began in the late autumn of 1852 and a year later, on 11th November, 1853, the 9½ miles of the railway were opened for mineral traffic. Passenger opening followed on 25th February, 1854. The line, which was worked by the Stockton & Darlington Railway, climbed for 2 miles from Ormesby to Nunthorpe at 1 in 44, and the Codhill branch, a mile to the east from Guisborough – the only one of the two branches actually laid down – was even steeper, finishing at 1 in 19.

Next, two rival schemes were promoted in 1854, one, the Stockton &
Cleveland Union Railway, for a line from Stockton-on-Tees to Stokesley,
with two branches, and the other, the North Yorkshire & Cleveland Railway, from a junction with the Leeds Northern at Picton across the Yorkshire Moors to join the York & North Midland Malton and Whitby line at
Grosmont. Parliament threw out the Stockton & Cleveland Union Bill,
but passed that of the North Yorkshire & Cleveland, which received the
Royal Assent on 10th July, 1854. After the North Eastern Railway had
been formed by the amalgamation of 1854, the N.E.R. took over the
interest of the Leeds Northern in this scheme.

Construction did not begin until 1855, and by 6th April, 1858, after
opening in stages, the line had reached Kildale, 14 miles from Picton.
From Battersby, just short of Kildale, the Ingleby Mining Company built
a 3½-mile branch which not only made directly towards the Cleveland
Hills, on a 1 in 50 gradient, but on reaching the foot of the steep northern
face went straight up to Burton Head with a rope-worked incline as steep
as 1 in 5 to 1 in 6. The operating wire ropes were 1,650 yards long, passing
round drums of 14ft diameter at the Drum House, 1,370ft above sea-level.
This branch also was opened for traffic on 6th April, 1858.

The North Yorkshire & Cleveland directors had their eye on it, for in
West Rosedale, to the south-west of Burton Head, a rich vein of magnetic
ore had been discovered, which the N.Y. & C. wanted to exploit. From the
West Rosedale mine the first 3,000 to 4,000 tons of ore had been carted by
road to Pickering and worked from there *via* Malton and Pilmoor to the
North Eastern main line and on northwards to various ironworks, such as
the Derwent Works at Consett, that wanted to experiment with it. But a line
across the moorland from Burton Head to West Rosedale would provide a
far shorter route, and this was built and opened in April, 1861. From
Blakey Junction, high up on the moor, a further branch was opened in
August, 1865, to a mine in East Rosedale.

Long before this, however, the North Yorkshire & Cleveland Railway
had been absorbed by the North Eastern Railway, which thus obtained
control of the Ingleby incline and the Rosedale branches and their ore
traffic. There might have been difficulty in this acquisition, for the West
Hartlepool Railway, by virtue of its friendly relations with the former
Leeds Northern, had provided £38,500 of the N.Y. & C. share capital. But
as at that very time the Hartlepool Company was needing capital for
another enterprise, it offered no opposition to being bought out.

The other enterprise just referred to was a bold scheme to obtain a share
in the lucrative Cleveland ore traffic. Blast-furnaces were now springing
up all over the place; indeed, by 1857 there were as many furnaces in blast
on Tees-side, including those now established at South Bank by Bolckow,
Vaughan & Company, as there had been in the whole of Durham and
Northumberland at the beginning of the decade. Among them was an
important plant built by Bell Brothers on land acquired from the West
Hartlepool Harbour & Railway Company at Port Clarence. The reason
for the choice of a site on the opposite bank of the Tees from the Cleveland

ore was the shorter haul needed for coal and coke from the Durham mines. In 1857, therefore, Ralph Ward Jackson and the Hartlepool party evolved a scheme for a new jetty at Port Clarence, a steam ferry to carry the ore across the Tees, another jetty at Cargo Fleet, and from there a 'Durham & Cleveland Union Railway' across the Eston Nab ridge to Guisborough; it would then continue by way of Brotton and round the bold headland known as Hunt Cliff to Skinningrove, with a branch to Staithes. At Skinningrove a rope-worked 1 in 6 incline would be needed to reach the bottom of the valley. It was proposed to bridge over the Middlesbrough & Redcar and Middlesbrough & Guisborough Railways and to lay in spur connections with each.

Needless to say, this projected intrusion into their preserves incensed Joseph Pease and his Stockton & Darlington party, and counter-measures were set on foot at once. The S. & D.R. planned a line of their own from Guisborough to Skinningrove, but direct from Brotton over the high ground behind Hunt Cliff, which would have involved some severe gradients. They also acquired the Upleatham and Skelton ironstone royalties, and proposed an extension of the Middlesbrough & Redcar Railway to Saltburn, to give a better connection to these mines. Finally, they projected a ¾-mile line from west of Middlesbrough across the Tees by a swing-bridge to connect with the Stockton branch of the Hartlepool Railway, which, they claimed, would give the Hartlepool Railway adequate facilities while still keeping a fairly long haul of the ironstone over Stockton & Darlington metals.

In May, 1858, a tremendous fight took place in Parliament over these rival proposals. The town of Stockton, jealous of the rising importance of Middlesbrough, opposed the swing-bridge. The town of Middlesbrough opposed the ferry. The Tees Conservancy Commissioners opposed both the bridge and the ferry. The owners of the land under which the iron ore lay supported the Durham & Cleveland Union scheme, as they considered that the competition of an outside company would do more to develop the resources of the district than if that development were left entirely to the Stockton & Darlington.

In the end, Parliament exercised something closely resembling the judgment of Solomon. The Durham & Cleveland Union Company were authorised to build their railway – to be known as the Cleveland Railway – but only between Guisborough and Skinningrove, that is, without the Cargo Fleet–Guisborough section or the Staithes branch. The Stockton & Darlington obtained authority for its extension from Redcar to Saltburn, with a branch to the Skelton mine, but not for the swing-bridge over the Tees nor any extension eastwards of its own line from Guisborough. But of greater importance to the Stockton & Darlington Railway was the fact that this Act, which like that of the Cleveland Railway received the Royal Assent on 23rd July, 1858, authorised the S. & D.R. to amalgamate with all the lines that it held on lease – the Middlesbrough & Redcar, Middlesbrough & Guisborough, Wear Valley, and – a line to which we shall come in a moment – the Darlington & Barnard Castle.

Nevertheless the Cleveland Railway promoters were not content to have their plans curtailed; like the Stockton & Darlington they also had acquired substantial ironstone royalties, in this case on the Ormesby and Normanby Estates, to the west of the Eston mines, and were determined to be independent in the movement of their ore. Their next move was to present to Parliament a Bill for a 'Cleveland Extension Railway', extending their Guisborough–Skinningrove line backwards over the course originally proposed to a jetty in the Tees at Cargo Fleet. The pretext was that this would make it possible to load ore expeditiously into barges for movement to ironworks up the river, or into sea-going ships for export; other advantages also were claimed.

The Stockton & Darlington Railway tried to checkmate this plan by proposing to lay in a curve west of Thornaby to connect their line directly with the former Leeds Northern (now North Eastern) main line just south of Stockton, so expediting the movement of Cleveland Railway ore to the Hartlepool Railway. This was quite acceptable to the N.E.R., which wished to be on equally friendly terms with both parties, but it proved no deterrent to the Hartlepool party. When the Cleveland Railway Extension Bill was presented to Parliament, it was passed by a Committee of the House of Commons, but rejected by the Lords on the ground that such a line would offer direct competition with the Middlesbrough & Guisborough line of the Stockton and Darlington.

The House of Lords Committee, however, threw out the hint that it ought to be permissible for the owners of mining royalties on the Ormesby and Normanby Estates to lay in branches to work their ore on to the Redcar branch of the S. & D.R., in the Cargo Fleet area, and thence *via* Middlesbrough, instead of it having to pursue the roundabout route *via* Guisborough. This gave the Hartlepool party their cue. Although the Stockton & Darlington received authority from Parliament to lay in its Hartburn curve, and in other ways to improve the facilities it offered to the Cleveland Railway for the movement of its ore, the Cleveland Railway acted on the House of Lords Committee's suggestion by presenting to Parliament in 1860 a Bill for an 'Upsall, Normanby & Ormesby Railway', including the Tees jetty at Cargo Fleet.

The Stockton & Darlington Railway tried to oppose this by claiming rights over the Tees foreshore for the full width of the Normanby Estates, but without success, and eventually the Hartlepool party got their way by the House of Commons Committee laying it down that no Act was needed for what essentially would be a private and not a public railway. That is to say, they could go ahead without further formalities. Still the Stockton & Darlington Railway were not prepared to give in tamely, and in their sustained opposition they now got the backing of the Tees Conservancy Commissioners.

The latter so objected to the jetty that as soon as work began on it in the autumn of 1860 they offered physical obstruction by mooring a line of barges on the site. As this was the Long Vacation, Ralph Ward Jackson of Hartlepool, unable to get redress by law, took matters into his own hands, and there began what at the time was known as the 'Battle of the Tees'. His men were clearing away the barges when a steam tug of the Commissioners bore down on them and a free fight developed, which Jackson's men won. Chains secured to large buoys were then installed to protect the site, but the following night three steam tugs arrived with instructions to damage the works, and this time there was a much more dangerous fight, with flying lumps of iron ore and even paving-stones. The police were then called in, and kept watch day and night until the work was finished.

Another blow for the Stockton & Darlington Railway was when in November, 1860, Captain Chaloner of the Guisborough Estates came to the conclusion that the Upsall, Normanby & Ormesby Railway would provide a shorter and cheaper route for his ore than the Middlesbrough & Guisborough line of the S. & D.R., and built a bridge over the latter to reach the line of his choice. By now Jackson had gained all that his Hartlepool party had sought in their Bill of 1858 and even more, and as what he had done reversed in large measure the parliamentary decision of that year, even to the extent that loaded ore-wagons were now to be carried across the Tees from Cargo Fleet to Port Clarence by a species of train-ferry, it was necessary to obtain retrospective sanction for what had been done.

In the Parliamentary Committee Rooms the Stockton & Darlington Railway representatives complained bitterly of the partiality which appeared to have been shown to their rivals, especially as the S. & D.R. had spent between £8,000 and £10,000 in improving the facilities for handling the Cleveland Railway's ore traffic, but all to no avail. The latter's 13-mile independent line from the Skelton New Mine direct to the Normanby jetty was completed and opened on 23rd November, 1861. Three months earlier, on 17th August, 1861, the Stockton & Darlington Railway had brought into operation its 5-mile extension from Redcar to Saltburn.

As for the activities of the North Eastern Railway in this area, the North Yorkshire & Cleveland line from Picton had been further extended in the Whitby direction, from Kildale to Castleton, and work was in progress on the link between this line and the Middlesbrough & Guisborough line, between Battersby Junction and Nunthorpe by way of Great Ayton. Not until 2nd October, 1865, did the opening of the last 7½ miles of the former from Castleton to Grosmont establish through rail communication by this direct route between Stockton-on-Tees and Whitby; the Battersby–Nunthorpe line was opened on 1st June, 1864, but for its first four years for mineral traffic only.

During these years important developments had been taking place also to the west of Darlington, in which the carriage of iron ore played a vital part and with which the Stockton & Darlington Railway was closely concerned. First of all, the traffic from and to the Derwent Ironworks at Consett had vastly increased. By 1857 the company owned 18 blast-furnaces, 543 coke ovens, rolling mills for wrought-iron sections and foundries, and every year, using some 600,000 tons of coal, 300,000 to 400,000 tons of iron ore and 110,000 tons of limestone, was turning out

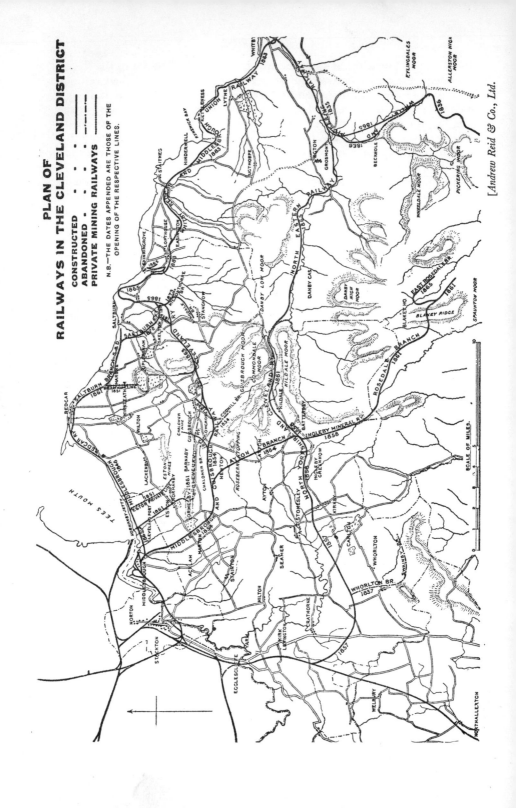

PLAN OF
RAILWAYS IN THE CLEVELAND DISTRICT

CONSTRUCTED . . .
ABANDONED . . .
PRIVATE MINING RAILWAYS

N.B.—THE DATES APPENDED ARE THOSE OF THE
OPENING OF THE RESPECTIVE LINES.

[Andrew Reid & Co., Ltd.

about 150,000 tons of iron or iron products. With the joint assistance of the Stockton & Darlington and North Eastern Railways it had survived the crash in that year of the Northumberland & Durham District Bank, to which it was heavily indebted, and though in financial difficulties for several years afterwards there was no interruption of its output.

Whereas in former years the Derwent traffic over the Stockton & Darlington line to the south had been mainly of its manufactures, there was now the heavy traffic in iron ore from its Upleatham mine near Middlesbrough to be handled in the opposite direction from near sea-level up steep gradients and several rope-worked inclined planes to the 1,154ft altitude of Burnhill before reaching the ironworks, and this was a different proposition altogether. On the 1 in 43 Howden incline, near Crook, a powerful locomotive called the *Duke*, specially built in 1854 for the purpose, assisted the ore trains in rear as they were pulled by wire ropes to the summit by the stationary winding engine.

Worst obstacle of all was the deep cleft at Hownes Gill, on the former Stanhope & Tyne line. Chapter V described the original method of working by ropes down and up the 1 in 2½ and 1 in 3 gradients of the two sides, when the wagons were lowered and raised singly. This extraordinarily cumbrous method continued until 1853, when after experiments it was found possible to dispense with the former turntables and cradles, and to run the wagons up and down three at a time, as many as 550 to 650 being dealt with in a day. From time to time, however loads fell out of the wagons because of the steep angle at which they were being handled, especially lengths of iron rails and sections on their way from Consett to the south.

Finally, in 1856, the Stockton & Darlington Railway had to make the inevitable decision to replace the inclines by a viaduct, and after a year and half's work and an expenditure of £15,756, this notable masonry structure was brought into use on 1st July, 1858. At its highest 150ft above the valley floor, it had 12 semi-circular arches and was 730ft long. Four years later a deviation line between Crook and Tow Law cut out the Sunnyside inclined plane, with its 1 in 13 to 1 in 16 inclination, and substituted for it a 4½-mile climb at 1 in 51–52.

The North Eastern Railway also was interested in obtaining independent access to the Derwent Iron Works with ore worked from its North Yorkshire & Cleveland line, and on 13th July, 1857, obtained parliamentary authority to build a line from Relly Mill Junction, at the Durham end of the Durham–Bishop Auckland branch, up the Lanchester valley to Blackhill. Because of the financial difficulties of the Derwent Iron Works at this time, previously referred to, construction was held up, but eventually this 12-mile line was completed and opened for traffic on 1st September, 1863. A notable feature of the branch was a great timber viaduct at Knitsley.

This vast increase in iron production was having an effect in another direction altogether. Cleveland iron ore in general is of a low grade, high in phosphorus, and to obtain iron of the best quality it was necessary that the blast-furnace charges should include an admixture of the purer haema-tite ores, of which the nearest supply was the West Coast deposits of Cumberland and North Lancashire. A considerable traffic thus had begun to come across the country from Cumberland to Durham by the only available route, the Newcastle & Carlisle Railway. This fact had not escaped the notice of the alert Stockton & Darlington directorate, which decided to revive the scheme of the early 1840s, already mentioned in Chapter XII, for a line across the Pennines through Barnard Castle and Kirkby Stephen, forking there into the branches to Tebay to the south, and Clifton near Penrith to the north, on the Lancaster & Carlisle Railway.

As the first stage, several of the Stockton & Darlington directors joined the board of a company formed to promote a line from Darlington to Barnard Castle, by way of Winston, Gainsford and Piercebridge. Once again they were to have to fight resolute opponents. Landowners whose property might be affected were up in arms; it was claimed that the line would give the S. & D.R. an unfair monopoly of the district; and a tech-nical objection concerning the width of the formation proposed for the line secured the rejection of the Bill. A second Bill was prepared by November, 1853, but now the implacable enemies at Hartlepool stepped in with an alternative plan, for a line from Bishop Auckland to Barnard Castle as the first stage of the Pennine crossing. The York, Newcastle & Berwick Railway (this was a year before the formation of the North Eastern Railway) had just let the contract for its Durham–Bishop Auckland branch, and so backed the Hartlepool project, as also did the towns of Newcastle, West Hartlepool and Durham and the Sunderland Dock Company.

Joseph Pease was the personal target of much of the attack, as an auto-crat who wanted to rule the entire area. Nevertheless he got his Act, on 4th July, 1854, and Ralph Ward Jackson and his party, notwithstanding their very substantial backing, this time suffered a defeat. The latter derived some consolation in that the Act for the Shildon Tunnel to St Helen's Auckland spur, which received the Royal Assent at the same time, required, *inter alia*, a reduction in the toll for freight passing through the tunnel from 6d. to 2d. a ton, to the advantage of the Hartlepool Railway. The Bishop Auckland & Barnard Castle Bill was rejected.

Amid public rejoicing the Darlington & Barnard Castle Railway was opened on 8th July, 1856, and by an Act of Parliament in 1858, not only was this line amalgamated with the Stockton & Darlington Railway, but also, as previously mentioned, the Wear Valley, Middlesbrough & Guisborough and Middlesbrough & Redcar Railways. Another important opening in 1856, on 13th September, was of the spur line of the Stockton & Darlington from the north end of Shildon Tunnel to West Auckland, mentioned in the last paragraph. This meant that coal from the Gaunless valley no longer had to be worked over the celebrated Brusselton incline, as it had done for over 30 years since the opening of the S. & D.R. in 1825, in order to reach Shildon.

In November, 1856, when the former York & Carlisle and Northumber-land & Lancashire Union schemes for new railways across the Pennines from Barnard Castle westwards, mentioned in Chapter XII, had fallen into abeyance, various interests, the Stockton & Darlington among them, promoted a Bill for a railway continuing the S. & D.R. Hagger Leases branch from Spring Gardens Junction, near the Lands Colliery, and joining the Darlington & Barnard Castle Railway at the latter town – so replacing the previous Bishop Auckland & Barnard Castle scheme – and proceeding from Barnard Castle to Kirkby Stephen and Tebay. It was to be called the South Durham & Lancashire Union Railway and to be worked by the S. & D.R., the latter to have the right to lease or acquire the line on guaranteeing a 6 per cent dividend to the preference share-holders.

Without opposition from any quarter, the Act received the Royal Assent on 13th July, 1857. A year later, on 21st May, 1858, Parliament sanctioned a scheme promoted by various gentlemen in Westmorland for a railway from Kirkby Stephen through Appleby to a junction with the Lancaster & Carlisle Railway at Clifton, south of Penrith; the Eden Valley Railway thus completed the original York & Carlisle and North-umberland & Lancashire Union proposals.

It is difficult to imagine that the capital of £533,000 originally authorised was sufficient to cover the building cost of the South Durham & Lancashire Union Railway, in view of the engineering works that were necessary to lay a line through the heart of the Pennines. Immediately after leaving Barnard Castle the line had to cross the Tees; this required a viaduct 732ft long, with five wrought-iron lattice girder spans carried on masonry piers at a maximum height of 132ft above the river, flanked by masonry arches. Next the line, bending for a short distance due southwards, had to cross the profound gorge of the Deepdale river, and here a 740ft viaduct with eleven 60ft spans was built, having similar lattice girders supported on wrought-iron trestles up to 161ft above the stream level.

Biggest of all the viaducts was on the westward descent from the summit, across the Belah valley between Barras and Kirkby Stephen; the maximum height of this was no less than 196ft, and in the total length of 1,040ft sixteen 60ft lattice girder spans on wrought-iron trestles were needed. These three viaducts alone accounted for more than £77,400 of the total expenditure. Also in crossing Smardale, between Kirkby Stephen and Tebay, a masonry viaduct had to be built to a maximum height of 90ft, 553ft long and with fourteen arches of 30ft span; five other masonry viaducts of lesser size were needed at other points.

Formidable gradients were unavoidable in carrying the line to its maximum altitude of 1,370ft at Stainmore Summit. Already, between Darlington and Barnard Castle, there had been 5 miles up mainly at 1 in 80–86 from between Winston and Gainford to Broomielaw. Then, a mile west of Barnard Castle, there began a 5½-mile climb at about 1 in 70 to Bowes, followed, after an easier 4-mile ascent, by 3 final miles at 1 in 68 to the summit. The ascent from the west was considerably more exacting. Out of Kirkby Stephen came 2 miles at 1 in 72, and then 6 miles right off at about 1 in 60. Tunnelling might have eased these inclinations considerably, but for the sake of economy Thomas Bouch, the engineer, preferred to work round the contours, at the expense of distance and steepness, which were both to complicate the operating problems after the line had been opened.

Mineral traffic began at various dates in 1861, but the formal opening for passenger traffic did not take place until 8th August of that year, after which two passenger trains ran in each direction daily. Two especially powerful 4-4-0 engines, the *Lowther* and the *Brougham*, with 16in by 24in cylinders and 6ft coupled wheels, were built in 1860 by Robert Stephenson & Co. for service over the line; in view of the probable severity of winter weather at such high altitudes, both were fitted with unusually large cabs, with two windows on each side.

Construction of the Eden Valley Railway was rapid; by 7th June, 1862, it was ready to begin operation; little engineering work of note had been required, other than the Skygarth and Musgrave viaducts, the former with four lattice girder spans of 98ft 3in each. During the time it was being built there had been a happening which later on considerably increased its importance. It was the Act of Parliament obtained in 1861 for the Cockermouth, Keswick·& Penrith Railway, which, in conjunction with the Cockermouth & Workington Railway, was to provide a direct route for a two-way traffic – haematite iron ore from West Cumberland to the blast-furnaces of County Durham and North Yorkshire, and Durham coke for the blast-furnaces of West Cumberland. For this sound reason, the Stockton & Darlington Railway subscribed £25,000 to the capital of the C.K. & P.R.

Running powers were obtained over what had now become the London & North Western main line from Eden Valley Junction, Clifton, to Penrith, and to avoid reversal in Penrith of the through trains, the Stockton & Darlington obtained powers also to build a 1-mile spur from Eamont Bridge Junction, a mile south of Penrith, direct to Red Hills Junction on the Cockermouth, Keswick & Penrith line. The year 1862 saw the amalgamation of the South Durham & Lancashire Union and the Eden Valley Railways with the Stockton & Darlington Railway, and also with the 2¼-mile extension from Frosterley to Stanhope of the Wear Valley Railway; a total of 59 route miles was thus added in this one year to the S. & D.R. system.

CHAPTER XV

Repelling the Would-Be Invaders

DURING the momentous years of railway development on Tees-side, described in the last chapter, matters were by no means at a standstill on Tyneside. One small railway had come into existence north of the Tyne which was destined to become quite prosperous; to remain independent, as an enclave within the heart of the North Eastern Railway, until twenty years after the formation of that company; and also to figure in the plans of another railway which had ambitions to penetrate N.E.R. territory. The Northumberland line in question was the Blyth & Tyne Railway.

In the days of the early wagonways laid to carry coal from the Durham mines to the sea, a number of similar wagonways had been laid in the southern part of Northumberland. One was the Seghill Railway, opened in June, 1840, and promoted in order that the Seghill Colliery owners might get their coal down to the Tyne without being dependent, as hitherto, on the even earlier Cramlington wagonway. Between Seghill and Holywell it was operated by steam locomotives, but stationary engines were used to work the incline from Prospect Hill to the staiths at Percy Main, which descended first at gradients of 1 in 55 to 1 in 70, and finally at 1 in 25 to 1 in 31. After various short branches had been built and worked privately, the decision was reached to incorporate, and on 30th June, 1852, the Blyth & Tyne Railway obtained its Act of Parliament.

After some severe fights against competing interests, the Blyth & Tyne obtained a second Act, on 4th August, 1853, to build a branch from Newsham (which had already been reached by an extension from Seghill through Hartley) by way of Bedlington to the then York, Newcastle & Berwick Railway at Morpeth; another line was authorised parallel with the coast from New Hartley southwards to Tynemouth, and a third from Bedlington to North Seaton, to tap mines in the Ashington area. By October, 1857, the Morpeth branch was opened for freight traffic and six months later for passenger trains.

Four years after this, in face of severe opposition from what had now become the North Eastern Railway, powers were obtained by the Blyth & Tyne to build a further branch from Backworth into the heart of Newcastle itself. This last, which crossed the Newcastle & Berwick main line at Benton, then turned south through Jesmond to terminate near Picton House, at New Bridge Street, as the station soon became known. The Newcastle branch was opened formally on 22nd June, 1864, and for public traffic five days later. From the start it enabled the Blyth & Tyne to compete successfully with the North Eastern's Newcastle–Tynemouth branch, acquired from the former Newcastle & North Shields Railway.

By now the Blyth & Tyne had a north-to-south main line from Blyth through Newsham, New Hartley and Seghill to Percy Main on the Tyne, with a branch from Newsham to Morpeth; intersecting this at Backworth was the west-to-east line from New Bridge Street, Newcastle, *via* Monk-seaton to Tynemouth; there were also the connecting line from Monk-seaton to New Hartley, the branch from Bedlington to North Seaton, and one or two minor colliery branches. By cutting through Prospect Hill the company had considerably eased the gradient down to the Tyne at Percy Main.

About this time the North British Railway in Scotland was displaying a good deal of restlessness, and more than one of its neighbours had reason to be concerned about its ambitions. As early as 1847 to 1849 the North British had extended a feeler south-westwards from Edinburgh through Galashiels to Hawick. By the middle 1850s the eyes of the Scottish company were on Carlisle and Newcastle, and the determination had been born to reach both with its own metals. In the winter of 1857–1858 the North Eastern directors approached those of the North British with a view to possible amalgamation, in order to forestall such competition, but terms could not be agreed, and the project came to nothing.

Then the North British began to move. In 1845 the Border Counties Railway Company had been formed, for a line branching from the New-castle & Carlisle Railway at Hexham, and proceeding up the valley of the North Tyne; this had reached Woodburn, $34\frac{1}{2}$ miles from Hexham. The North British planned to extend its Edinburgh–Hawick line as a new Border Union Railway south from Hawick into Liddesdale, in order to reach Carlisle, and to finance an extension of the Border Counties line, branching from the latter at Reedsmouth, $3\frac{3}{4}$ miles short of Woodburn, and proceeding up the North Tyne valley to join the Border Union at Riccarton. So an alliance was formed between the N.B.R. and the Border Counties, leading to amalgamation in 1860, well before the completion of the con-nection between the two, which was not ready for use until 1862.

Meantime the North British Railway had backed another scheme, for a line up the Wansbeck valley from Morpeth, intended eventually to effect a junction with the Border Counties Railway. By 1862 the Wansbeck Valley Railway had reached Scotsgap; by 1863 it had been purchased by the North British; by 1865 the N.B.R. had completed the necessary exten-sion to the junction with the Border Counties, which it had acquired five years earlier, at Reedsmouth. Now, therefore, the North British Railway had its own independent route, even if circuitous and very steeply graded, from Edinburgh to Morpeth *via* Hawick, Riccarton and Reedsmouth.

The next move of the N.B.R. was to enter into traffic arrangements with the Blyth & Tyne, branching as it did from the opposite side of the North Eastern main line at Morpeth and giving independent access to Newcastle. As Tomlinson writes in *The North Eastern Railway*, the smaller company was 'not a little astonished at receiving so much flattering attention' from the North British authorities in Edinburgh. But any designs that the N.B.R. may have had to take possession of the Blyth & Tyne came to nothing, as also did a scheme to make a new line northwards from Scotsgap through Rothbury and Whittingham to Wooler, with an eventual extension to Jedburgh. This plan was opposed so strenuously by the people of Alnwick, who feared diversion of traffic from their town, that the North British had to abandon the major part of it, though they did obtain an Act to build a branch as far as Rothbury, which they opened in 1870.

The North British Railway had now obtained a substantial foothold in Northumberland, and independent access of a kind to Newcastle and the ports at the mouth of the Tyne. But this was only a part, and, indeed, a minor part of the N.B.R. ambitions. The Border Counties Railway opened a whole vista of possibilities. To combat these ambitions of a company which hitherto the North Eastern had regarded as an ally, but which now had become definitely hostile, the N.E.R., in 1858, had approached the board of the Newcastle & Carlisle Railway, which until then it had held under lease only, with a view to amalgamation, and terms had been agreed in 1859. But certain dissatisfied shareholders of the Newcastle & Carlisle, backed by the North British, had found a legal flaw in the agreement between the former and the North Eastern, with the result that under a new agreement the Newcastle & Carlisle resumed independent management of its line, including reacquisition from the N.E.R. of its rolling stock. The opposition of the North British and its allies was strong enough to defeat the N.E.R. – N. & C.R. Amalgamation Bill in the parliamentary session of 1860.

Now the North Eastern Railway had to face a new and serious threat to Tyneside from the south. A company was formed in 1859 to build a 13½-mile railway from Scotswood, on the Newcastle & Carlisle line, up the Derwent Valley past the ironworks at Consett to a junction with the Stockton & Darlington Railway at Hownes Gill. By the spring of 1860 the Newcastle & Derwent Valley Railway scheme had expanded to a much more comprehensive Newcastle, Derwent & Weardale Railway, starting from Gateshead, and from there proceeding *via* Redheugh and Swalwell up the Derwent Valley to Consett; the Stockton & Darlington line would then be avoided by building an independent line through Tow Law to the South Durham & Lancashire Union Railway at Bishop Auckland, though a connection with the S. & D.R. would be laid in at Hownes Gill. But a connection was also proposed with the Byers Green branch of the Stockton & Darlington's traditional enemy – the West Hartlepool Harbour & Railway Company. It was proposed, further, to link up with the North Eastern Railway at Gateshead and the Newcastle & Carlisle at Derwenthaugh.

The dangers of this scheme to the North Eastern Railway were not so much in the realm of local as of through traffic, for two-thirds of the share capital of the new company was to be provided by the North British and the London & North Western Railways. The L.N.W.R. had always been aggrieved by the fact that the N.E.R. insisted on carrying its traffic from Liverpool to Newcastle by way of Normanton, which deprived the North Western of any share of its haulage, and favoured the Lancashire &

Yorkshire Railway instead. The L.N.W.R. claimed that the correct route
was *via* Leeds and the Leeds Northern, which was considerably shorter.
The North Eastern also had blocked the route from Liverpool by way of
Carlisle and over the Newcastle & Carlisle from there to Newcastle – one
of the objections, incidentally, which had been used by the opposition to
secure the defeat in 1859 of the North Eastern and Newcastle & Carlisle
amalgamation Bill in Parliament.

The purpose of the London & North Western Railway was clear; it was
to open up a new branch from its main line at Tebay to Newcastle by way
of Kirkby Stephen, Barnard Castle, Bishop Auckland and Crook. More
than that, with the enthusiastic co-operation of the West Hartlepool Harbour & Railway Company, a through London & North Western route
would become available to Hartlepool, where the L.N.W.R. proposed to
purchase land and build warehouses, and also to acquire a quarter of the
share capital of the West Hartlepool Railway. So this, it will be seen, was
a threat of the first magnitude to the North Eastern; it hinged, of course,
on the acquisition or control by the L.N.W.R. of the South Durham &
Lancashire Union Railway, which as yet had not passed into the possession of the Stockton & Darlington Railway. As for the North British Railway, the Newcastle, Derwent & Weardale line would enable it to move
ironstone from the Bellingham area direct to the Consett and Tow Law
ironworks without any use of North Eastern metals.

The North Eastern Railway directors now had to move, and to move
fast. Work on the branch from Durham to Consett *via* Lanchester had
been held up, as previously described, by the difficulties of the Derwent
Iron Works consequent on the Northumberland & Durham District Bank
crash; a new Act had to be obtained before construction could be recom-
menced and expedited. Hitherto, the N.E.R. had given no attention to the
Derwent Valley also as a means of access to Consett, but now was compelled to do so, and immediately began surveys for a rival line up the
valley to link up at Consett with the Lanchester branch. Negotiations
were begun at the same time with the Stockton & Darlington board as to
a possible amalgamation with the N.E.R., and as the former now realised
that eventually they might have to face a choice between the London &
North Western and the North Eastern Railways, these advances of the
N.E.R. were not unfavourably received.

The South Durham & Lancashire Union Railway board also showed a
disposition to sit on the fence rather than to fall into the arms of the
Newcastle, Derwent & Weardale promoters, who thus felt the ground cut
from beneath their feet. However, the latter pressed forward with their
Bill, even to the extent of getting the preamble proved by the House of
Commons in the 1861 session, whereas the North Eastern Railway's Bil
for a branch from Blaydon to Consett was thrown out. The N.E.R. representatives, on the other hand, had little difficulty in proving that a route
such as that proposed from Tebay to Newcastle *via* Kirkby Stephen,
Barnard Castle, Bishop Auckland and Consett would be extremely expensive to operate for through traffic between Liverpool and Newcastle,

because of the length and steepness of its gradients, and that it could offer no comparison with the existing route *via* Normanton. If the N.E.R. had lost its own Bill, it experienced the relief of seeing its opponents' Bill rejected also by the House of Lords.

Moreover, in the following year, 1862, the North Eastern Railway got its Act for a Derwent Valley line practically without opposition. Steep gradients were involved; indeed, for 7½ miles from Rowlands Gill to just beyond Blackhill a practically uninterrupted 1 in 66 climb was needed. There were also four substantial brick and stone viaducts with 6oft span arches – two over the Derwent of nine and seven arches respectively, each with a maximum height of 8oft; one six-arch viaduct over the Fogoes valley near Lintz Green 9oft high; and the biggest a ten-arch structure up to 12oft high over the Pont valley. This branch was opened for mineral traffic on 18th June, 1867, and for passenger traffic on 2nd December of the same year.

With the collapse of the Newcastle, Derwent & Weardale scheme the rosy dreams faded which the West Hartlepool Harbour & Railway had had of a lucrative association with the London & North Western Railway. On the contrary, by 1861 the West Hartlepool Company found itself in serious financial difficulties. The L.N.W.R. had expended £100,000 in buying the whole side of one of the West Hartlepool docks, with its warehouses, but the attempt of this company to secure a footing on the North East Coast was now doomed to failure. Worse than this, however, the West Hartlepool Company's own finances were in a sorry mess. Debenture interest to the extent of more than £126,000 was unpaid, and in February, 1862, the Court of Chancery appointed a receiver. Investigation showed that whereas the amount of share and loan capital that had been authorised by various Acts was some £2,800,000, the amount actually raised and spent had been no less than £3,733,393; the capital authorised had been spent to the full on the harbour, docks, warehouses, railways and rolling stock, but nearly a million more had gone on the acquisition of collieries, steamships, shares in other companies, and in other ways. The net deficiency on the revenue account for the year ending 31st December, 1861, was £153,596.

As the result of disclosures of various financial irregularities, Ralph Ward Jackson, who had been in charge of West Hartlepool affairs, had to resign from the board. In a measure it was the story of George Hudson all over again, though in this case the downfall was that of a man who had derived no personal profit from his actions, but whose zeal for his company and his town had led him to financial indiscretion on a large scale. Nevertheless, Hartlepool owed much to his enterprise. What eighteen years before had been merely a barren coastline of sandhills backed by agricultural land by 1862 had become a substantial port, with a harbour covering 44 acres, three deep-water docks aggregating 32 acres in area, two large graving docks, a timber area comprising 24 acres of water space and 20 acres of timber yards, warehouses with a total floor area of 13 acres, and 25 miles of railways in and around the docks and as approaches. A short connecting line built on piles across the Slake had been opened in January, 1862, to restore the railway communication between West Hartlepool and Hartlepool that had been severed in 1845. Hartlepool itself had grown into a thriving town with some 16,000 inhabitants.

Some relief was obtained by the new West Hartlepool directorate by the sale, at a considerable loss, of the company's fleet of steamers; similar attempts were made to dispose of the collieries, but the prices quoted by possible purchasers were so low that it was decided for the time to retain these. It was then realised that parliamentary sanction would be needed for a rearrangement of the capital, and without litigation the directors obtained the agreement of the stockholders for the conversion of the debentures into preference stock, thereby reducing the interest payable. The Act of 1863 gave authority to raise £100,000 in order to repurchase from the London & North Western Railway the docks property that had been sold to that company; it also directed that the West Hartlepool's collieries must now be sold.

The affairs of the associated Cleveland Railway were in a similarly unsatisfactory state, but the directors themselves redeemed out of their own pockets those of the debentures that they were unable to get cancelled, and by calls on the shareholders the corner was turned. Overtures which the North Eastern Railway had made in 1860 to both these companies as to possible amalgamation had come to nothing, for their financial condition at that time had been such that the terms could not have been other than unfavourable to them; but it was clear that this fusion could not now be delayed much longer.

There had been other threats to the North Eastern at about this time. One city on its system with which the company had not the happiest relations was Hull, no doubt because the N.E.R. had the monopoly of its rail approaches. For this reason various other railways had their eyes on Hull, and not without encouragement from that city took steps to obtain, if they could, independent access to it.

In 1862, three projects were on foot for approach to Hull from the south-west through Goole. One was the Hull & West Riding Junction Railway, which failed for lack of financial support. The second was the Doncaster, Goole & Hull Junction, promoted by the Lancashire & Yorkshire Railway, for a line extending its own main line from Liverpool and Manchester to Goole across the Ouse to Staddlethorpe, on the N.E.R. Leeds–Selby–Hull line. The third was a proposed Hull Extension of the South Yorkshire Railway, to leave this company's Doncaster–Frodingham–Grimsby line at Thorne and also run through Goole to Staddlethorpe. Behind the latter there was the Manchester, Sheffield & Lincolnshire Railway, which was to absorb the South Yorkshire Company in 1864, and also the Great Northern Railway, which similarly hankered after direct access of its own to Hull.

A fierce fight developed in Parliament between the companies promoting the two last-mentioned schemes and the North Eastern Railway, which had before Parliament at the same time its own Bill for a line

Eight-coupled mineral locomotive designs began with Wilson Worsdell's Class 'T' in 1901, with piston-valves, and the similar Class 'T1', with slide-valves, 50 in all.

Next followed the superheated Class 'T2', under Raven's supervision, of which 152 were built from 1913 to 1921.

The final 0-8-0 development was Class 'T3', with three-cylinder simple propulsion, the first of which appeared in 1919.

[*All, Locomotive Publishing Co.*]

The first North Eastern Atlantic type, No. 649 of the Wilson Worsdell Class 'V', of which the pioneer, No. 532, was turned out in 1903.

No. 696 of the second Wilson Worsdell Atlantic series, the slightly less powerful Class 'VI', which appeared in 1911.

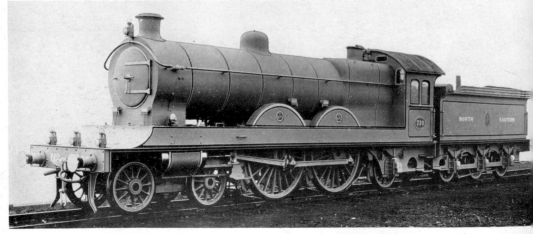

W. M. Smith's masterpiece – No. 730, one of two four-cylinder compound Atlantics built in 1906 under Wilson Worsdell's superintendence.

[*All, Locomotive Publishing Co.*

Above, No. 2002 of the original Class 'S', first of the Wilson Worsdell 4-6-0 classes, with single-window cab (to shorten the engine for turntable reasons), built in 1899.

Left, No. 2111 of the series of five built with 6ft 8in coupled wheels (the only true N.E.R. 4-6-0 express engines).

Later engines of Class 'S' had cabs of the normal two-window type.
[*All, Locomotive Publishing Co.*

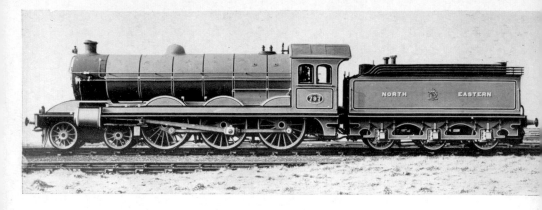

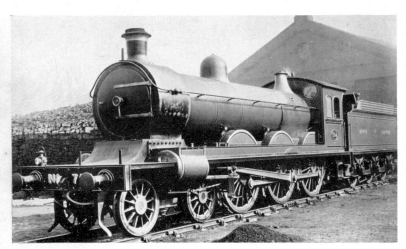

Above, Raven's develo[p]ment of the 'S' mix[ed] traffic 4-6-0s was Cla[ss] 'S2', with 5ft 6in boil[er] of which No. 797 is illu[s]trated. An intermedia[te] stage (*left*) was the mod[i]fication of Class 'S' wi[th] raised running-plate fro[m] cylinders back to cab.
[*W. J. Reyno[lds*]

Below, Class 'S3' 4-6[-0] No. 825, fitted wi[th] Stumpf 'Uniflow' cylin[ders.
[*All, Locomot[ive] Publishing C[o.*]

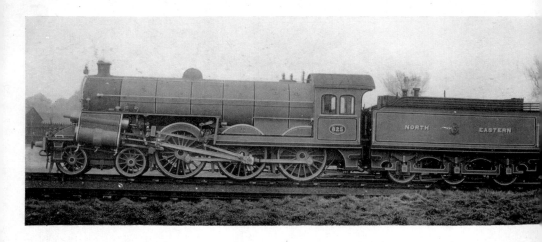

from Staddlethorpe through Goole to Thorne; the contest proved expensive, as it cost the contestants some £100,000 in all. In the end both the Doncaster, Goole & Hull Junction and the South Yorkshire Hull Extension Bills were defeated; the North Eastern Bill passed the Commons but by no more than a single vote was thrown out by the Lords.

On 23rd July of the following year, 1863, however, the North Eastern Railway obtained its Act, after having come to terms with its competitors. The South Yorkshire Railway was conceded running powers for coal trains over the new line from Thorne to Hull – powers which, of course, passed into Manchester, Sheffield & Lincolnshire Railway hands in the following year – while the North Eastern in return was granted running powers over the South Yorkshire from Thorne into Doncaster. A new agreement was come to with the Lancashire & Yorkshire Railway that traffic from the L. & Y. line to and from Hull should be carried at the same rate *via* Goole as it had been hitherto *via* Normanton and Selby; the L. & Y.R. also was to have running powers over the N.E.R. from Goole to Hull, balanced by N.E.R. running powers over the L. & Y.R. from Normanton to Barnsley.

One major engineering work was needed in building the 15½ miles of line between Thorne Junction and Staddlethorpe. It was the crossing of the River Ouse just north of Goole, just before the river widens to become the estuary of the Humber, and as the river is navigable this required an opening bridge. At the time of its construction the opening span of the Skelton bridge was the largest double-line swing-bridge, with one exception, in the world. The movable centre span, hydraulically operated, was hog-backed in form, 250ft in length, and rotated on a 30ft diameter turn-table; it weighed 670 tons. It was flanked by five fixed plate girder spans, each 116ft long between the centres of the supports, the whole forming a viaduct 830ft in length. At Goole spur lines were laid in, partly by the Lancashire & Yorkshire and partly by the North Eastern, to bring the former's trains on to the North Eastern line at Boothferry Junction, just short of Goole passenger station. Owing to the time taken to complete the Skelton bridge, the Thorne–Goole–Staddlethorpe line was not opened until 30th July, 1869; Goole benefited greatly by being now on a direct main line to and from London.

Meantime yet another dangerous threat, aimed at Hull, had developed from the south. This was a project in 1865 for a Hull, Lancashire & Midland Counties Railway, which would give the Manchester, Sheffield & Lincolnshire, Great Northern and Great Eastern Railways completely independent access to Hull. The new line, which had the support of the Hull Corporation and other public bodies in the city, would leave the Boston–Lincoln loop line of the Great Northern Railway at Bardney and cut northwards to reach the Lincoln–Market Rasen–Barnetby branch of the Manchester, Sheffield & Lincolnshire Railway at Snelland. The latter would then be used until just before it curved to the east at Barnetby; new construction would continue from here, with spur connections from both the Sheffield–Grimsby and Doncaster–Frodingham–Grimsby lines of the M.S. & L.R., to Barton-on-Humber.

A high-level viaduct would then be required across the Humber, from the north end of which, at Hessle, the North Eastern Railway Selby–Hull line would be paralleled into the city. A link-up was also proposed with what proved to be the abortive Leeds, North Yorkshire & Durham Railway (mentioned in Chapter XVI) by way of Market Weighton, Wharram and Rillington, with a branch to Bridlington. The cost of this ambitious scheme, and particularly of the great viaduct across the Humber, would have been enormous; it is hardly surprising that the lack of adequate financial support caused it to be dropped.

It is difficult to understand why the Hull authorities through these and subsequent years should have followed a course as antagonistic as they did to the North Eastern Railway. The latter had not used its monopoly to take advantage of Hull. It might have been a matter for argument whether its freight rates favoured Hull, or the reverse, but the N.E.R. certainly could not be charged with indifference to Hull interests. On the contrary, in 1865 it had obtained parliamentary powers to subscribe £50,000 towards the cost of constructing the Albert Dock, without laying down any conditions as to preferential treatment in the dock's use.

But when, in October, 1865, the N.E.R. directors, with a view to acquiring the whole of the Hull Docks, convened a conference of representatives of the Hull Corporation, the Hull Chamber of Commerce, the Hull Dock Company, and all Hull steamship owners, though the last-mentioned without exception were in favour of the N.E.R. plan, the Hull Corporation opposed it, and proposed instead that the docks should be vested in a body of trustees for the benefit of the city. Moreover, the Corporation shortly afterwards deposited a Bill in Parliament for this purpose, but now the opposition of the North Eastern Railway, the Hull Dock Company, and a number of citizens who feared an increase of rates if dock operation by the trust should prove unprofitable, was sufficient to secure defeat of the Corporation's Bill in the House of Commons. At the same time the N.E.R. directors, who also had deposited a Bill to authorise their proposed acquisition of the docks, decided in view of probable future difficulties with the Corporation not to proceed with their Bill either.

Elsewhere in North Eastern territory there had been a threat of less consequence from the Midland Railway, which proposed in 1860 to cut through from Leeds into Wharfedale, and reach Ilkley, thereby forestalling a branch for which the North Eastern Railway already had made a survey. However, by an amicable arrangement between the two boards it was decided that the Midland should build a new line from Apperley Bridge to Guiseley, and then, forking north of Menston, that this railway should join at Milner Wood and Burley Junctions a line to be built jointly by both companies from Otley to Ilkley; the North Eastern Railway would build its own short link from Arthington, on the former Leeds Northern Railway, to join the new joint railway at Otley. These lines were completed and opened in 1865; in 1878 the Midland Railway opened a spur line from

Shipley to Guiseley, and thereby provided a direct route from Bradford to Harrogate.

Such happenings stress the able management of North Eastern affairs during some particularly difficult years. It is not surprising that the growing prosperity of North Eastern England should have been attracting the envious eyes of other railways, but as we have seen the N.E.R., not without some setbacks, had succeeded in repelling attacks from more directions than one. The London & North Western Railway had been decisively defeated and the North British Railway's incursion into Northumberland had been confined within fairly innocuous limits. Four attempted invasions of Hull from the south had been repelled, and it was not until some twenty years later, as we shall see in Chapter XXI, that in 1885 a 'stranger' began operation over a completely independent railway into and out of that city. By the pressure of events, also, the lines still independent within the heart of the North Eastern territory had been brought to the point of absorption into the larger system.

Credit for these achievements must go largely to two extremely able men who during this period were at the head of the North Eastern Railway – Harry Stephen Thompson (later Sir H. S. Meysey-Thompson, Bart.) and George Leeman. Both had joined the North Eastern Board at the time of the incorporation of the Company in 1854, Thompson from the York & North Midland Railway and Leeman from the York, Newcastle & Berwick. Within a year Thompson had become Chairman and Leeman Deputy Chairman of the Company, positions which they retained for 19 years; when Thompson retired in 1874, Leeman took his place and during his reign the office of Deputy Chairman temporarily lapsed. During the period covered by this chapter Thompson had under him an equally able General Manager in the person of Captain William O'Brien.

The principles on which Thompson conducted North Eastern affairs were well summed up in his speech to the first half-yearly meeting of the shareholders in February, 1866, when he said that 'the directors had framed their policy upon this assumption, that they held the district for so long, and so long only, as the majority of thinking men in the district believed that they were as well served by the North Eastern as they could be served by other companies'. So, under this most competent guidance the stage had been set, as we shall see in the next chapter, for a considerable increase in the size and influence of the North Eastern Railway.

CHAPTER XVI

A Greater North Eastern

THREE years, from 1862 to 1865, sufficed to incorporate into the North Eastern Railway the three principal railways within its borders that up till that time had still remained independent. In 1859, as we saw in the last chapter, the North Eastern and Newcastle & Carlisle boards had agreed to amalgamation, but such was the opposition by the London & North Western Railway, North British Railway and other interested parties that the Bill was thrown out by Parliament. By 1862, however, the circumstances had changed completely. The N.E.R. had seen the defeat of the Newcastle, Derwent & Weardale scheme, and had checkmated both its railway rivals by obtaining the Act for its own Derwent Valley branch in 1862. Its opponents, therefore, were now willing to come to terms.

These were increased facilities to the L.N.W.R. in regard to traffic to and from Newcastle, in return for which the North Eastern was to be allowed to move its passenger traffic from its own small and inconvenient London Road Station at Carlisle into the joint Lancaster & Carlisle, London & North Western and Caledonian Station – a change offering considerable advantages to through passengers. The North British Railway, which had acquired running powers from its Border Counties line into Hexham Station of the Newcastle & Carlisle Railway, was to have those powers extended into Newcastle; but the North Eastern secured considerably the better of this bargain by obtaining in exchange running powers over the North British from Berwick into Edinburgh. In this way all opposition was disarmed, and an Act authorising the N.E.R. and N. & C.R. amalgamation received the Royal Assent on 17th July, 1862.

Included in the Newcastle & Carlisle property was the branch to Alston which had been authorised as far back as 1846 in the interest of lead-mining. The first $4\frac{1}{4}$ miles, to Shankhill, had been opened in 1851, and the opening throughout was on 17th November, 1852. To climb from 405ft altitude at Haltwhistle to 905ft at Alston, in 13 miles of distance, involved some steep gradients, the worst of them a mile at 1 in 56 between Slaggy-ford and Alston. Nine stone viaducts in all were required through this rugged country, the biggest of them Lambley Viaduct, with nine 58ft arches and a maximum height of 110ft. At various times the Alston branch had figured in trans-Pennine proposals. One, in 1846, was a line from Frosterley in the Wear Valley to Alston, Milton and Carlisle. There were later schemes for lines from both Middleton-in-Teesdale and Stanhope-in-Weardale to Alston, but none of these proposals could find sufficient financial backing, and they soon died a natural death.

The following year, 1863, there was an amalgamation of even greater importance. As we have seen, during the contest over the Newcastle, Derwent & Weardale project the Stockton & Darlington Railway, realising that if London & North Western ambitions were fulfilled it might eventually come under the control of the latter, felt that control by the North Eastern would be a far preferable alternative, and in 1859 had reacted not unfavourably to advances from the N.E.R. board. The Stockton & Darlington had benefited equally by the defeat of the Newcastle, Derwent & Weardale Bill, and as was mentioned in Chapter XIV had amalgamated with both the South Durham & Lancashire Union and Eden Valley Railways, so coming now into complete control of the line across the Pennines from Barnard Castle to Tebay and Penrith.

Thus it was that, whereas in 1860 or 1861 a Bill authorising the amalgamation of the North Eastern and Stockton & Darlington Railways might have met with the fiercest of opposition, the same Bill, adding some 200 route miles of line to the North Eastern system, now went through both Houses of Parliament unopposed, save for a petition against it by the West Hartlepool Harbour & Railway; this was withdrawn, however, when the larger company offered certain reciprocal facilities. An important proviso laid down in the Act was that for the ensuing 10 years Stockton & Darlington affairs should be managed by a committee sitting in Darlington before the N.E.R. itself took over the management. Stockton-on-Tees had the protection of a clause which bound the N.E.R. to continue to maintain the railway sidings alongside the town quays on the River Tees. So this important Act received the Royal Assent on 28th July, 1863.

It was now obvious that the West Hartlepool Harbour & Railway could not remain independent for much longer. The financial difficulties of this company and its associated Cleveland Railway at this time were described in the last chapter and their 1863 Act for the rearrangement of capital did not bring all their troubles to an end. The North Eastern Railway had made advances in 1860 with a view to amalgamation, which at that time were rejected by Ralph Ward Jackson and his friends, but by 1862, as we have seen, he had crashed, and the opposition thus had been weakened correspondingly.

The Cleveland Railway board was the first to capitulate. On the basis of a guaranteed dividend of 5½ per cent per annum on a share capital of £203,700, they agreed to amalgamation, and also to the N.E.R. building a connecting line from Saltburn to their own at Brotton, and to the building of branches to serve the neighbouring ironstone mines at Liverton, Kilton and Lingdale. In the same year, 1865, the Cleveland Railway's line from Brotton round Hunt Cliff into Skinningrove was completed, with the curious zigzag, on gradients finishing with one as steep as 1 in 28, down to sea-level at the bottom of the deep Kilton Valley. But the building of a high viaduct across the same valley held up the working of the trains into Loftus, and this extension had passed into North Eastern hands well before its completion.

The West Hartlepool Harbour & Railway soon followed the Cleveland Railway into the North Eastern system. The basis of agreement in this case was that the N.E.R. would guarantee to West Hartlepool debenture and bond holders, on the exchange of their holdings for preference shares, dividends rising in stages from $3\frac{1}{4}$ per cent in July, 1865, to 4 per cent in July, 1868, and thereafter in perpetuity. West Hartlepool Ordinary shareholders were guaranteed the same dividends, but on shareholdings reduced in value to just under £77 for each £100. In view of the financial condition of their company so shortly before, the West Hartlepool shareholders thus had made an extremely good bargain, but because of the attempts that had been made by other companies, the London & North Western in particular, to obtain a foothold in this port, the North Eastern Railway had been wise to safeguard the position in this way.

As yet the problem had not been faced of consolidating the stocks of the various constituent parts of the N.E.R., but their proprietors were certainly doing well. York & North Midland shareholders had had their dividends increased from $2\frac{1}{2}$ to $5\frac{5}{8}$ per cent in this period, those of the York, Newcastle & Berwick from $3\frac{7}{8}$ to 6 per cent, and those of the Leeds Northern, drawing nothing at the time of the amalgamation, were now earning £3 13s. 9d. per cent. Newcastle & Carlisle shareholders had increased their dividends from 5 to 8 per cent, and those of the Stockton & Darlington, who in 1864 were already being paid at the handsome rate of $8\frac{1}{4}$ per cent, had now advanced to $8\frac{3}{4}$ per cent. The prudent management of North Eastern affairs, which had achieved such excellent results, had been beyond praise.

Such prosperity continued to attract the covetous gaze of other railway companies, and it must not be thought that the success of the N.E.R. in resisting invaders had brought their invasion attempts to an end. After the defeat in 1862 of the Newcastle, Derwent & Weardale scheme, the following year saw a proposal for a most ambitious Leeds, North Yorkshire & Durham Railway, behind which with little doubt, though out of sight, was the London & North Western, still smarting from its defeat at West Hartlepool. The L.N.Y. & D. was to cut a path from Leeds *via* Wetherby and through the Thirsk area directly towards the Cleveland Hills, the promoters obviously having their eyes on Cleveland iron ore. From Hemsley the line would proceed up Bilsdale, where there were untapped ironstone deposits, and then, tunnelling through the crest of the Cleveland Hills at Ingleby, it would continue northwards through Stokesley and Stockton-on-Tees to join the West Hartlepool & Harbour Railway Company's line – up to that time still independent – at Cowpen Bewley.

This might have given the L.N.W.R. access to West Hartlepool after all, but at the cost of a circuitous route and some extremely severe gradients. To increase the traffic prospects, branches were proposed from Helmsley to Pickering and Scarborough, and an iron ore branch from Kirbymoorside to Farndale. At eleven different points junctions with the North Eastern Railway were envisaged. The cost of the 125-mile project was estimated at the almost impossibly low figure of £1,500,000, as was proved when Parliament rejected the Bill on these very grounds. It raised its head again in 1864 in the form of an even more formidable project; this was in conjunction with a proposed Tyne, Wear & Tees Railway, which in North Durham would have used the metals of the little 6-mile Londonderry, Seaham & Sunderland Railway (opened in the same year) to reach the Tyne, and would then have bridged the river to link up with the Blyth & Tyne Railway. By way of Morpeth the North British Railway could have been reached independently of the N.E.R. altogether.

But it is hardly surprising that this fantastic proposal petered out. Indeed the North Eastern Railway found little difficulty in dealing with the principal men with local interests who were behind the plan. The expenses that they had incurred were paid, and the N.E.R. undertook to prepare Bills for new lines which would provide the facilities through the more populous districts without railway facilities which would have been served by the proposed line. One was the link between Knaresborough and Boroughbridge which had been sanctioned as far back as 1847 but never built. A second was a line from Leeds to Wetherby, there joining the Church Fenton to Harrogate line of the former York & North Midland Railway.

Short spur lines would be built to connect the Boroughbridge–Thirsk and Thirsk–Malton lines at Pilmoor, and the Thirsk–Malton and Malton & Driffield Junction Railway at Malton, so providing new through routes from Leeds to Scarborough, Whitby and Bridlington. It was also proposed to revive the plan for a branch from the Thirsk–Malton line at Gilling to serve Helmsley, from there curving round to the east to join the Malton–Whitby line at Pickering, a scheme which had been rejected by Parliament in 1864. But owing to financial difficulties that arose in 1867, and labour troubles in the same year, to which we shall come later, all these projected lines were held up for some years.

During this period there had been other threats from the south-west. These had their focus at Leyburn in Wensleydale, which had been reached by a separate company's extension from Bedale of the York, Newcastle & Berwick branch from Northallerton in November, 1855, taken over by the North Eastern in 1859. West of Leyburn there was a very large area of country, thinly populated because of its mountainous nature, that was still entirely without railway communication. As Chapter XII has related, in the middle 1840s there had been various proposals to penetrate it, such as the Liverpool, Manchester & Newcastle and the Northern Counties Union Railways, and it was some of these ideas that were now revived, with the London & North Western, Midland and Lancashire & Yorkshire Railways behind them, all intent if they could on the penetration of North Eastern territory.

The Midland Railway had obtained a lease in perpetuity of the North Western Railway (nicknamed the 'Little North Western' to distinguish it from the London & North Western Railway proper), which had opened from a junction with the Midland at Skipton through to Lancaster in June, 1850. It was now proposed to branch from this near Settle and to proceed up Ribblesdale and through to Garsdale, then turning east down Wensleydale through Hawes to Leyburn; from here the line would proceed north-east through Richmond and Darlington to join the West Hartlepool Harbour & Railway at Carlton. Such was the Midland idea of reaching the north-east coast, backed by the Lancashire & Yorkshire Railway, which would have ready access to such a line, either *via* Colne and Skipton or *via* Blackburn and Hellifield.

The London & North Western Railway sponsored another competing proposal. This was for a line from Sedbergh, on its recently-opened Low Gill and Ingleton branch, up Garsdale and down Wensleydale to Leyburn, and from there through Middleham and Masham to a junction with the former Leeds Northern at Melmerby, with a branch from Hawes down to Settle. It is difficult, however, to understand what precise purpose this East & West Yorkshire Union Railway would have served. A third project was a Skipton, Wharfdale & Leyburn Junction Railway, from Gargrave (between Skipton and Hellifield) on the 'Little North Western' through Kettlewell and over the Pennines to Spennithorne, on the N.E.R. between Bedale and Leyburn, which would have given a fairly direct route between North Lancashire and the North-East, but at the cost of some shocking gradients.

However, the North Eastern Railway was successful in warding off all these threatened invasions. It was helped by the fact that the Midland Railway, whose patience had been strained to the breaking point by the way in which the London & North Western had been treating its Scottish traffic *via* Ingleton and Tebay, had decided to have its own independent route to Carlisle, and in 1865 had obtained an Act for the construction of its Settle and Carlisle line. This would follow the course proposed for the North of England Union Railway as far as Garsdale, and on the understanding that the Midland would apply for powers to make a branch from Garsdale to Hawes, the North of England Union promoters agreed to withdraw their Bill.

Under a certain amount of pressure the Skipton, Wharfdale & Leyburn Junction promoters decided to terminate their line at Grassington and not to attempt to cross the Pennines into Wensleydale. Finally, the East & West Yorkshire Union Company agreed to limit its proposal to a line between Hawes and Melmerby only, provided that the N.E.R. provided half the share capital required. In the event, it was left to the N.E.R. alone to make this line, with the section from Leyburn to Melmerby abandoned; the Midland was to have running powers over it from Hawes to Leyburn and the North Eastern similar powers from Hawes at least as far as Settle.

As a measure of compensation to Masham, which would have been on the East & West Yorkshire Union route between Leyburn and Melmerby, the North Eastern Railway in 1871 obtained an Act for a $7\frac{1}{2}$-mile branch from Melmerby to Masham, which was completed and opened for traffic on 9th June, 1875. Meantime there had been a much more important development in this area. It will be remembered that in 1848 the then York & North Midland Railway had opened a branch from Church Fenton, Tadcaster and Wetherby over the great Crimple Viaduct to a terminus near the Brunswick Hotel at Harrogate. The year 1862 saw the abandonment of this station and of a mile of its approach line, replaced by a new line across the 'Stray' to a fine new station in the centre of Harrogate, opened on 1st August of that year. Not only so, but this line was continued for $1\frac{1}{2}$ miles down a 1 in 66 gradient to join the former Leeds Northern main line, which had made a circuit of the town on the east side through Starbeck, at Bilton Junction.

This extension, with the spur which had been laid in from east of Pannal on the Leeds Northern up to Crimple Junction (at the south end of the viaduct) now put Harrogate, instead of Starbeck, on a through main line from Leeds to the North, which was destined to become of considerable importance in later years. A second spur, between south and east at Bilton, from now on made it possible for trains from York through Knaresborough to continue into Harrogate, instead of terminating at Starbeck.

There were other happenings at about this time which were to assist materially in developing the East Coast Route to Scotland. Powers which had been obtained in 1848 for a direct line down the Team Valley from Durham to Gateshead had never been exercised, and the trains were still travelling from Ferryhill by way of Sherburn – to the east of Durham City – and Penshaw to Pelaw and Gateshead before crossing the Tyne. The Act of 1862 renewed these powers, and authorised a line branching from the Sunderland–Bishop Auckland line at Newton Hall Junction, just north of Durham, and proceeding through Chester-le-Street and Birtley direct to Gateshead.

This still left a gap in the future main line, however – from Tursdale Junction, north of Ferryhill, through Croxdale to Relly Mill Junction, south of Durham. By 1868 the $12\frac{1}{2}$ miles of the Team Valley line, with its eleven-span stone viaduct across Chester-le-Street, had been opened; but it was not until 1872, after delay for reasons given in Chapter XVII, that the 6 miles from Newton Hall Junction to Relly Mill Junction, with a deep cutting south of Croxdale and the Croxdale Viaduct across the River Wear, had been completed. By these important developments with the later King Edward Bridge across the Tyne, the distance from Darlington to Newcastle eventually was shortened to 36 miles.

The other important East Coast main line improvement was, at long last, the direct route from Doncaster to York. Opposition to this came only from the Lancashire & Yorkshire Railway, which thus stood to lose the traffic over its line from Askern to Knottingley, but the Act was obtained without difficulty in 1864. Great Northern agreement was obtained by the concession of the same running powers into York as the G.N.R. had enjoyed up to that time *via* Knottingley. Some 27 miles of new construction were needed, first for $14\frac{1}{4}$ miles from Shaftholme Junction, $4\frac{1}{2}$ miles north of Doncaster, to a junction with the Leeds, Selby & Hull line just short of Selby Station; the metals of the latter were then used through Selby Station and over the Aire swing-bridge to Barlby Junction, a little farther north; and $12\frac{3}{4}$ further miles of new line were needed through Escrick to Chaloner's Whin Junction, 2 miles south of York on the former York & North Midland line.

A connecting north-to-east spur was laid in where the new line crossed the Wakefield–Goole line of the Lancashire & Yorkshire Railway near Henshall. The one engineering feature of note was another swing-bridge, over the River Ouse at Naburn, about 4 miles from York, hydraulically operated. This important line was opened for traffic in January, 1871, and with the completion of the Tursdale Junction–Relly Mill Junction spur in the following year the East Coast Route of today had been completed, apart only from the King Edward Bridge of much later years which would permit running through Newcastle without reversal.

Various other developments during the period reviewed in this chapter need brief mention. One was the opening on 28th March, 1864, of an independent line to Hornsea, on the Yorkshire coast, for which an Act had been obtained in June, 1862. This was a 13-mile branch from Wilmington, on the Hull & Holderness Railway. The latter, a line $18\frac{1}{2}$ miles long from Hull to Withernsea, had been authorised by an Act of 8th July, 1853, and had been opened for traffic on 24th June, 1854; it had been worked by the N.E.R. from the start, but remained independent until amalgamated with the North Eastern in the same month that the Hornsea branch began operation. By 1866 the Hull & Hornsea Railway was in considerable financial difficulties, which prompted a request to the N.E.R. for amalgamation also. After negotiation, terms were agreed, and the North Eastern acquired the H. & H.R. by an Act which received the Royal Assent on 16th July of that year.

The previous year, 1865, saw the opening of the $6\frac{1}{2}$-mile section of railway between Castleton and Grosmont, completing the route from Stockton-on-Tees to Whitby *via* Battersby Junction. In the same year the $4\frac{1}{2}$-mile deviation between Goathland and Grosmont, cutting out the rope-worked Beckhole incline described in Chapter VI, came into use, greatly expediting the journey from York and Pickering to Whitby. Another addition in this area was a short east-to-north spur at Rillington, junction of the Whitby branch with the York–Scarborough main line, which made it possible to run between Scarborough and Whitby without reversal, and fast trains began to make this journey in $1\frac{1}{2}$ hours.

Thus, despite the threats of competing lines that had failed to mature, through this period the North Eastern Railway had been going from strength to strength. With the acquisition in 1865 of the West Durham Railway (a short colliery branch which as mentioned in Chapter XII had been one of the principal feeders of the Clarence Railway) and a year later of the Hull & Hornsea Railway, the N.E.R., 12 years after its incorporation in 1864, had acquired every independent railway in the County of Durham, and, indeed, in the entire area between the Humber and the Tyne, and had expanded into one of the most influential railways in the country, with over 1,200 route miles of line. Only the Blyth & Tyne Railway in Northumberland, linked up as it was at Morpeth with the North British incursion from across the Border, remained as a minor source of embarrassment.

CHAPTER XVII

Through Strain to Prosperity in the 1860s

IN the middle 1860s the North Eastern Railway passed through two difficult periods; the first was industrial and the second financial. In 1866, a
time of unrest in the labour world, a general movement took place among
locomotive men throughout the country to secure improved conditions
of service and better pay. A lead was taken by drivers and firemen on the
London, Brighton & South Coast Railway in the south, and those of the
North Eastern Railway in the north. In January, 1867, a deputation of the
N.E.R. men waited on the directors and presented a wide range of
demands.

In general, it was claimed that the working day for enginemen should
be a run of 150 miles for passenger drivers and firemen or 120 miles for
those on goods and mineral trains, or, alternatively, 10 hours of duty;
that overtime should be calculated on the basis of 120 or 100 miles for
these two categories or an 8-hour day; that Sunday work should be on a
time-and-a-half basis at the same rates. The actual pay demanded was 6s.
per day for drivers for the first six months, 6s. 6d. after twelve months, and
7s. from the end of the second year; 3s. 6d. per day for firemen for the
first twelve months, 4s. after two years and 4s. 6d. after three years. The
enginemen also claimed to be relieved of the duty of cleaning their engines,
and for a weekly 'shed day' to be substituted. Further claims were submitted in regard to systematic promotion of firemen to the position of
drivers on the basis of seniority and length of service, and also in matters
relating to superannuation and the right of appeal in cases where there
had been punishment for rule-breaking.

The directors conceded the 10-hour day, which had been the principal
object of the men's application, but when the men found that the weekly
'shed day' had not been agreed, they claimed that there had been a breach
of faith on the part of the Company, and on 10th April, 1867, they struck.
Unfortunately for the strikers, in the prevailing depression the authorities
found little difficulty in engaging men who were familiar with the working
of locomotives, and by arranging for members of the staff to accompany
these recruits until they had become familiar with the lines, the signals and
the rules, it was possible to introduce a provisional timetable with a fair
service of trains. Soon such a stream of applications had been received
that the place of the strikers had been filled, and in a relatively short time
operation was restored to normal. Some of the first strikers were prosecuted
for breach of contract, but on pleading guilty were discharged, though
with loss of any wages due to them; a few only were taken back; of the
remainder many emigrated to America, where they were able to find

employment. This was an unhappy episode in North Eastern Railway history.

The second crisis through which the Company passed was in the following year, 1867, and was due to the action of a critical shareholder; it was sufficiently serious to cause a temporary fall of no less than £750,000 in the market value of N.E.R. stock. This shareholder was a barrister named Henry J. Trotter, of Bishop Auckland, who by a series of letters to newspapers aroused uneasiness on the part of investors as to the financial methods that were being pursued by the North Eastern directors. He claimed that stock values were being inflated by the payment of bigger dividends than had been fairly earned, and in support of his contention he adduced the fact that in the half-year ended 30th June, 1866, the Great Northern Railway had shown in its accounts a far greater expenditure per mile for permanent way maintenance and renewal than the North Eastern had done over the same period. He also insinuated that the last N.E.R. dividend might not have been paid at all had not a loan been obtained at the last moment to provide the necessary sum.

At a special shareholders' meeting called in November, 1867, the directors took the opportunity of refuting Trotter's allegations. It was shown that the North Eastern method of dealing with the cost of track maintenance differed from the Great Northern; whereas the G.N.R. debited both maintenance and renewal against revenue in the first half-year, the N.E.R. charged maintenance only, charging renewals for the whole year against revenue in the second half together with maintenance over the second six months. The story that dividends had been paid with the help of a hastily raised loan was dismissed as 'pure fiction'. Having got his teeth in, Trotter was very reluctant to let go; but after the Company's auditors had declared that they had dealt with no accounts more efficiently and honestly compiled than those of the North Eastern Railway, the shaken public confidence in the integrity of the North Eastern board was restored, and the depressed stock quotations soon returned to their normal level.

Nevertheless, the Trotter attack was not without its effect. It led to a decision by the directors, not merely to add to each half-yearly report to the shareholders an abstract of all capital expenditure during the six months and also a review of future liabilities on capital account, but also for the time being to cut down capital expenditure on new works. Construction would be completed on work already in progress, but other extensions which had already been authorised would be held up for the time being.

Some of these deferments were mentioned in the last chapter; among them was the portion of the future East Coast main line from Ferryhill to Durham. Works postponed were the Cross Gates, Leeds to Wetherby line; the branches from Gilling to Pickering and Knaresborough to Boroughbridge; the line up Wensleydale to Hawes; and, most important of all, the new station which was being planned for York.

Among the works then in progress which were carried to completion was the line from Thorne to Staddlethorpe, giving a direct route from Doncaster to Hull (described in Chapter XV), which was brought into use on 30th July, 1869; also the Team Valley section of the East Coast main line, from Newton Hall Junction, Durham, to Gateshead, mentioned in Chapter XVI, which was opened in 1868, for freight traffic on 2nd March but not for passenger traffic until 1st December. Another line which was to prove of considerable importance in the future was the 5-mile spur from Church Fenton, on the former York & North Midland line, to Micklefield, on the Leeds & Selby line, which enabled York to Leeds trains to avoid the use of Midland Railway metals from Methley into Leeds, shortened the rail distance between the two cities from 31½ to 25½ miles, and from now on permitted fast travel throughout. It is, perhaps, surprising that so many years had elapsed before this direct access to Leeds from York became available; the delay had been the aftermath of Hudson's deliberate policy to deprive Leeds, if he could, of main line status.

This line, opened on 1st April, 1869, was part only of a far larger enterprise, which came into use on the same day – Leeds New Station; a name by which it continued to be known for more than half-a-century. The North Eastern Railway had joined forces with the London & North Western Railway in building a station worthy of the city of Leeds. The construction of the station and its approaches involved no small engineering problems. From the original Leeds & Selby terminus at Marsh Lane the line was carried westwards on a series of masonry viaducts and bridges – save for an embankment some 90 yards long, where it crossed the burial ground of St Peter's Church, to avoid disturbance of the graves – until it reached a point abreast of the Midland Railway Wellington Station. Here Leeds New Station was built, entirely on arches, and in part above the River Aire.

The station was provided at its east end with four bay platforms from 270 to 330ft long for North Eastern trains, and at its west end with a four-track bay for the L.N.W.R. 648ft in length; in addition, one through platform ran the whole 870ft length of the station. The station was covered by an overall roof supported on wrought-iron columns, with its biggest span 92ft across. West of the station the new line had first to cross a canal basin with a bridge of 85ft span and then the Leeds & Liverpool Canal itself, which required a bridge 200ft long and with a main span 127ft across. About 100 yards west of the station a junction was effected with the Midland Railway. Owing to the site chosen, no elaborate frontage was possible to Leeds New Station, access to which from Boar Lane could be obtained only through the entrance gate of the Midland station.

About this time a great deal of work was going on in the replacement, by structures of masonry and wrought-iron, of bridges of earlier days which had been built in timber for cheapness. These included the viaducts of the York and Scarborough line over the Derwent between Huttons Ambo and Malton; over the Esk in the Vale of Goathland between Goathland and Whitby; and over the South Tyne on the Newcastle & Carlisle line. This work had been completed by 1869, and was being followed by similar reconstructions of the lengthy Scotswood bridge across the Tyne on the Newcastle & Carlisle and the big Ouseburn Viaduct between Newcastle and Heaton on the main line to the north.

At this time of restricted expenditure an important task had to be faced at Middlesbrough. The Cleveland iron trade was growing at such a rate that the enlargement of Middlesbrough Dock had to be undertaken without delay, for the larger ocean-going ships could not be brought through the dock gates, which were only 30ft wide. In consequence, these ships were being diverted to Hartlepool, and even to Hull, to load, and the ironmasters were being compelled to add from 3s. to 11s. per ton to their costs to cover the rail carriage involved. An expenditure of £100,000 was authorised for this purpose, but £120,000 had been spent when the work at last was finished in 1874. It increased the dock area from 6 to 12 acres, provided a new entrance 58ft wide, and quayage having a total length of 1,626ft, allowed vessels with a draught of up to 23ft at spring tides and 15ft at neap tides, and was well equipped with appliances for the rapid discharge of iron ore and loading of pig iron.

Among other openings at about this period one short line which had proved very expensive to build was the Quayside branch at Newcastle. Leaving the Newcastle–Berwick line at the old cattle dock, just beyond the Manors Station, this dived down on a gradient as steep as 1 in 27 to 1 in 30 through tunnels and cuttings on a semi-circle to the quayside on the north bank of the Tyne, where it joined the lines of the Newcastle Corporation near the Hamburg Wharf. The Quayside line was opened on 1st June, 1870. A start had been made on the loop line from Gilling to Helmsley and Pickering, and this came into service as far as Helmsley on 9th October, 1871, together with the curve north of Raskelf which gave direct access from the York direction to the Thirsk and Malton line.

A private line of interest a little farther to the north was the 5¾-mile Merrybent & Darlington Railway, which branched from the Darlington and Barnard Castle line 3½ miles from Darlington, and proceeded southwards, crossing the River Tees by a substantial lattice girder bridge with three 75ft spans to reach copper mines and limestone quarries near the village of Barton. This was opened on 1st June, 1870, and was worked by the North Eastern Railway, but its chequered existence led to bankruptcy in 1878; in 1890, however, it was purchased by the N.E.R. Another private line 4¼ miles farther west was the Forcett Railway, leaving the Darlington–Barnard Castle line between Piercebridge and Gainford stations, authorised in 1865; this, also, was worked by the N.E.R., but never passed into North Eastern hands, though it became part of the London & North Eastern Railway in January, 1923.

As to other lines, in 1865 the North Eastern Railway had agreed to subscribe £10,000 towards the capital of a small independent line projected up the lead-mining Allendale valley from Hexham southwards to the town of that name, which obtained its Act on 19th June of that year. The crossing of the valleys of the small Balder and Lune streams involved the company in some expensive engineering work; over the former valley a masonry viaduct of nine 30ft arches was required, with a maximum height of 100ft, and over the latter one of five 50ft arches, 60ft high. The branch was opened in stages between August, 1867, and January, 1868, though not for passenger traffic until 1st March, 1869. For most of its independent life the Hexham & Allendale Railway was in low water financially, and finally, by an Act dated 13th July, 1876, was acquired by the North Eastern Railway on the basis of a payment of £6 for each £10 share.

But before this happened, another and more important acquisition had taken place, of the only line still remaining independent – apart from the southern tentacles of the North British Railway and the leased Hull & Selby Railway – between the Humber and the Tweed. This was the Blyth & Tyne Railway. Its continued independence had been due to its competent management. From the original wagonway of 1853 it had expanded in 20 years to a prosperous railway with 43½ route miles of line, carrying over a million passengers annually, and competing on level terms with the N.E.R. for the traffic between Newcastle and North Shields, Tynemouth and even Morpeth. Between 1853 and 1873 its passenger revenue had increased from £4,600 to £53,570 per annum, and its freight and mineral traffic, with the help of its coal-shipping staiths at Howdon on the Tyne and at Blyth, from £13,200 to £129,230. Though wayleaves made considerable inroads into its profits, it had been able to pay dividends rising to a maximum of 12½ per cent. Probably its most notable record was that of having operated for twenty years without having lost the life of a single passenger or caused any injury other than the most trivial.

In view of such financial standing, the N.E.R. had no alternative other than to pay an appropriate price. The bigger company therefore offered, in addition to paying all preference interest, to guarantee a dividend of 10 per cent on the £315,000 of ordinary stock, and also to hand over £50,000 in cash in return for the reserve funds and all surplus property other than the railway and the staiths. Preference shareholders with 10 per cent stock and ordinary shareholders received £250 of North Eastern 4 per cent preference stock for each £100 of their holdings, and those with 5 per cent preference stock £125 for each £100. Agreement was reached in January, 1874, and ratified by Act of Parliament dated 7th August, 1874. By the acquisition of the Blyth & Tyne Railway, and also of the Hull & Selby Railway, which after 26 years of lease dating back to York & North Midland days was purchased by the N.E.R. on 1st September, 1871, the North Eastern system had expanded to a total of 1,378 route miles of line.

Early in the 1860s the N.E.R. began to develop a policy of reduced fares. On 1st January, 1860, a reduction was made in return first and second class fares; a year later second class passengers were admitted to all express trains, and supplementary 'express fares' were abolished. 1st July, 1865, saw the beginning of a series of fare reductions designed, over a period of three years, to reduce first class fares from 3d. to 2d. a mile, second class from 2d. to 1½d. a mile, and third class from 1½d. to 1d. a mile; the last-mentioned was the obligatory 'Parliamentary' fare by at least one train a day on each route, but was now to be applied generally. Second class passengers from now on were treated to cushioned compartments. At the same time there were reductions of 10 to 20 per cent in the rates charged on moving coal for shipment, and freight rates in general were reduced.

The crisis following on the Trotter attacks previously described, with the curb on finance that resulted, caused a temporary reversion, in January, 1866, to the old fares, but the full concessions were restored on and from 1st January, 1870 – that is, 2d. per mile first class and 1½d. per mile second class (plus the Government duty of 5 per cent in each case), and 1d. per mile third class; first and second class return tickets were issued at 50 per cent above the single fare.

The North Eastern Railway by 1870 had attained an enviable state of prosperity, probably exceeding that of any other railway in the country. Chapter XVI described some of the complicated financial arrangements that had followed amalgamation, with the shares of the various main constituents all still maintaining their independent existence and drawing, on an agreed basis, their separate dividends. In the year between January, 1869, and January, 1870, quotations for Berwick stock, drawing 6½ per cent, had advanced from 100 to 126; York stock, with 6¼ per cent dividend, had gone up from 88 to 123½; and Leeds stock, with 4³⁄₁₆ per cent, from 55½ to 83. The dividends being paid on the Darlington, Carlisle and Thirsk & Malton stock were 9, 8⅝ and 5 per cent respectively. Some of these stocks, 'Berwicks' in particular, were more readily marketable than others.

While the net revenue of the railway as a whole was divided in certain fixed proportions between the various groups of shareholders, the varying claims of preferential and guaranteed stockholders had some extraordinary results. In his book, *The North Eastern Railway*, W. W. Tomlinson has pointed out that 'an increase in net revenue which gave an additional 20s. to the Berwick shareholders added 24s. 0½d. to the York dividend, 20s. 4d. to the Leeds, 25s. 6d. to the Darlington and 24s. 2d. to the Carlisle. Upon the dividend likely to be paid depended the solution of the question whether a section would gain or lose by consolidation. At 5 per cent the Berwick, Carlisle and Darlington sections were losers, and the York and Leeds sections gainers; at 6 per cent the Berwick and Carlisle were losers and the York, Leeds and Darlington gainers, and at 7 per cent the York and Leeds were losers and the Berwick, Carlisle and Darlington were gainers.'

This was an extremely thorny problem for the North Eastern Board to handle; the difficulty was that of fixing the critical turning point at which there would be a reasonable balance between all the various interests. Eventually it was fixed at 6¼ per cent, and on that basis the directors' proposal was to offer North Eastern Railway stock to the following values for every £100 held by the stockholders: Darlington £136, Carlisle £133,

One of the most successful of the Raven designs – his three-cylinder Class 'Z', which for many years worked all the principal East Coast services, first built in 1911. [*Locomotive Publishing Co.*

The most powerful express locomotive type built for the N.E.R. – Raven three-cylinder Pacific No. 2403 *City of Durham*. The first of these five engines appeared in 1922.   [*F. R. Hebron*

Above, William Worsdell's smallest N.E.R. locomotive design — a $15\frac{1}{2}$-ton 0-4-0 dock shunter of 1890. *Left*, one of William Worsdell's 0-6-2 tank engines built originally as two-cylinder compounds between 1888 and 1890.
[*Both, Locomotive Publishing Co.*

A Worsdell 'E' class 0-6-0 shunting tank, which in its modified 'E1' form remained standard until the end of N.E.R. history, and of which building continued even after nationalisation.
[*E. R. Wethersett*

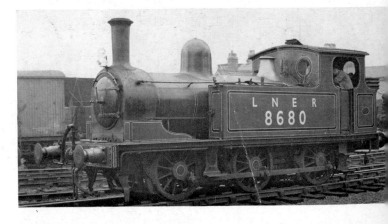

One of Raven's handsome tanks of Class 'D', with three cylinders and the unusual 4-4-4 wheel arrangement.

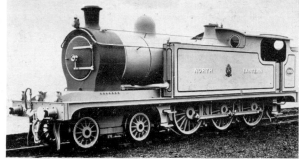

A Class 'W' 4-6-0 tank built under Wilson Worsdell in 1907 for the heavily-graded coast route between Saltburn, Whitby and Scarborough.
[*Both, Locomotive Publishing Co.*

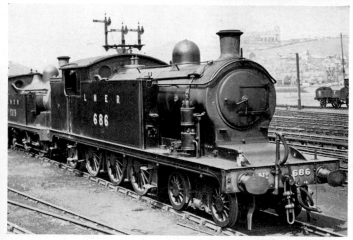

A Class 'W' tank rebuilt as a 4-6-2 to increase the bunker capacity.
[*H. C. Casserley*

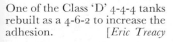

One of the Class 'D' 4-4-4 tanks rebuilt as a 4-6-2 to increase the adhesion.   [*Eric Treacy*

Above, one of the first three-cylinder simple locomotives built for the North Eastern Railway – Wilson Worsdell's Class 'X' 4-8-0 tank of 1909 for marshalling yard work.
[*Locomotive Publishing Co.*

Left, an 'X' class tank on humping duty at the Erimus Yard, Newport. [*P. W. B. Semmens*

Below, one of the massive three-cylinder 4-6-2 tanks for short-distance mineral work.
[*Locomotive Publishing Co.*

Berwick £100, York £98, Leeds £65 and Malton £10. The approval of the shareholders was received at a meeting held on 3rd December, 1869, and the Act embodying the consolidation scheme received the Royal Assent on 12th May, 1870.

The total amount of stock thus consolidated was £16,211,467, and it became known as 'North Eastern Consols'. By June, 1870, the market value of the stock had risen to 149, and an increase in receipts for the half-year made it possible for the directors to declare a dividend on their new 'Consols' of $7\frac{1}{4}$ per cent, rising in the second half-year to $8\frac{1}{2}$ per cent. So in the first full year of the consolidated stock the fortunate shareholders earned $7\frac{7}{8}$ per cent on their capital. High-water mark was reached in the following year, when in round figures a gross revenue of £5,000,000 and expenses of £2,250,000 only left net receipts totalling £2,750,000, and made it possible to pay an $8\frac{1}{4}$ per cent dividend in the first half-year and 10 per cent in the second, or $9\frac{1}{8}$ per cent for the full year. It is small wonder that by 3rd January, 1872, 'North Eastern Consols' were being quoted on the Stock Exchange at the record figure of $187\frac{1}{2}$.

At the time of the amalgamation in 1854 which brought into existence the North Eastern Railway, Parliament had not been too happy about such fusions. Moreover, about the time when the N.E.R. was reaching the zenith of its prosperity, as just described, a Parliamentary Committee was set up to enquire into the whole question of railway amalgamations. Their report, when published, proved to be an emphatic justification of such measures.

'The balance of advantage to the public as well as to the shareholders may even well be thought to be on the side of amalgamation', it claimed. 'The case of the North Eastern is a striking illustration. That railway, or system of railways, is composed of 37 lines, several of which formerly competed with each other, and before their amalgamation they had, generally speaking, high rates and fares and low dividends. The system is now the most complete monopoly in the United Kingdom; from the Tyne to the Humber, with one local exception' – the Blyth & Tyne, which was absorbed three years later – 'it has the country to itself, and it has the lowest fares and the highest dividends of any large English railway; it has little or no litigation with other companies. Whilst complaints have been heard from Lancashire and Yorkshire, where there are so-called competing lines, no witness has appeared to complain of the North Eastern, and the general feeling in the district it serves appears favourable to its management.'

Such was the tribute paid by Parliament to the progressive North Eastern Railway. For the time being things were going well, extremely well. But the early years of the 1880 decade, as we shall see in Chapter XVIII, found various bodies in the area rather less 'favourable to its management', and difficulties arising which considerably affected the Company's prosperity.

Coastal and Other Improvements

By the early 1870s many modern developments in equipment and operation were beginning to appear on the North Eastern system. Up to 1871,
although the block system of signalling had been installed between
Shildon and Darlington as early as 1865, it had not been extended to a
total of more than 48 miles of line. But in May, 1871, following on two
serious accidents in the previous two years – one at Thirsk and the second
at Brockley Whins, both due to human forgetfulness – it was decided by
the directors that the whole of the North Eastern lines should be operated
under the absolute block system. Steps were taken forthwith both to begin
the installation of the equipment, and also to train signalmen, pointsmen
and others in its use. Both the two accidents mentioned might have been
prevented by interlocking, and the first steps were taken to remedy this
deficiency also.

The North Eastern Railway was probably the pioneer in the matter of
marshalling trains by gravity. From 1859 the work at Tyne Dock had been
carried on entirely by gravity, from the reception of the full coal wagons
to their marshalling into empty trains for return to the collieries. There
had also been some more or less haphazard gravity marshalling for some
years at Shildon, but in 1869, with a rearrangement of the old tracks and
the laying in of new groups of sidings, systematised gravity marshalling
became general, on a scale probably greater than at any other yard in the
country. By now the Shildon yard had over 10½ miles of tracks, extending
over 16 acres, and was dealing with some 2,000 wagons daily, consigned
to about 200 different destinations, and yet sorted at a cost of but little
over ¼d. per ton of the minerals thus dealt with.

Freight traffic all the time was increasing by leaps and bounds. By 1870,
some 10,000,000 tons more of freight and minerals were being carried by
the North Eastern Railway than 10 years earlier. The night sky of Tees-
side flamed with the charging of the open-top blast furnaces which had
sprung up in large numbers on both sides of the estuary, and there were
many other plants operating farther inland in County Durham. Moreover,
to the smelting of iron there was now being added the still more important
manufacture of steel.

In 1856 Henry Bessemer had read to the British Association his epoch-
making paper on the inexpensive production of steel by the converter
process, which in the 1870 decade had been introduced by a number of
Tees-side firms. Then in 1878 there came the first public announcement
of the discovery by Thomas and Gilchrist that by lining the converter with
dolomite the embrittling phosphorus could be separated in the converter

from iron which had been smelted from low grade phosphoric ores, such as those of Cleveland. This opened the door to the making of basic Bessemer steel, and so was of immense importance to Tees-side.

The first firm to put the process into production was Bolckow, Vaughan & Company of South Bank, an eastern suburb of Middlesbrough, a town which had now developed from a group of houses on some marshland into an industrial centre of great importance. A quarter of a century later, with the introduction of the Siemens-Martin open-hearth steel process, and much more accurate control of the product, basic open-hearth steel-making almost completely replaced Bessemer acid and basic steel production, and in consequence the transport of haematite iron ore across the country from the West Coast came to an end.

It is interesting to note that the first steel rails in North Eastern tracks were laid in April, 1862, on the High Level Bridge at Newcastle; from then onwards they were introduced gradually at locations where the heaviest rail wear was experienced, and also to the manufacture of switches and crossings. Elsewhere considerable use had been made of iron rails which had been hardened by a special 'steeling' process patented by a firm named Dodds, to a total extent of about 100 miles of main line track, but a number of breakages due to brittleness led to its discontinuance, and very soon the wear problem was being solved by the substitution of steel for iron.

Better staff relations came about at the beginning of 1872 by a reduction in the standard hours worked by signalmen and certain grades of drivers and firemen. In the spring of the same year improved scales of pay were granted to signalmen, guards, ticket-collectors, porters, shunters and certain other grades. But with these increases and a very serious rise in the cost of materials the ratio of working expenses to gross receipts began to change very materially. During the first half of 1872 gross receipts increased by $8\frac{1}{4}$ per cent, but expenses by $13\frac{1}{2}$ per cent. The most staggering rise was in the price of locomotive coal, which in 1872 was being quoted by the collieries at no less than three times the figure in 1871.

All the railways in Britain were affected, and they decided to take common action by increasing passenger fares and freight rates, by an average of from $12\frac{1}{2}$ to 15 per cent. By the end of 1872, while North Eastern gross receipts were $7\frac{3}{4}$ per cent up, working expenses had increased by $19\frac{3}{4}$ per cent; no less than £87,000 additional had been paid during the year for coal and coke. Nevertheless the North Eastern directors found it possible to declare a dividend of 9 per cent for the year 1872, and in 1873, when the increase in working expenses had slowed down considerably, there was a reversion to 10 per cent. Never again were North Eastern Railway dividends to be as high as those of the years 1871 to 1873 inclusive.

A great deal of construction work was going on at this time. After 17 years of use the old Newcastle & Carlisle goods station at Forth Banks had been replaced by the much larger Forth Goods Station at Newcastle, opened on 3rd March, 1871; other new goods stations were being built at

Middlesbrough and Marsh Lane, Leeds. The passenger stations at Darlington and Thirsk had been rebuilt, and improvements carried out at Newcastle Central Station to bring the low platforms up to coach floor level;
a new island platform on the south or Tyne side of the station had been
opened in 1871. At long last, also, a start had been made on the building,
outside the city wall, of a fine new station at York to replace the original
terminal.

In the 1870s active steps were being taken to connect Saltburn, Whitby
and Scarborough around the Yorkshire coast – a problem envolving
engineering work on a considerable scale owing to the way in which the
high ground bordering the coast with substantial cliffs was intersected at
various points by deep valleys. Out of Saltburn, for example, the 3¼-mile
line connecting the Darlington and Saltburn branch with the former
Cleveland Railway at Brotton had to cross the valley of the Skelton Beck
by an eleven-arch brick viaduct 783ft long and with a maximum height of
some 150ft. Incidentally, owing to this branch taking off short of the
Saltburn terminus, when passenger service was begun in 1875 between
Saltburn and Loftus the trains required to back out of the station to
Saltburn Junction before proceeding southwards.

The North Eastern Railway had opened the last stretch of the Cleveland
line into Loftus in 1867, after completion had been delayed by the construction of the high viaduct across the Kilton Valley, between Skinningrove and Loftus, 678ft long and with twelve 45ft lattice girder spans on
masonry piers which at their highest were 150ft above the stream. A good
many years later the stability of this viaduct was threatened by ore mine
workings, and it was encased by an immense embankment tipped from one
side of the valley to the other.

On 16th July of the previous year, 1866, an independent company
called the Whitby, Redcar & Middlesbrough Union Railway had obtained an Act to build a line along the coast from Whitby to link up with
the North Eastern Railway at Loftus. Work was begun, but by 1874
construction had proved so expensive that the company had come to the
end of its financial resources, having spent some £240,000. Approach was
therefore made to the N.E.R. Board to take the line over and complete it.
This the latter agreed to do, on the basis of a lease in perpetuity at a
minimum rental of £4,500 per annum, 50 per cent of the gross receipts
in return for operating it *plus* 4½ per cent on the capital required for completion, and an option to purchase after 10 years. The arrangement was
confirmed by an Act dated 19th July, 1875.

Five viaducts were required, the most notable of them the one over the
Dale House Valley at Staithes, 700ft long, 152ft high at its maximum, and
with six 60ft lattice girder spans supported on tubular-iron columns in
pairs filled with concrete and braced together. Eight years after construction, the viaduct was strengthened by the addition of two horizontal
lattice bracings. There were also some 60ft spans flanking the bigger spans
on either side. In later years, owing to the exposed position of this viaduct,
a wind gauge was installed at one end, and if gales off the North Sea

exceeded a certain velocity the passage of trains over it was temporarily suspended.

There were other viaducts at Upgang, Newholm, East Row, and Sandsend, and two tunnels, one between Kettleness and Sandsend measuring 1,651 yards in length. The rail journey between Saltburn and Whitby has had few scenic rivals in the North of England, with its succession of views of the open sea, deep wooded ravines, and inland the moors. At times the track was almost on the edge of the cliffs; indeed, at several points the North Eastern Railway engineers varied the original route by carrying it farther inland for safety reasons.

But the Whitby, Redcar & Middlesbrough Union Railway proved a most unprofitable enterprise. It was hoped that beds of iron ore between Loftus and Whitby would be tapped and would help to provide the line with traffic, but this never happened. Not until December, 1883, was it opened for traffic, and by then the construction of its 16½ miles had cost a total not far short of £700,000, or about £42,000 per mile. The net receipts from its operation were not sufficient to pay even the rental charge of £4,500 per annum, let alone to provide any net revenue between the N.E.R. and the owning company. Eventually the original company, which had spent £240,000, as already mentioned, disposed of its interest to the North Eastern for no more than £25,000.

Meantime another line had been creeping northwards from Scarborough to join the line from Saltburn at Whitby. In earlier years there had been various projects for coastal railways northwards from Scarborough, and these finally materalised in the 20-mile Scarborough & Whitby Railway, which obtained its Act on 29th June, 1871. Construction of this proceeded at an even slower pace than from Loftus to Whitby, and 13 years elapsed from the cutting of the first sod to the opening on 16th July, 1885. To effect an end-on junction with the line from Loftus at Whitby West Cliff Station, the Scarborough line had to cross the deep Esk Valley by a massive thirteen-arch masonry viaduct, 915ft long and up to 120ft high. In the valley below was the North Eastern Pickering and Whitby line, to which the line from Saltburn descended from the West Cliff station in order to reach Whitby terminus. Trains from Scarborough terminating at Whitby therefore had to reverse at West Cliff before making the descent.

Like the Saltburn–Whitby line, that from Whitby to Scarborough had equal scenic attraction, with its views in particular of Robin Hood's Bay and from the high ground at Ravenscar, but at the expense of some of the most formidable switchback gradients to be found anywhere in the North Eastern system. As at Saltburn the exit from Scarborough to this line also, rather curiously, was by reversal at a junction ½-mile out of Scarborough terminus, from which there was a fairly level mile to Cloughton. But from here there was not another level stretch the whole way to Saltburn.

First there was the tremendous climb to Ravenscar summit, 631ft above the sea, beginning with 2½ miles averaging about 1 in 75 and then 2¼ miles as steep was 1 in 41; even worse was the 3¾-mile descent to between Fyling Hall and Robin Hood's Bay, almost all at 1 in 39. Next came 1¾ miles at

1 in 43 up from the last-mentioned station, and 3 miles down averaging
1 in 45 to the Esk Valley Viaduct at Whitby. The gradients between there
and Loftus were not quite as steep though 2½-mile stretches at 1 in 57 to
61, up from Sandsend to Kettleness, down to Staithes, up to Grinkle and
down past Loftus to Skinningrove, called for plenty of hard work. Many is
the train that has stalled on the fearsome climbs from both directions to
Ravenscar.

Again an unprofitable railway had been built. It had cost a total over
£649,800, or £27,000 per mile – not so expensive, certainly, as the Loftus
and Whitby line, but too costly for the traffic it managed to attract. The
North Eastern Railway undertook to operate the Scarborough & Whitby
Railway for 50 per cent of the gross receipts, but after working it for some
years on these terms they found that they were doing so at a loss. In 1898,
therefore, they decided that purchase of the undertaking was the best
course to pursue, and they succeeded in doing so by a payment in N.E.R.
stock of £261,633, or roughly two-fifths of the cost of construction. The
opening of the Scarborough & Whitby line in 1885 completed coastal
railway communication from Bridlington through Scarborough and Whitby to Saltburn and Redcar.

During the 1870s Middlesbrough was in course of being provided with
one of the finest passenger stations anywhere in North-Eastern England,
befitting its growing importance. This was opened to the public on 1st
December, 1877, and was of no small architectural distinction. A carriage
drive led from Zetland Road, at the west end, to a raised enclosure, with
shops beneath, extending to Linthorpe Road; the station buildings
fronted this enclosure, with a glazed arcade provided to enable carriages
and cabs to unload their passengers under cover. The station itself had
two platforms 600ft long, with additional tracks between, and the whole
covered by a single arched roof extending to a height of 60ft above the
rails.

Other developments were in progress farther to the north. As yet there
was no direct coast route between Hartlepool and Sunderland, and the
journey between Middlesbrough and either Hartlepool or Sunderland
was still of a most circuitous description. Middlesbrough and Billingham
stations, 3 miles apart on a direct line, were 9¼ miles apart by rail;
between Redcar and West Hartlepool 7½ miles direct across the water
extended to 24¾ miles by rail journey. There had been various plans at
different times to bridge over or tunnel under the Tees estuary; indeed, in
1874, the North Eastern Railway had actually obtained powers for a
tunnel; but none of these schemes had come to anything. In 1872, however, to shorten the distance between Sunderland and Middlesbrough, the
North Eastern Railway applied for powers to make a new line southwards from Wellfield, ¾-mile north-west of Castle Eden, to by-pass both
Hartlepool and Stockton, on the west side, and to proceed to a junction
with the Darlington and Middlesbrough line at Bowesfield, a little to the
west of Thornaby.

In effect this was to be a continuation of the Haswell branch of the former Durham & Sunderland Railway, and of the Hartlepool Railway continuation of the latter to the point where it joined the former Hartlepool Railway main line at Castle Eden. The latter was to be crossed just west of Castle Eden, and where the new railway also crossed the Stockton to Ferryhill line, at Carlton, spur connections would be laid in to give a direct run from the Sunderland direction to both Stockton and Port Clarence, and, on the opposite side, a direct run for coal and minerals between Ferryhill and Middlesbrough. These powers were granted without opposition, and the railway was opened from Wellfield to Bowesfield Junction on 1st May, 1877.

In the first decade of the present century the Wellfield route was used by several express trains daily, including the through Newcastle–Bournemouth trains in each direction, and an afternoon train from Newcastle to Manchester and Liverpool, non-stop between Sunderland and Stockton by the north-to-east Carlton spur. The chief operating difficulty was the stiff climb from Ryhope southwards to Seaton, beginning at 1 in 60 and for 1¼ miles as steep as 1 in 44.

Four weeks after the Wellfield–Bowesfield opening a new line was opened through West Hartlepool, making a direct connection between West Hartlepool and the terminal station in East Hartlepool. But 27 years were to elapse before the opening of the coast line from Hart, 2 miles from Hartlepool on the Castle Eden line, through Horden and Easington to a junction with the former Londonderry, Seaham & Sunderland line at Seaham Harbour, thereby completing the coastal chain of railway communication from Bridlington throughout to Sunderland.

In Sunderland itself there was also a major development during this period. It was the opening, on 4th August, 1879, of the Monkwearmouth Junction line, crossing the Wear by a notable single span bridge and giving access, by means of tunnels on both sides with an aggregate length of 1,000 yards, to a new Central Station in Sunderland. The bridge had a clear span of 300ft, with a headroom of 86ft above high-water, and was of a bowstring girder type, with vertical stiffeners and ornamental ironwork making circular or elliptical openings between each pair. The station buildings, beautified by a clock tower, fronted on the High Street; the platforms, 16ft below street level, were covered throughout their length of 600ft by an overall roof of 95ft span.

On the north bank of the Wear an independent company had obtained an Act in 1871 for a line from Monkwearmouth to Southwick and Hylton, there linking up with the former Pontop & South Shields; this was opened for traffic on 1st July, 1876, and worked from the outset by the North Eastern Railway. But it proved another unfortunate enterprise financially; it never succeeded in paying a dividend, and in 1883 passed into the hands of the N.E.R. at a cost of £130,000 for its 4¼ miles of line.

Another privately promoted line which got its Act in 1871, on 16th June, was the Scotswood, Newburn & Wylam, designed to branch from the Newcastle & Carlisle line just east of where the latter crossed the Tyne by Scotswood bridge, to serve Newburn, Heddon-on-the-Wall and other places on the north bank, and then itself to cross the river and rejoin the Carlisle line between Wylam and Prudhoe. The line was completed and opened in stages between 1875 and October, 1876. It had one engineering feature of considerable note – the wrought-iron bridge over the Tyne at West Wylam, with a span of 240ft.

This was one of the first bridges in the country to embody the principle of the arch rising high above the railway (or road), and with the bridge floor suspended from it by vertical ties – an idea that was to find its maximum expression many years later in the famous 1,650ft span of Sydney Harbour Bridge in New South Wales, Australia – and it came through some very severe stress tests with flying colours. The cost of its construction was £16,000. From the first the Scotswood, Newburn & Wylam line was worked by the North Eastern Railway, and yet once again it proved to be a line which could not be operated at a profit and provided no dividend for its shareholders. So, like the Hylton, Southwick & Monkwearmouth it passed into the hands of the N.E.R. in the same year, 1883, at a price of £155,746 for its 6½ miles.

Construction had been proceeding very slowly with the railway up Wensleydale, which had been the scene of so many conflicting proposals. Though the continuation of the branch from Northallerton to Bedale had been opened as far as Leyburn for freight in 1855 and for passengers in the following year, no progress was made beyond that point for over a decade, until it was known whether the Midland Railway plan for an independent main line from Settle to Carlisle was to materialise. When the construction of the latter became certain, and it also became clear that the independent Hawes & Melmerby Company would never be able to raise sufficient funds to build their line, the North Eastern Railway took over, and in 1869 obtained from Parliament the necessary extension of time.

The Midland Railway agreed to grant running powers over its branch from Garsdale to Hawes, and the North Eastern reciprocally was willing for Midland trains, if desired, to work through to Leyburn. So it was that on 1st February, 1877, the line was opened for 13 miles from Leyburn to Askrigg; the remainder, from Askrigg to an end-on junction with the Midland Railway at Hawes, where the two companies built a joint station, came into use on 1st October, 1878.

In the following year, after 4 years spent in construction, another new line was opened which in later years was to assume a considerable importance. As far back as 1863 there had been an agitation in Leeds for a railway to Wetherby which the London & North Western Railway, hovering in the background, could envisage as forming a link in one of its many attempts, described in Chapter XV, to penetrate North Eastern territory. In 1865 the project, now taken over by the newly incorporated North Eastern Railway, took more definite shape as part of a possible route from Leeds to Scarborough *via* Knaresborough, Boroughbridge, Pilmoor and Malton, thus avoiding York.

An Act was obtained in 1866 for 10¾ miles of new line from Cross Gates, on the Leeds–York main line, to Wetherby, on the Church Fenton to

Harrogate line, but economies following the Trotter attack of 1867 (Chapter XVII) caused construction to be held up; it was not resumed until 1875, and any idea of extension beyond Wetherby was abandoned. The value of this link, opened for traffic on 1st May, 1876, was that it brought into use a new route from Harrogate, and thereby from the North, into Leeds. Though with its gruelling climbs – 5 miles at 1 in 86–91 from Spofforth up to Harrogate going north, and 3¼ miles at 1 in 66–90 from Bardsey to Scholes coming south – severe speed restrictions and 3¾ miles additional distance, a considerably harder route than that *via* Arthington, the Wetherby line had made it possible for express trains between Newcastle and Liverpool to pass through Leeds without reversal. Three of these trains in each direction still so use it today, diesel-headed, and with no change of locomotive in Leeds.

Meantime there had been important developments farther to the south. In 1872 the restless merchants and shipowners of Hull, as a result of a sudden increase in shipping traffic which overtaxed the limited North Eastern terminal accommodation to such an extent that the sidings became blocked with loaded wagons and the unloading and loading of ships was badly delayed, began agitating once more for railway access independent of the N.E.R. The latter took steps without delay to lay down additional sidings, but a cry that the trade of the port was in danger provided all the needed stimulus to the plan for independence.

A company was therefore launched, with the title of the Hull South & West Junction Railway, to build an independent line to Hessle and there to turn south, this time tunnelling under rather than bridging over the Humber with a bore just over 1½ miles long to Barton. From here the line would proceed south to join the main Sheffield–Grimsby line of the Manchester, Sheffield & Lincolnshire Railway at Brigg, with a spur connection to the latter's Doncaster–Frodingham–Barnetby line near Appleby. The estimated cost was £960,000, and 10,000 Hull people signed a petition in favour of the line. The Bill got through the House of Commons, but the Lords had doubts as to the feasibility of the engineering involved, of the tunnel in particular, and much to the satisfaction of the North Eastern Board threw the Bill out.

However, the Hull agitation was not without its results. On 11th July, 1873, an agreement was signed by the North Eastern and Manchester, Sheffield & Lincolnshire Companies granting the latter running powers from Thorne Junction to Hull, for passenger, freight and mineral trains; on 1st August, 1873, the first M.S. & L. passenger train made its appearance in the Hull Paragon Station. The N.E.R. also built for the M.S. & L. a large warehouse on Kingston Street for the exclusive use of the latter company, for which a fixed annual rental was paid.

Next came a new agreement with the Midland Railway over a plan which would avoid the constant delays to through traffic to and from the North Eastern line due to the restricted accommodation at Normanton, both passenger and freight. This agreement was to seek powers to build a new joint line direct from Swinton, north of Rotherham, through Pontefract to a junction at Ferrybridge with the spur line from Knottingley to Burton Salmon, where the former York & North Midland line would be rejoined. Opposition from the Manchester, Sheffield & Lincolnshire and Great Northern Railways was bought off by the grant of running powers to both over the new line, the M.S. & L. being permitted to lay in a connection at Swinton which would enable its trains to run from its Sheffield Victoria Station through to York.

The Act for the Swinton & Knottingley Joint Railway was thus obtained without further trouble, and with its opening on 1st July, 1879, a route which in later years was to become a traffic artery of the greatest importance between North-Eastern England and the Midlands, the South and the West, came into existence. Great Northern access to it was provided by connections laid in, both from south to west (from the Sheffield direction towards Leeds) and from east to north (from the Doncaster direction towards York) where the Swinton & Knottingley line crossed the Great Northern and Manchester, Sheffield & Lincolnshire Joint West Riding & Grimsby line at Moorthorpe.

As mentioned in Chapter XVII, two of the four last remaining links in the East Coast main line of today had been opened during this decade – the direct line from Shaftholme Junction, north of Doncaster, through Selby to Chaloner's Whin Junction, 2 miles south of York, on 2nd January, 1871, and the short length from Tursdale Junction, north of Ferryhill, to Relly Mill Junction, Durham, on 1st March, 1872. The third link was the loop between Severus and Holgate Junctions, outside the city wall at York, which for the first time permitted through running without reversal of the East Coast trains, and, with the loop, a magnificent new York Station. At the time of its construction this was the biggest station in Britain, and the disgruntled shareholder who described it as 'a monument of extravagance' would have been astonished could he see the size to which it was compelled to grow in later years to accommodate the unceasing increase of traffic.

The station was built on a curve throughout its length, and the great curved roof, 81ft in span, 42ft in height to the crown of the arch, and 800ft long, has always been an object of admiration. This covered four through lines and two main platforms, the longer of which had a length of no less than 1,500ft; on both sides of the station and at both ends there were bay platforms, covered by subsidiary roof spans. On the city side of the station a handsome building was erected to house the booking hall and other station offices. The station was opened for traffic on 25th June, 1877, and on 20th May of the following year the station amenities were added to by the opening of the palatial five-storey Royal Station Hotel, with beautiful pleasure grounds running down to the River Ouse and a delightful view across the river to York Minster beyond. The building of the station, as we saw in the last chapter, had been delayed, for financial reasons, but when at last it came into use it was an asset of which both the North Eastern Railway and the City of York might well be proud.

One final opening of this period was on Tyneside. Various teeming communities east of Newcastle, on the north bank of the winding river, were not touched by the direct line of the former Blyth & Tyne Railway from Newcastle to North Shields. Powers were therefore obtained in 1871 for a new 'Riverside' branch, taking off from the Newcastle–Berwick main line at Byker Junction, between Manors and Heaton, following the curves of the river on a very circuitous course, and joining the North Shields line at Percy Main. The task proved a lengthy one, owing to the heavy engineering work involved, tunnels, cuttings, substantial retaining walls, bridges and embankments following one another in rapid succession, and it was not until 1st May, 1879, that the Riverside line was completed and opened for traffic.

CHAPTER XIX

The Troubled 1870s and After

WHILE the North Eastern Railway was making the advances described in Chapter XVIII, matters were not going so happily in the industrial or the financial realms. In that chapter it was stated that never again after 1873 was so high a dividend as 10 per cent to be paid, and we have now to review the reasons for the subsequent decline. After six years of peaceful labour relations, trouble broke out again in 1874. This time it was at Tyne Dock, where the trimmers and the teemers, whose normal weekend lasted no longer than from midnight on Saturday to the uncomfortably early hour of 3 o'clock on Monday morning, asked to be able to cease work at 4 p.m. on Saturday, and not to have to resume until 6 a.m. on Monday.

The coal-owners objected that this would interfere, both with the regular supply of coal to gasworks in London and also to the speedy return of empty wagons to the collieries, and the N.E.R. directors therefore refused to agree to the request. As a result, the men struck work on 2nd February. But once again, like the drivers and firemen in 1867, the men were unfortunate; replacements were quickly obtained from Darlington, and by the end of February practically all the vacant places had been filled.

Labour unrest on a much wider scale now began to affect North Eastern Railway receipts. A depression had begun to set in, and the inflated prices for the products of the area – such as coal, for example, which as mentioned in Chapter XVIII had trebled in price between 1871 and 1872 – were now falling. Wages in the coal and iron industries were therefore reduced, those of the blast-furnacemen in March and of the Durham coal-miners a month later; the miners struck work but their strike lasted no more than a week. Not so with the Cleveland ironstone miners, however; to fight their reduction in wages of $11\frac{1}{2}$ per cent they struck for almost the whole of May and June, seven weeks in all, many of the blast-furnaces in the area having to be damped down in consequence.

The reduction in the carriage of coal and iron severely affected the North Eastern Railway revenue from mineral traffic, which fell by £27,090 in the first half-year of 1874; over the whole year, despite various economies, increased expenses, chiefly higher wages, resulted in the dividend falling to $8\frac{1}{4}$ per cent. We have taken note already of the way in which the North Eastern Railway Board held up various developments, because of the financial conditions in the 1870s; whereas from 1874 to 1876 expenditure on capital account had averaged about £2,000,000 annually, in 1877 the amount was halved, in 1878 reduced to £750,000 and in 1879 to £500,000.

The next strike began at the end of 1877, when the Northumberland coal-miners came out on 18th December and remained out until 14th February, 1878. As a result, in the first half of 1878 the railway receipts fell off by about 5 per cent, though the loss was largely countered by further reductions in working expenses. In July, 1875, to help the iron-masters over the depression period, the N.E.R. had reduced their carriage charges for coal, coke, ore and limestone to the blast-furnace plants by 7½ per cent, and in November, 1878, they conceded a further 7½ per cent for the next five months, eventually extended until the end of 1879. But these concessions were not sufficient to prevent a number of bankruptcies among the many firms, both small and large, that were by now making iron in County Durham and North Yorkshire.

Industrial unrest still was not at an end; on 5th April, 1879, the Durham coal-miners followed those in Northumberland by going out on strike, and remained out until 19th May. The result of all these troubles was that in the first half-year of 1879 North Eastern revenue reached its *nadir*. All receipts were down – from the carriage of minerals most of all, and even of passengers, more than half-a-million fewer third class passengers being carried. So the dividend on North Eastern Consols, which had been 10 per cent in 1873, had dropped to 5 per cent by the first half-year of 1879, though from then on there was a slight recovery. But the effect of the depression during this decade is seen in the fact that between 1875 and 1879 N.E.R. gross receipts fell by over £1,000,000, or by 15·6 per cent – 3·6 per cent in passenger takings, 5 per cent in general freight and 7 per cent in minerals.

During this depressing period, however, there had been one bright interlude. It was the celebration, on 27th and 28th September, 1875, of the Jubilee of the world's first steam-operated public railway – the Stockton & Darlington. The North Eastern Railway Board decided to allocate £5,000 to the cost of an appropriate commemoration, and to this the Corporation of Darlington, which was decided on as the *venue*, added £1,000. The various events agreed on were an exhibition of locomotives illustrating the development of locomotive power from 1825 to 1875, a banquet for guests invited to represent all the world's principal railways, the unveiling in the town of a statue of Joseph Pease and the presentation of his portrait to the Corporation, and excursions to various places in the area.

The Locomotive Exhibition was held in the North Road shops and ranged from *Locomotion No. 1* of the Stockton & Darlington to the latest Fletcher 2-4-0 of the '901' class, and one of Patrick Stirling's 8ft 4-2-2 express engines from the Great Northern Railway. The way in which horses used their 'dandy carts' of early days was demonstrated in the North Road yard. The town of Darlington was beautifully decorated, and, favoured by fine weather, the great banquet was held at the Feethams Ground, near Bank Top Station, followed by illuminations and a fine firework display.

At the banquet T. E. Harrison, the Chief Engineer, remarked that 'the people living in 1925 will look back to the railways of 1875 with as much curiosity as those taking part in the Jubilee Celebration were doing to the railways of 1825'. Though possibly this was not the most accurate of forecasts, Harrison's audience would certainly have been deeply interested had they been able to witness the vastly more imposing locomotive procession with which the Centenary of the Stockton & Darlington Railway was celebrated in 1925, after the North Eastern Railway itself had become merged in the London & North Eastern Railway.

Although the North Eastern Railway Board, as we have seen, slowed down its development work during the 1870s, owing to the depressed conditions, it had refused to bring the work to a complete stop, and during the following decade extension continued. On 21st July, 1873, Royal Assent had been given to an Act authorising the Leeds, Castleford & Pontefract Junction Company to tap the mining area south of the Leeds and Selby line by a branch from the latter, at Garforth, for 8¼ miles southward to Castleford. The N.E.R. had been authorised to subscribe to its capital, and by an Act of 13th July, 1876, to take over its powers, which it did by exchanging £75 of its own Consols for every £100 of L.C. & P.J. stock. So it was the North Eastern which completed the line and opened it for traffic on various dates in 1878.

Other extensions were spurred on by the plans of rival companies, which still threatened to invade North Eastern territory. In 1881, for example, a 'Central Northumberland Railway' was promoted to tap the agricultural country between Newcastle, Scotsgap, Rothbury, Whittingham, Wooler and Coldstream, and also, in conjunction with the North British Railway (whose existing line between Scotsgap and Rothbury would be used) to form a new route from Newcastle to Edinburgh. But this proposal came to nothing when in 1882 the North Eastern obtained an Act to build a 35½-mile line from Alnwick to a junction with its Tweedmouth & Kelso branch at Coldstream, following much of the same route. Five years were occupied in construction, and the line was opened throughout on 5th September, 1887. A new station was built at Alnwick, but still terminal, trains from Alnmouth to Wooler and Coldstream requiring to reverse direction in it. A very circuitous course was needed to get the line over the high ground between Alnwick and Whittingham, and to reach the summit level of 655ft required a 4-mile climb at 1 in 50, followed by 3 miles down at the same inclination to just beyond Edlingham. Despite severe gradients through much of its length, the line needed some very heavy earthworks, both embankments and cuttings, through the hilly country traversed on the flanks of the Cheviots.

Speculative interests in the south still had their eyes on a possible infiltration of North Eastern territory from the Skipton direction, by way of Kettlewell into Wensleydale, and in 1883 proposed an extension of such a line through to Darlington, Stockton and Middlesbrough. The North Eastern Railway promptly promoted two lines over parts of the same route, one from Spennithorne on the Northallerton–Leyburn branch to Scorton on the Richmond branch, and the other from Darlington Bank

Top Station through Dinsdale to a junction with the original Darlington North Road to Stockton line of the Stockton & Darlington at Fighting Cocks, designed to improve the communication between Darlington and Middlesbrough.

Nothing came of the former (or of the Skipton–Kettlewell scheme) owing to the objection of landowners, but the Darlington to Fighting Cocks line was sanctioned, completed and opened on 1st July, 1887. With it was opened the fine new Bank Top Station at Darlington, looped off the through running lines, and built on the island platform principle, with the offices in the centre, flanked by very lengthy down and up main platforms, and with bay platforms for branch trains at both ends. Three roof spans, each 60ft wide and 100ft long, provided platform coverage, and the western elevation of the station was graced by a lofty clock tower, visible from a large part of the town.

Next came a scheme for a 'West Durham & Tyne Railway', promoted by a prominent coal-owner named Sir George Elliott, together with other coal-owners in the districts of Tanfield and Pontop. They wanted a direct line from the Pelton area, between Chester-le-Street and Consett, down to the Tyne at Dunston, just east of Gateshead, where shipping staiths were proposed, to reduce the cost of working their coal north-eastwards to Tyne Dock for shipment. Such improvements had been made by the Tyne Commissioners to the navigation of the river, including dredging and the replacement of the old arch road bridge by a swing-bridge almost underneath the High Level Bridge, that steamers of up to 1,500 and 1,600 tons could now move as far up the river as Elswick. It was also calmly proposed to apply for running powers over various North Eastern lines, including that from Lamesley to Tyne Dock and even for passenger trains into Newcastle Central Station.

When the Bill came before Parliament in 1886, the North Eastern Railway was able to claim that it had by no means neglected the area concerned. On 1st January, 1886, it had completed and brought into use a deviation between Annfield Plain and Pelton, which had done away with the Stanley, Edenhill and Waldridge inclines of the Stanhope & Tyne Railway, thereby expediting the movement of coal. The shipping facilities at Tyne Dock were of a high order, and the rates, fixed when coal was at its lowest level of price in the 1860s, had never been increased. Nevertheless, the House of Commons Committee, against the opposition of the North Eastern, passed the Bill, on the ground that the coal-owners ought to have the option of shipping at Dunston if they so wished.

But fortunately the House of Lords took the view that to build a new line would be an unjustifiable waste of money. On the understanding that the North Eastern would build shipping staiths of their own at Dunston, and lay in connecting lines which would give direct access to these staiths, the Bill was thrown out. Not until 1893 were the new staiths ready, with three shipping berths, each 26oft apart and each with two sets of side-tipping spouts, the whole having a length of 1,709ft. On the same date, 16th October, the connecting Dunston Extension railway was brought into use; it left the Team Valley main line at Ouston Junction, Low Fell, and ran for 2½ miles down to the staiths, with spur connections to the other lines on the south bank of the Tyne between Redheugh and Blaydon.

Another line completed throughout at this time was the Annfield Plain deviation with its tremendous climb from the junction with the main line, just south of Birtley, to a mile beyond Annfield Plain, 8 miles almost entirely at 1 in 50, conquering a difference in level of 654ft; this was opened throughout on 13th November, 1890. Five years before this on 1st December, 1885, a further extension of the Ferryhill and Spennymoor branch had been opened to Bishop Auckland, so greatly improving the connection between the Hartlepools and West Durham.

About this time considerable developments were taking place at the Northumberland port of Blyth. Coal had been shipped here from 1874 onwards, but in small vessels only, owing to the shallowness of the harbour; in 1881 work began on deepening the channel and the water at the loading berths, and in 1882, a year in which no more than 93 vessels all told loaded at North and South Blyth, a Board of Commissioners was appointed to take in hand the work of improvement. The North Eastern Railway assisted by building, at a cost of £25,000, a new set of staiths, 1,100ft long, with the latest loading equipment, brought into use on 28th February, 1884. So between 1883 and 1884, the shipments of coal at South Blyth rose from 42,176 tons to 252,780 tons.

In the following year a new West Pier, 2,470ft long, built by the Commissioners, was brought to completion. A short connection from Ashington Colliery to the former Blyth & Tyne Railway at Ashington gave Ashington coal a direct route to Blyth instead of the former circuit *via* Morpeth, Bedlington and Newsham. In 1887, despite the Northumberland miners' strike, coal shipments at South Blyth were up to 466,983 tons, and with the traffic constantly increasing, the North Eastern Railway built a further range of staiths, 1,237ft long, and with four spouts, brought into use on 1st May, 1888, providing direct access to these with a new 1½-mile loop line from Newsham.

Still the shipments increased, until by 1893 South Blyth was handling some 2,000,000 tons of coal a year, and additional accommodation had become imperative. Powers to construct additional staiths, in this case at North Blyth, were obtained in this year, but when in 1894 the North Eastern applied for authority to build a short spur from Newsham to Cramlington, on the main line, only 2½ miles apart, which would have shortened considerably the journey between Blyth and Newcastle, the House of Lords insisted on such onerous conditions, to satisfy the claims of certain landowners whose wayleaves over the former Blyth & Tyne might have been affected, that the railway company withdrew the Bill.

Among other openings during this period was the Scarborough to Whitby line, described in Chapter XVIII, in 1885, and the long-deferred 'Scarborough, Bridlington & West Riding Junction Railway', cut down finally to a line from Bridlington to Market Weighton only, but thereby opening up a direct route from the South and the Midlands to Bridlington

A Royal train leaving York for the north in the first decade of the century behind Class 'S' 4-6-0 No. 2010, with a coach of unusual aspect behind the tender.

More than twenty years later Raven Pacific No. 2401 *City of Kingston-upon-Hull* starts northwards from York with a heavy East Coast express.   [*Locomotive Publishing Co.*

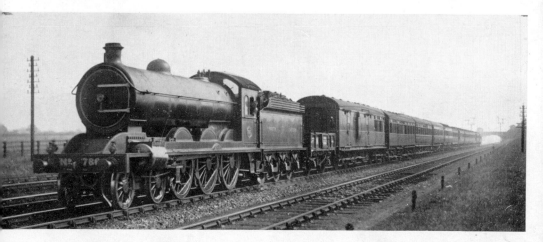

An express of mixed corridor and non-corridor stock headed by Class 'S2' 4-6-0 No. 786.   [*Locomotive Publishing Co.*

Above, the 'Fastest Train in the British Empire', on its 43-min. run from Darlington to York with an unusually heavy load, passing Beningbrough at 75 m.p.h. behind 'R' class 4-4-0 No. 1207.   [*H. Gordon Tidey*

Below, the racing stretch of the former North Eastern Railway line from Darlington to York over which the fastest start-to-stop run in Great Britain is still made, now in 35 min., at 75.6 m.p.h., and the 'Flying Scotsman' and 'Talisman' are timed in 32 min. pass-to-pass, at 82.7 m.ph.   [*British Railways*

Above, Wilson Worsdell's Class 'V1' two-cylinder Atlantic No. 901 at the head of an Anglo-Scottish express, composed of typical clerestory-roofed bow-ended East Coast Joint Stock.
[*R. J. Purves*

Below, Raven Class 'Z' three-cylinder Atlantic No. 2171 at speed when under test with the North Eastern Railway dynamometer car. [*Locomotive Publishing Co.*

Above, one of William Worsdell's 2-4-2 passenger tanks of Class 'A', first introduced in 1886.

[*Locomotive Publishing Co.*

Left, an unusual duty for one of Wilson Worsdell's 'O' class 0-4-4 tanks – assisting a modern British Railways Class 'A1' Pacific up the 1 in 44 of Seaton bank with an express diverted from the direct Sunderland–West Hartlepool main line.

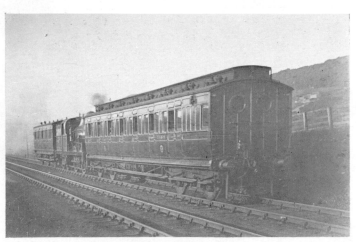

Left, a North Eastern 'auto-train' – a push-and-pull unit worked by a Fletcher 'BTP' 0-4-4 tank.

[*H. Gordon Tidey*

via Selby. The inception of this scheme, as described in Chapter XII, was in 1865; the line was actually opened in 1890. In 1892 an independent company obtained powers to extend the Weardale branch for 9½ miles from Stanhope to Wearhead, and started work, but as with other previous minor lines in the area there were financial difficulties, which resulted in the North Eastern Railway taking over the project in 1894, and completing and opening the extension on 21st October, 1895.

Work was going on at this time on the enlargement of Newcastle Central Station. The first part of the extension to be completed was an imposing hotel, opened in October, 1892; the work on the station itself, which included additional platforms on the south side, a new entrance and booking hall, and other additions, was completed and brought into use in June, 1894. At the same time a widening to four tracks past the Manors and Heaton to the junction with the North Shields branch came into operation. In 1894 also another widening, from Neville Hill to Marsh Lane, Leeds, was brought to completion.

CHAPTER XX

Developing the East Coast Route to Scotland

ONE further railway opening of major importance had taken place in the 1880s, not of a part of the North Eastern Railway, but in North Eastern territory; what this was, however, will need for its description a chapter to itself. Meantime something needs to be said about the North Eastern Railway as the central link in the East Coast Route to Scotland. The North British Railway, across the Border, was proving to be a somewhat fickle partner. The penetration of the N.B.R. into Northumberland has been described in Chapter XV; next came the opening of the North British Waverley route from Edinburgh to Carlisle in 1862, as a result of which the North Eastern Railway found that in 1863 its freight traffic from Edinburgh to London had dropped to no more than a fraction of what it had been before.

From 1st June, 1869, therefore, the North Eastern Railway decided to begin to exercise the running powers over the North British from Berwick to Edinburgh, which as described in Chapter XVI it had obtained as a *quid pro quo* for North British running powers from Hexham into Newcastle. So from the date just mentioned the East Coast expresses were worked through between Newcastle and Edinburgh by North Eastern locomotives. At the end of the same month the long-standing English and Scotch Traffic Agreement between the East and West Coast Companies came to an end; negotiations for a further agreement to pool the traffic fell through, owing to uncertainty as to what the position might be when the Midland Railway had completed its Settle and Carlisle line, but it was agreed that the same rates and fares should be charged for through Anglo-Scottish freight or passenger traffic by either route.

The new agreement, however, had no provisions as to how many trains might be operated, and on 2nd August, 1869, the Great Northern and North Eastern Railways, without reference to the North British and aided by the powers of the N.E.R. to run through to Edinburgh, announced a new express from King's Cross at 8 p.m., due in Edinburgh at 6.5 a.m. Now by the Scotch Amalgamation Acts of 1865 and 1866 the North British and Caledonian Railways were bound to provide through connections between Edinburgh and Aberdeen, *via* Stirling and Perth, with all East Coast trains from London, and the new night express had thus to be served. In consequence, passengers who had left London at 8 p.m. from now on could reach Perth at 8.59 a.m., Aberdeen at 12.20 p.m., and Inverness at 2.45 p.m.; a Glasgow arrival also had become possible by 7.45 a.m. over the Edinburgh & Glasgow Railway. The immediate response of the West Coast was to put on an 8 p.m. express of their own from

Euston to Glasgow, arriving at 7.10 a.m. Thus began the rivalry in East and West Coast times, which was to last for a quarter of a century and culminate in the famous 'Races' of 1888 and 1895.

Furthermore, in the matter of comfort rather than journey time, the competition became intensified in 1873 by the East Coast Companies putting in service their first sleeping cars, which from 1st September were attached to the 8.30 p.m. express from King's Cross to Edinburgh and Glasgow, returning to London by the 9 p.m. from Glasgow and the 10.30 p.m. from Edinburgh.

The next complication came about late in 1874, with the announcement by the Midland Railway that from 1st January, 1875, to secure economy in the use of rolling stock, it intended to abolish second class and to provide third class accommodation on all its trains. From the same date, first class fares were to be reduced to 1½d. per mile, or 50 per cent above the third class rate, and in this the North Eastern Railway and its partners had to follow suit. Then, on 1st May, 1876, there came the opening of the Midland Railway's Settle & Carlisle line, and with it the inauguration of new routes from London to both Edinburgh and Glasgow, as a result of which the Great Northern and North Eastern Railways had to take further action.

From 1st July, 1876, the 'Flying Scotsman' in each direction, at 10 a.m. from King's Cross and from Edinburgh, had its overall time cut from 9½ to 9 hours, thereby beating the West Coast day service by 1 hour 25 minutes and the best Midland train by 1¾ hours. The East Coast flyer still continued to carry first and second class passengers only, but as far back as 1872, when the 'Flying Scotsman' had been accelerated to make the run in 9½ hours, a second train, with third class coaches included, had been put on at 10.10 a.m., with a running time of 10½ hours. In the 1876 accelerations this latter time was cut to 10¼ hours and that of the night mail from 9¾ to 9½ hours; the 1866 Act compelled the Caledonian Railway to provide a Perth connection to the latter, which brought passengers who had left King's Cross at 8.30 p.m. into Perth by 8.40 a.m. – with a 20-minute lead over the West Coast 'Special Scotch Mail' from Euston – and into Aberdeen by 12.40 p.m.

Through these years important developments were taking place north of Edinburgh also. It was beginning to dawn on the North British management that it had more to hope for from its association with the North Eastern and Great Northern Railways than from that with the Midland, however useful the latter might be as a feeder of traffic. Moreover, if it was to obtain any adequate share of receipts from the traffic between Edinburgh and Perth, Dundee and Aberdeen, this would never be possible while passengers had still to submit to the discomforts and delay of ferry crossings across the Firths of Forth and Tay; otherwise it would continue to remain largely dependent on the Caledonian Railway. As far back as the 1860s, therefore, the possibility was being faced of throwing bridges across both firths. In anticipation, the North British Railway in 1862 had acquired the Edinburgh, Perth & Dundee Railway, and in 1863 had secured powers to build railways from Ratho, on the Edinburgh–Glasgow line, to South Queensferry, and from North Queensferry, on the opposite side of the Firth of Forth, to Dunfermline, in the Perth direction.

Not until 1870 was the Act obtained to build a girder bridge across the Tay from Wormit to the eastern suburbs of Dundee, while various plans for bridging the Forth (including an Act of 1865 which was never implemented) culminated in the Forth Bridge Railway Act of 1873. The Forth Bridge undertaking was of such magnitude that the North British Railway could not possibly face it alone. A separate Forth Bridge Company was therefore formed with the North British, North Eastern, Great Northern and Midland Railways – the last-mentioned in anticipation of the opening of its Settle & Carlisle line – guaranteeing an annual dividend on the capital.

The story of the Tay and Forth Bridges has been fully told in *The North British Railway*, by C. Hamilton Ellis, and there is no space in which to review it in detail here. Suffice it to say that Thomas Bouch's original Tay Bridge, begun in the summer of 1871, completed early in 1878 at a cost of £350,000, and opened on 1st June of that year, lasted no more than 18 months, the central portion being demolished by a furious gale on the night of December 28th, 1879 – one of the outstanding disasters of railway history. The New Tay Viaduct Act, for a far more substantial bridge to the design of W. H. Barlow, received the Royal Assent in July, 1881, and after the expenditure of roughly £1,000,000 this bridge was opened for traffic on 20th June, 1887.

Up to 1878 progress on the Forth Bridge had been extremely slow, and the Tay Bridge disaster brought the work to a standstill, for the Forth Bridge design also had been prepared by Bouch and the contractors were no longer prepared to proceed. Indeed, in 1880 the Forth Bridge Company applied for powers to abandon the undertaking, but the English railways interested, the North Eastern included, opposed any such abandonment. In the end John Fowler's celebrated design for a cantilever bridge was accepted; the four railways then met the representatives of the Forth Bridge Company at York, and the latter agreed to withdraw their Bill for abandonment and to apply for fresh powers, which were granted. The financial basis was an agreement by the four railways to substitute for their former conditional guarantee of interest on the capital expenditure an absolute guarantee of a perpetual 4 per cent, to be borne in the proportions of 18¾ per cent each by the Great Northern and North Eastern Railways, 30 per cent by the North British, and, remarkable to relate, the biggest contribution of 32½ per cent by the Midland Railway.

Work was begun on the new design early in 1883, and on 4th March, 1890, the Forth Bridge, which still today ranks as one of the engineering wonders of the world, was opened ceremonially by the Prince of Wales. It had cost some £3,000,000. The North British Railway, needless to say, was the principal beneficiary, for although it would still have to use 38 miles of Caledonian tracks from Kinnaber Junction, Montrose, to reach

Aberdeen, it was now completely independent of the latter company in its access to Dundee and Perth. The journey from Edinburgh to Perth had been reduced from 59 to 48 miles, to Dundee from 90 to 59 miles, and to Aberdeen from 159 to 130 miles; and, of course, all through traffic from the Great Northern, North Eastern and Midland Railways benefited proportionately in time and operational cost.

Mention was made earlier in this chapter of the way in which contests began between the East Coast and West Coast Companies as to which route could provide the fastest service between London and Scotland, and how, after that a further complication came about by the opening in 1876 of the independent Midland Railway route from London to Scotland. The competition culminated in two 'Races'. Although the various railway managements concerned blandly denied that anything in the nature of racing was in progress, the public was under no illusion that these were sporting events of the first magnitude, and public excitement, in the 1895 Race in particular, rose to a very high pitch. In the days in which we live, it seems well-nigh incredible that railway managements, with the safety of the travelling public in their hands, could have countenanced the risks that must have been taken, more particularly in excessively high speeds round curves, to attain the shortest journey times that were achieved, but so it was.

Here again are stories which have been told at such length – as, for example, in O. S. Nock's book *The Railway Race to the North* – as to need no recapitulation in detail, and the barest description must suffice. The 1888 Race to Edinburgh resulted from the decision of the East Coast Companies in November, 1887, to admit third class passengers not merely to the slower 'Flying Scotsman' relief train, which by then had come down to a 10-hour run, but to the 9-hour 'Flying Scotsman' itself; until then the 10 a.m. from Euston to Edinburgh, which did carry third class passengers, had never come below 10 hours. Suddenly, in June, 1888, the London & North Western and Caledonian Companies announced an acceleration of their 10 a.m. expresses in each direction to the same 9-hour time as the 'Flying Scotsman', and the Race was 'on'. Acceleration followed acceleration until by the middle of August the trains concerned had been speeded up to 7¾ hours in each direction. The fastest time achieved over the East Coast Route, which included the lunch stop always made at York – on this occasion of 26 minutes – was 7 hours 27 minutes, beating the best West Coast time by 11 minutes. From then on the railways concerned came to an agreement that the time of the day trains should be fixed at a minimum of 8½ hours, ½-hour less than the previous East Coast time and 1½ hours less than that of the West Coast.

Competition in speed did not flare up again until well after the opening of both the Forth and Tay bridges. It started modestly enough with an acceleration by no more than 10 minutes of the 8 p.m. express from Euston, to bring it into Aberdeen at 7.40 a.m., only 5 minutes behind the corresponding night express from King's Cross. This happened on 1st June, 1895, and a month later the East Coast countered by announcing that their 8 p.m. down would reach Aberdeen at 7.20 a.m., 20 minutes earlier. Within a fortnight the West Coast at one stroke cut 40 minutes from their schedule, advertising an Aberdeen arrival at 7 a.m. As in 1888, acceleration succeeded acceleration in quick succession, but on a far more drastic scale, until by the latter part of August the West Coast express was being booked to reach Aberdeen, 540 miles from Euston, at 5.35 a.m., and the East Coast train, after 523½ miles of running but on the whole a more difficult route, at 5.40 a.m.

Both flyers, cut down to very light loads and with relief trains following to make the stops that the racing trains were missing out, by now were gaining time handsomely even on these drastically accelerated schedules. The climax came on the nights of 21st and 22nd August, 1895. On the former the 105-ton East Coast 8 p.m. from King's Cross was the first into Aberdeen, at 4.40 a.m., one hour early, having covered the 523½ miles in 520 minutes, five intermediate stops included; on the following night the West Coast train, reduced in weight to no more than 70 tons and with three stops only, put in an appearance at 5.32 a.m., having covered 540 miles in 512 minutes, at an average of 63·3 m.p.h. throughout. These closing weeks had been all the more exciting in that the competing trains had had to use the same metals, those of the Caledonian Railway, over the final 38 miles from Kinnaber Junction to Aberdeen.

By these concluding times, the West Coast Companies had cut their schedule of three months earlier by no less than 3 hours 18 minutes, while the East Coast had cut theirs by 2 hours 55 minutes. Such times between London and Aberdeen have bever been beaten or equalled from that day to this; even with the steam-hauled streamlined 'Coronation' express of 1937–1939 or the present-day diesel-operated 'Flying Scotsman' and 'Talisman' schedules of 6 hours between King's Cross and Edinburgh – 19 minutes less than the best time in the 1895 Race – no faster regular timing than 3 hours has ever been attempted between Edinburgh and Aberdeen. On the North Eastern line the shortest time achieved over the 80½ miles from York to Newcastle, with its slow finish round the Gateshead curve and over the High Level Bridge into Newcastle Central Station, was 78 minutes; from Newcastle to Edinburgh Driver Nicholson, with N.E.R. 'M' class 4-4-0 No. 1621, made the amazing time of 113 minutes for the 124½ miles to Edinburgh, but at the expense of what must have been some pretty reckless speed over the curves at Morpeth, Alnmouth, Tweedmouth to Berwick, and Portobello.

This was nothing to the shocking risks that must have been taken by the North British drivers, however, in running the 59¼ miles from Edinburgh to Dundee, with their succession of steep switchback gradients and sharp curves, in the even hour, and the 71¼ miles on to Aberdeen, nearly as bad and with stretches of single track in addition, in 77 minutes. By common consent, the Race then came to an end; some very fast timings remained, but in the following year a disaster to the 8 p.m. from Euston, which actually was derailed with severe loss of life on the sharp curve north of Preston Station, caused the schedules over both routes to be eased out to such a degree that the 'Race to Aberdeen' soon was no more than a memory.

A curious interlude in North Eastern–North British relationships began in the year 1894, just before the 1895 Race. The N.B.R. was about to face the reconstruction of its Waverley Station in Edinburgh, and considered that the time had come for 'foreign' locomotives to be barred from what was so exclusively North British territory. Chief among these intruders, of course, were the North Eastern locomotives which, authorised by the running powers secured by the N.E.R. in 1869, were still working the East Coast expresses through between Newcastle and Edinburgh. The N.B.R. thus gave the N.E.R. what was, in effect, six months' notice 'to quit', but the N.E.R. had no intention of complying with this ultimatum. The North British, therefore, filed an application with the Railway & Canal Commission that an order should be issued to the North Eastern to hand over these trains to the N.B.R. at the 'frontier' station of Berwick. The Commission ruled, however, that the North Eastern was acting within its rights, as the possessor of running powers, and they could do nothing in the matter.

Having got its teeth in, the North British was reluctant to let go, and began legal proceedings in the Scottish courts, which were carried finally from the Scottish Court of Session to the House of Lords. This august body ruled that no specific legal rights existed on either side, and that if the two companies could not come to an amicable agreement they had better refer the matter to the Railway & Canal Commission, which they did. But while the Commission was considering this knotty point the North British decided to take matters into its own hands and to work the East Coast trains between Berwick and Edinburgh with its own locomotives, which it began to do on 14th January, 1897. In order to 'keep face', and as the N.B.R. could hardly expect the N.E.R. to accelerate its running to allow for the engine-changing stop at Berwick of the trains hitherto non-stop between Newcastle and Edinburgh, the North British had to do all the time-cutting over the 57½ miles of its own line between Berwick and Edinburgh. This meant some very hard running for the N.B.R. Holmes 4-4-0 express engines, which had to be used in pairs on the heavier trains, so that this North British insistence proved quite an expensive business to that company.

However, this working lasted only for just over a year. In February, 1898, the Railway & Canal Commission gave its ruling, which was an order that the North Eastern Railway should be permitted to work ten trains daily through to and from Edinburgh, including all the non-stop workings between Newcastle and Edinburgh, and that the remaining eight should be worked by North British locomotives between Berwick and Edinburgh. It is of interest that a month later the N.E.R. brought into use, for the benefit of these trains, its first set of water pick-up troughs, between Lucker and Belford; its second set, between Northallerton and Danby Wiske, followed in 1901. One outcome of this N.E.R.–N.B.R. *imbroglio* was that, by arrangement with the Caledonian Railway, the

North Eastern for a time ran through coaches between Newcastle and Glasgow by way of Carlisle and the Caledonian route, a distance of 163 miles only as compared with 172 miles *via* Berwick and Edinburgh, thus making the North British pay in another small way, by loss of traffic, for its intransigence. But the N.B.R. had learned its lesson, and there was no further trouble of this kind.

A pale reflection of the 1888 and 1895 Races was seen in the summer of 1901, when the Midland Railway, in an attempt to obtain a larger share of the Anglo-Scottish traffic, decided on an acceleration of its service between St Pancras and Edinburgh, which called, of course, for North British co-operation over the Waverley route. From 1st July, 1901, the 9.30 a.m. from St Pancras was advertised to reach Edinburgh Waverley at 6.5 p.m., 10 minutes ahead of rather than behind the 10 a.m. 'Flying Scotsman' from King's Cross, and no more than 20 minutes slower in overall time from London.

There seemed here a parallel with the opening of the 1895 Race to Aberdeen and speculation arose as to whether Portobello East Junction might become another Kinnaber, with the signalmen having to decide which of the two expresses to allow to precede the other over the last 3 miles into Waverley. In any event it seemed possible that the 'Flying Scotsman' might be delayed if the Midland train were running slightly behind time. But in the very first week the North Eastern Railway put the matter beyond doubt by reaching Waverley from 6 to 13 minutes early every night. The Midland train, however, arriving up to 16 minutes late nightly, never got nearer its booked time than 6.6 p.m., whereas the 'Flying Scotsman', on this first night, was in by 6.2 p.m. Despite the excitement of the newspapers, no Race developed out of this modest beginning.

Though out of its chronological order, there was one further major and costly development of later years that can most appropriately be dealt with in this chapter. Earlier chapters have described how the original East Coast main line ran from Doncaster to York by way of Knottingley and Church Fenton, and from Ferryhill to Gateshead *via* Penshaw, Washington and Pelaw, and how the present routes between these points came into use in considerably later years – from Durham down the Team Valley to Gateshead in 1868, from Shaftholme Junction, Doncaster, *via* Selby to York in 1871, from Newton Hall Junction, Ferryhill, to Durham in 1872, and the new through station which avoided reversal at York in 1877.

But until 1906 it was still necessary for all East Coast trains to reverse direction in Newcastle Central Station, obtaining access to it over Robert Stephenson's High Level Bridge across the Tyne, which by now was becoming badly congested with traffic. One more great bridge remained to be added to the High Level Bridge, the Royal Border Bridge at Berwick and the Forth and Tay Bridges to complete the East Coast Route and to make possible the non-stop running of more modern times between London and Edinburgh. It was the King Edward Bridge across the Tyne gorge.

The decision to build the bridge was taken at the turn of the century and the work began in 1902, to the designs of C. A. Harrison. As compared with the six main spans of the High Level Bridge, the King Edward Bridge was content with four, the two centre ones 300ft across, flanked by side spans of 191ft on the south side and 231ft on the north. It was wider than its older rival, carrying four railway tracks as compared with three, and so requiring a bridge floor 50ft wide, fanning out in width on the south side to permit a Y-shaped connection with the existing main line between Bensham and Gateshead. The main lattice girder spans were supported on massive piers of Norway granite, the centre one carried down to a depth of 69ft below high-water to find a firm foundation. In all, the bridge proper, excluding approaches, required 5,782 tons of steel and 330,000 cu. ft of granite.

On the north side the new tracks had to cut right through one end of the Forth Goods Station to reach a junction with the Newcastle & Carlisle line at the west end of the Central Station. This curve was on a sharp radius of 10 chains, but at King Edward Bridge Junction, at the south end, an even sharper curve of 7 chains radius was unavoidable. The Y-junction here and the similar one at Gateshead from now on made it possible for trains between Newcastle and either the main line to the south or the Sunderland direction to enter or leave either end of Newcastle Central Station. It was a fitting sequel to the opening of the High Level Bridge by Queen Victoria that a little over half-a-century later her son, King Edward VII, on 10th July, 1906, in person declared open the bridge which ever since has borne his name.

CHAPTER XXI

Hull and the Stranger within the Gates

WE come now to the 'further event of major importance' referred to at the beginning of Chapter XX as having taken place during the 1880s. Earlier chapters have described the many attempts made by other railway companies, in most cases promoted independently but often with the backing of the major railways in other parts of the country, to penetrate the compact and prosperous territory served by the North Eastern Railway. As we have seen, apart from invasions across the Border into Northumberland by the North British Railway, which never developed into any threat sufficient to cause serious concern, all these attempts had failed. Either the plans had been abandoned for lack of support, or the Bills had been thrown out by Parliament, or the North Eastern Railway had succeeded in buying off the would-be invaders or combining with them in some project likely to be of mutual value, such as the Swinton & Knottingley Joint Railway.

We have noted also that not a few of these incursions were aimed at Hull, or Kingston-upon-Hull, to give the city its full name, and with every encouragement from the restless burgesses of that city, a kind of 'fifth column' that never ceased to be dissatisfied with its treatment by the N.E.R., and was always on the look-out for ways and means of obtaining some competing railway access. By 1880 the various railways which had attempted to reach Hull with their own lines had all settled down with reasonable satisfaction; every facility had been given by the N.E.R. to the Manchester, Sheffield & Lincolnshire Railway to develop its Hull traffic, and although the Great Northern and Lancashire & Yorkshire Railways had obtained running powers into the port, they were so well content with their treatment that up till then neither had attempted to exercise these powers. Of these companies the M.S. & L.R. and L. & Y.R., with the N.E.R., had provided part of the capital of the Hull Dock Company, and had representatives on the Board of the latter.

From 1872 onwards the N.E.R. had spent some £450,000 in providing additional sidings and warehouse accommodation, and had obtained powers to lay in a branch from the Hull & Withernsea line to the site of a projected new dock between 2 and 3 miles east of Hull, at Salt End. This was to have been built by the Hull Dock Company, which also at the time was constructing the William Wright and St Andrew's Docks at a cost of about £400,000; but such exacting conditions were laid down by the Hull Corporation in connection with the Salt End dock and its associated works that the Dock Company, after getting its Bill through both Houses of Parliament, decided to proceed no further with the scheme.

It was in these circumstances that the Hull, Barnsley & West Riding Junction Railway scheme was born, at a meeting in the Station Hotel, Hull, on 28th May, 1879. Its promoters were Colonel Gerard Smith, a Hull banker, and a well-known London solicitor named Robert Galland. The course proposed for the new railway followed in general that of two earlier projects, the Hull & Barnsley Junction of 1845 and the Hull & West Riding Junction of 1862. But in addition to a new railway from the South Yorkshire coalfield in the Barnsley area to Hull, the plan was also to include a new deep water dock on the Humber designed expressly for the shipment of coal.

It had always been a grievance of Hull that equal rates were charged by the N.E.R. for traffic between all the North-East coast ports and the principal Yorkshire cities, and also that the more northerly ports, Hartlepool in particular, could provide return cargoes for ships discharging timber, grain and merchandise, whereas it was maintained that the North Eastern Railway and the Hull Docks Company had never catered properly for coal shipment. For this reason the Hull Corporation strongly supported the Hull & Barnsley project, agreeing to subscribe £100,000 to the capital – a very modest sum, however, in relation to the estimated cost of £4,000,000 – and to sell 126 acres of land to the new company. It was characteristic of the Corporation, however, to lay it down that without Corporation consent the new company should not be able to sell, lease or transfer its property to any other company, or even to enter into any arrangement for joint operation – a provision with little doubt aimed at any possible acquisition by the North Eastern.

By January, 1880, the Hull & Barnsley plans were ready, and by June the Bill was before the House of Commons Committee. It was somewhat amusing that in arguing before the Committee that Hull had been neglected by the North Eastern Railway and its trade handicapped by crippling railway rates and dock dues, the promoters submitted tabular statements as to exports and imports that hardly supported their own case. Between 1870 and 1878, while timber imports at Hartlepool had increased by 9 per cent, those at Hull had gone up by 36 per cent. Despite the claim as to inadequate facilities at Hull Docks for shipping coal, from 1870 to 1879 Hull shipments had gone up from 193,000 to 463,800 tons, whereas those at Grimsby, on the other side of the Humber, directly connected with the South Yorkshire coalfield by the Manchester, Sheffield & Lincolnshire Railway, had advanced only from 290,600 to 332,600 tons. The N.E.R. claimed that even if the proposed Hull & Barnsley Railway managed to draw away from their own line all the traffic passing at that time between Hull and the area of Yorkshire to be served by the H. & B.R., it would be unable to pay a dividend on the heavy capital expenditure involved – a forecast which later proved to be justified.

The Hull Dock Company was solidly behind the N.E.R. in its opposition to the Hull & Barnsley Railway Bill, as it feared the effect that the competition of a new dock might have on its own traffic and its shares. But it was unfortunate for the N.E.R. that at the very time that the Hull &

Barnsley Bill was under examination, new docks at the Hartlepools were completed and brought into use. These brought the total water facilities at the Hartlepools up to seven docks, four timber ponds, two tidal harbours and two tidal basins, having between them a water area of some 200 acres served very adequately by quays, sidings and timber yards with a total area of another 150 acres. By comparison, Hull had a total water area of 114 acres only, with a further 11 acres under construction; the coal-shipping facilities were inferior by comparison with those at the Hartle-pools and the port charges were higher. This comparison was sufficient for the preamble of the Hull & Barnsley Bill to be proved by the House of Commons Committee, and notwithstanding some opposition in the House of Lords, it was passed and received the Royal Assent on 26th August, 1880.

Construction of the Hull & Barnsley Railway and of its Alexandra Dock proceeded with unusual speed, despite formidable financial difficulties. Indeed, work was suspended for a time owing to the railway being unable to raise the necessary funds by the issue of 5 per cent preference stock; eventually Parliament took the unprecedented step of allowing the Company to borrow £2,500,000 to supplement its authorised capital of £3,000,000, the total, it will be noted, being £1,500,000 in excess of the original estimate. So three successive openings took place in July, 1885 – the Alexandra Dock on 16th, the railway for mineral traffic on 20th, and for passenger traffic on 27th to and from its new Cannon Street terminus in Hull.

The new line had a second Hull Station on the Beverley Road and also served the suburb of Willerby; then it threaded the southern spur of the Yorkshire Wolds by the biggest engineering work on the line – Drewton Tunnel, just under 1¼ miles long – crossed a whole succession of North Eastern lines without connecting with any and proceeded to a junction with the Manchester, Sheffield & Lincolnshire at Stairfoot, just east of Barnsley, with a spur to the Midland main line at Cudworth. Before very long the last-mentioned was being used to provide a through passenger service between Hull and the Midland station at Sheffield. By the time of opening, the Hull & Barnsley capital had been increased to £6,000,000, and the borrowing powers to £3,500,000. In later years various branches were opened, as described at the end of this chapter.

As soon as the Hull & Barnsley had commenced operation, a ruinous rate war began, the Hull & Barnsley, the North Eastern and the Hull Dock Companies all taking part. Within a year carriage and dock charges had all been reduced, and while the N.E.R. could stand the strain, the two other participants could not. On the Hull & Barnsley opening day Colonel Gerard Smith, its principal promoter, had foreseen for it a 'pro-mised land of commerce'; actually in its first five months the H. & B.R. had earned no more than £54,848 gross, or £6,170 net revenue, a fraction only of the amount that would be needed to pay the debenture interest, let alone any dividend on the ordinary shares. Already Hull Dock shares were being quoted at no more than £34 per £100 share, while those of the

Hull & Barnsley Railway had fallen as low as 14½. Evidence that other companies were concerned at the turn matters were taking was seen in the fact that from 12th April, 1886, the Lancashire & Yorkshire Railway decided to join the Manchester, Sheffield & Lincolnshire Railway in exercising its running powers into Hull, in its case reaching N.E.R. metals at Goole; setting up its own carting establishment in the city, the L. & Y.R. thus became much more active than before in competing for Hull traffic.

Now the 1880 Act of the Hull, Barnsley & West Riding Junction Railway & Dock Company had included provision to build a short spur from its line to the Alexandra Dock, at Sculcoates, to connect with the adjacent North Eastern line. This branch had been all but completed in 1887 when the Hull & Barnsley management laid it down that no competitive North Eastern traffic should be worked over it to or from Alexandra Dock, but only traffic from or to points which could not be reached over the Hull & Barnsley line. The N.E.R. tried to secure parliamentary compulsion on the H. & B.R. to complete the branch, but without success. Indeed, up to the end of independent N.E.R. history the North Eastern never had any direct access to the Alexandra Dock.

By this time the Hull & Barnsley was falling deeper and deeper into debt. The Midland Railway had some interest in the smaller company, which by means of the junction at Cudworth now provided the shortest route between the Midlands and Hull, and in 1887 an approach was made by the Hull & Barnsley directors to the Midland Board with a view to possible amalgamation. The Midland, by no means reluctant to obtain a foothold on the North East Coast, agreed to absorb the smaller company on the basis of a reasonable percentage of the gross receipts, and also the exchange of H. & B. debentures for 3½ per cent debentures of the Midland Company. But the condition was that the existing rate war must be brought to an end. This brought violent opposition from the South Yorkshire coal-owners who were likely to be affected, and who naturally had profited by the low carriage charges. The Hull Corporation also opposed, as such an arrangement would defeat the Corporation's original proviso that the Hull & Barnsley should not be sold, leased or otherwise transferred to any other company without the Corporation's consent. However, it was the Hull & Barnsley's own shareholders who decided the issue, for they refused in any event to agree to the proposal.

In June, 1888, the Hull Corporation made another move. The Hull Docks Act of 1861 had laid it down that the Dock Company would be under obligation not to oppose any decision to which the Corporation might come, if it so desired, to form a Dock Trust to control the whole of the Hull Docks. This was the plan that the Corporation now formulated, including in it the Alexandra Dock of the Hull & Barnsley Company; the Corporation would settle the debts both of the Dock Company and the railway, and would aim at making the Hull & Barnsley the principal artery for all rail access to the city. The Dock Company strongly opposed this scheme, as also did the Hull & Barnsley Railway, which would thus lose its most valuable property. Instead, the Dock Company in 1889 presented a Bill to Parliament for a new working arrangement with the North Eastern Railway, but Hull interests got this Bill thrown out by Parliament on the ground that it included no guarantee by the N.E.R. as to the future improvement or extension of the docks.

Next the Hull & Barnsley directors, whose company was now in very low water financially, made an approach to the North Eastern Railway Board as to whether the latter would consider an amalgamation. The N.E.R. agreed, on the basis that the H. & B. debenture holders would be paid off, with all their arrears of interest, as well as other creditors; the ordinary shareholders would receive ¼ per cent on their holdings in 1890, rising to 1½ per cent in 1894, and thereafter with an annual bonus if the dividends on the North Eastern's own Consols should rise above 6 per cent. These terms were more generous than they might appear, seeing that up till then the holders of Hull & Barnsley ordinaries had received no dividend at all. Even Colonel Gerard Smith, foremost of the original promoters of the Hull & Barnsley scheme, recommended acceptance, but the H. & B. shareholders, eternally hopeful, turned this scheme down also.

While this time-wasting and money-wasting struggle was dragging on, the position at Hull Docks was becoming more and more acute. The growing fishing trade badly needed better quay and water accommodation, and also bunkering facilities for the steam trawlers, which by now were rapidly replacing the former sailing craft. More deep-water facilities also were required, and in particular a deep-water entrance to the Albert Dock. In 1891 a plan was formulated for the acquisition of the Dock Company by the North Eastern Railway, with the N.E.R. offering some £1,936,000 worth of N.E.R. Consols in exchange for £3,570,000 stock of the Dock Company and also assuming the latter's debt of £304,000; the N.E.R. also proposed to spend £1,000,000 on a new deep-water dock rather than waste money on improving the entrance to the Albert Dock.

Many Hull interests now welcomed this proposal, but it was opposed by the Hull & Barnsley Company in that a new dock would prejudice the trade at their Alexandra Dock. Moreover, it put the Hull Corporation in a dilemma. They shared the view of the H. & B.R. as to the projected new dock, but felt that, if they opposed it, the N.E.R. would have little interest in spending money on the improvement of the existing dock installations. In the end, however, it was the contention of the Hull & Barnsley Railway that this scheme might lead to their eventual extinction which led the House of Commons to throw out the Bill, even though it had been passed by the Lords.

The North Eastern Railway directors now realised that they would get nowhere unless some agreement were reached with the Hull & Barnsley Railway as to future developments. In 1893, therefore, they brought forward once again the proposal for amalgamation with the Hull Dock Company. But this time, as a preliminary, they agreed with the H. & B.R. that there should be no reduction in dock dues save by agreement or arbitration between the two companies. They also agreed that if the North

Eastern attempted to build a new deep-water dock to the east of the H. & B.R. Alexandra Dock, the H. & B.R. should have the right to require that it be located on vacant land owned by the H. & B.R., and that, if the latter so desired, it should be built as a joint undertaking by the two companies. On this basis, the N.E.R. submitted a new Bill to Parliament to authorise the acquisition of the Hull Dock Company.

The Hull Chamber of Commerce was strongly in favour of these North Eastern proposals, but the Hull Corporation continued to act as the nigger in the wood-pile. It both resented the North Eastern Railway having dropped its previous new dock project, and also regarded any agreement between the North Eastern and Hull & Barnsley Railway as contravening the intention behind the Hull & Barnsley Railway Act of 1880, which was to ensure complete Hull & Barnsley independence. Whereas the H. & B.R. Board was apprehensive that the N.E.R., if it acquired control of the Hull Dock Company, might reduce the dock charges to a starvation level, for competitive purposes, the Corporation took precisely the opposite view, that the N.E.R. and H. & B.R. together might do the opposite, and by jointly agreeing to raise their dock dues might seriously weaken Hull's trading position. Opposition to the North Eastern Railway Bill came even from the River Tyne Commissioners, on the ground that the N.E.R. might attempt to divert shipping trade from the Tyne to the Humber as some compensation for its proposed heavy expenditure at Hull.

At long last, however, the opposition was defeated. This time prominent representatives of Hull trading interests, who formerly had been strong opponents of North Eastern policy, came out in support of the Bill, which was passed by both Lords and Commons with the one stipulation that in addition to the purchase price for the Hull Dock Company, the N.E.R. should spend at least £500,000 in improving the dock accommodation and facilities. So the Act received the Royal Assent on 24th August, 1893, 13 years after the passing of the Hull, Barnsley & West Riding Junction Railway and Dock Act of 1880. By it the North Eastern Railway acquired eight docks and various basins, three of the latter tidal, and with a total water area of 100 acres, together with 40 acres of timber ponds. The total cost was about £2,250,000.

The first step taken by the N.E.R. towards docks improvement was in the interests of the fishing trade. It was the decision to build a basin 10 acres in extent, with jetties and three slipways, at St Andrew's Dock, for the exclusive use of trawlers, at a cost of between £70,000 and £80,000; work on this scheme got under way by June, 1894. The next steps towards dock improvement were not likely to be easy. Any attempt to increase the deep-water accommodation would be construed as aimed at competition with the Hull & Barnsley Railway, whose Alexandra Dock was the port's only deep-water dock, to this railway's considerable advantage. Dredging was going on at the time to deepen the Victoria Dock, but by the terms of the 1893 agreement with the H. & B.R. the N.E.R. was prevented from building another deep-water dock without Hull & Barnsley agreement.

For a second time, therefore, the Boards of the two companies came together to discuss a possible amalgamation. Seeing that once only in nine years had Hull & Barnsley shareholders received a dividend, and of no more than a modest ⅜ per cent, the terms that the North Eastern offered were distinctly generous – £100 of N.E.R. 3 per cent debentures for each £100 of H. & B.R. first debentures and £115 of the former for each £100 of H. & B.R. second debentures – but again the Hull & Barnsley shareholders refused to play, and the Hull Chamber of Commerce, the Hull Corn Trade Association and various other interests in the city, which put pressure on the Hull Corporation, were all suspicious of a future North Eastern Railway monopoly and were correspondingly antagonistic. A Bill to authorise the amalgamation had been deposited in Parliament but was withdrawn by the N.E.R. when the strength of the opposition became manifest.

Matters then dragged on until 1897, when the North Eastern Railway presented another Bill to Parliament, this time for a new river-wall, enclosing additional quay accommodation, from the William Wright Dock to the Victoria Dock basin, new lock entrances to the Albert and Humber Docks, and a new 10-acre dock on the site of the island wharf, at an estimated cost of £781,000. Opposition now came from unexpected quarters. On the grounds that the new works might interfere with Humber navigation, the Humber Conservancy Commissioners, the Aire & Calder Navigation, and even the Great Central Railway (as the Manchester, Sheffield & Lincolnshire had now become), were all ranged against the N.E.R., with, it need hardly be added, the Hull Corporation. The Conservancy Commissioners, however, withdrew their opposition on the N.E.R. agreeing to carry out certain dredging work in the navigable channel of the Humber, and agreement on certain matters was come to with the Corporation also; but the Parliamentary Committee decided that what the Commissioners and the Corporation originally demanded must be insisted on. Once more, therefore, the N.E.R. withdrew their Bill.

In 1898 the same dreary process was gone through all over again. A new North Eastern Railway Bill sought authorisation for an extension eastwards of the Victoria Dock, for the benefit of the timber trade, with an enlarged storage space for timber, and also new sidings to serve the shipping of coal from the Victoria Dock jetty. This plan hinged upon the purchase from the Corporation of some land known as the 'western reservation', and on learning this the Hull & Barnsley Railway deposited a Bill of their own to forestall the N.E.R. by acquiring the piece of land in question. The Hull Corporation now proceeded to queer the pitch by demanding that the North Eastern Railway take steps to substitute overbridges or underbridges for the many N.E.R. level crossings in and around the city, though at the same time refusing to share in the cost of such work. The Humber Conservancy Commissioners also raised again the matter of responsibility for the maintenance of the navigable channel of the river. So yet another N.E.R. Bill was abandoned by its promoters.

The North Eastern Railway Board now realised that there was only one way out of the *impasse*. It was to combine with the Hull & Barnsley

A typical third-class brake of North Eastern Railway standard non-corridor stock for local services, with clerestory roof.

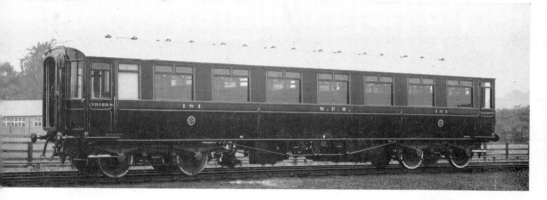

One of the handsome corridor coaches of the type built for the Newcastle–Liverpool and Leeds–Glasgow service.

A standard non-corridor third-class coach of a later type, with elliptical instead of clerestory roof.　　　　　　　　[*All, British Railways*

Above, a North Eastern express, headed by 'Z' class Atlantic No. 736, which includes one of the straight-sided coaches built after the visit of N.E.R. officers to the United States. *Below*, interior of first-class dining saloon, Newcastle–Liverpool and Leeds–Glasgow stock.

[*British Railways*

Moving minerals in the north-east. *Above*, a coal train near Morpeth, headed by a Class 'P3' 0-6-0. [*J. W. Wright*

Left, a Class 'T2' 0-8-0 assisting in rear an ore train on the climb from Tyne Dock to Consett. [*P. Ransome-Wallis*

Below, in modern days a train of empty ore hoppers drifts down from Consett past Annfield East box behind a 'T3' three-cylinder 0-8-0. [*J. M. Rayner*

The former Locomotive Yard signalbox at York, one of the largest manually operated boxes in Great Britain. *Above*, the interior, with its 295 levers set in one continuous frame. *Below*, the lengthy exterior. The box, replacing an earlier one, came into use in 1909.

[*British Railways*

Railway, under the terms of the 1893 ageement, in building a new joint deep-water dock to the eastward of the Hull & Barnsley's Alexandra Dock. Part of the agreement was that the two companies would have running powers over appropriate sections of each other's lines in and around Hull. True to form, the Hull Corporation opposed the Bill, presented to Parliament in the 1899 session, but this time without success, and the Hull Joint Dock Act became law in the same year.

Fifteen years elapsed before King George V in person opened, on 26th June, 1914, the new joint dock, to be known as the King George V Dock in honour of this Royal occasion. It was a worthy addition indeed to the shipping facilities at Hull. Entered through a lock 750ft long and 85ft wide, the main basin was 1,050ft by 1,000ft in size, giving the largest vessels room to manoeuvre on entry and exit. From the main basin there extended a north-west arm 1,350ft long by 325ft wide, and a north-east arm 1,555ft long by 450ft wide, at the inner end of which were two graving docks, 550ft by 72ft and 450ft by 66ft respectively. In all, the new dock provided 8,162ft of quayage and a total water area of 53 acres.

Inside the dock area there was a maximum depth of 38ft and a minimum of 31ft. The northern side of the new dock was very completely equipped for the shipment of coal, with the quays arranged in *echelon* form in order to provide berths for the maximum number of ships simultaneously. Reinforced concrete warehouses on an extensive scale and a reinforced concrete grain silo of 40,000 tons capacity, served by portable elevators and band conveyors, formed part of the new installations. Another joint North Eastern and Hull & Barnsley enterprise was a new oil jetty at Salt End, eastwards of the new dock, extending for 1,500ft into the River Humber and with a depth of water alongside of 30ft at low tide.

By these notable additions to its port facilities, Hull now possessed 10 railway docks, with a total water area of 158 acres; two river piers with a quay length of 3,850ft; 101 cranes, the largest with a lifting capacity of 100 tons; 34 coaling appliances, capable of shipping all but 10,000 tons of coal an hour; 51 warehouses with an aggregate storage capacity of some 138,000 tons; 890,000 cu ft of refrigerated storage space; and 340 acres of open storage ground. One of the quays just referred to was the Riverside Quay with its passenger station, parliamentary powers for which were secured in 1905; these were brought into use on 11th May, 1907.

By the same 1905 Act the North Eastern Railway was authorised to run its own steamer services between Hull and a number of continental ports, and in the following year it acquired a half-share with the firm of Thomas Wilson & Company in steamers plying between Hull and Hamburg, Antwerp, Ghent and Dunkerque. Jointly with the Lancashire & Yorkshire Railway the North Eastern also began in 1907 to operate a tri-weekly passenger and freight service between Hull and the Belgian port of Zeebrugge, the two companies having acquired a special steamer, the *Duke of Clarence*, for this purpose. A boat train, run in connection with this service, carried through coaches both from Glasgow, *via* Edinburgh, Newcastle, York and Selby, and from Liverpool Exchange (Lancashire

& Yorkshire) *via* Manchester, Wakefield and Goole, to Riverside Quay.

So it was that peace eventually descended upon the Hull railway scene, after all but 20 years of strife from the passing of the Hull, Barnsley & West Riding Junction Railway & Dock Act in 1880 to the agreement in 1899 between the Hull & Barnsley and North Eastern Railways to build their joint King George V Dock. Tenacious to the last, the Hull Corporation in 1910 opposed a working agreement that had been negotiated between the two railway Boards, just as it had obstructed every previous move for closer railway co-operation. It was not until the last year of North Eastern independence, 1922, that the two railways carried through an amalgamation, and by the following year both had been swallowed up in the capacious maw of the London & North Eastern Railway.

By the time of losing its separate identity, the Hull & Barnsley Railway – the shortened title which became official by a 1905 Act of Parliament – had expanded considerably from its original size. In September, 1894, an independent company – the South Yorkshire Junction Railway – had opened an $11\frac{1}{2}$-mile branch from Wrangbrook Junction, on the H. & B.R. main line, south-eastwards to the Denaby and Cadeby Collieries at Conisborough, and this was worked from the outset by the Hull & Barnsley Railway. Eleven years later the traffic over the branch was increased by a connection with the newly-opened Dearne Valley Railway, over which the H. & B.R. secured running powers. The year 1902 saw the opening of another branch from Wrangbrook Junction, this time constructed by the Hull & Barnsley, for 9 miles south-westwards to Hickleton and Wath, with various colliery connections.

Of equal, if not greater, importance was the line promoted by the Hull & Barnsley Railway in 1909 to gain direct access to the Bullcroft, Bentley and Yorkshire Main Collieries, which at that time were being sunk to the north-west of Doncaster, and to continue to link up with a new line which was being constructed at the same time by the Midland and Great Central Railways between the Rotherham area and Shireoaks. By the Act of 1909 the Great Central Railway became joint owner with the Hull & Barnsley of the 21 miles of new line, while from Braithwell Junction, at its southern end, the Hull & Barnsley joined the Midland and Great Central in joint ownership of 5 miles (including branches) of the Thrybergh Junction (Rotherham) to Brantcliffe Junction (Shireoaks) of the joint line just mentioned, as far as Laughton Junction, Dinnington. Here came convergence with the South Yorkshire Joint Committee's line previously mentioned, with which the new railway had pursued a roughly parallel course.

Known generally as the Gowdall & Braithwell Railway, the joint Hull & Barnsley & Great Central Line left the H. & B. main line at Aire Junction, just short of where the latter crossed the East Coast main line, and turning southward, paralleled the latter until crossing over it at Shaftholme. On this section a notable engineering work was the opening bridge over the Aire & Calder Navigation, of the Scherzer rolling-lift type. The course from Shaftholme onwards was to the west of Doncaster, where a short branch with a triangular junction was laid in to a passenger terminal called York Road. Connections were then made with the Great Central Doncaster avoiding line at Sprotborough, and from here the new line continued southwards to its termination at Laughton Junction. The Gowdall & Braithwell Joint Line was opened on 1st May, 1916.

These Hull & Barnsley extensions, as well as the spur connections that had been laid in at various points where the Hull & Barnsley crossed the network of other railways in this area, gave the H. & B.R. direct access to a large number of South Yorkshire collieries, and helped greatly towards the modest prosperity of the company in its later years. Indeed, from the financial crisis of 1887, which for a time put the Hull & Barnsley in the hands of a receiver and manager, by 1913 the railway had recovered sufficiently to be able to pay a dividend of 3½ per cent on its consolidated ordinary stock. By this time, and on through the 1914–1918 war, it was certainly performing a useful function in the movement of coal between Yorkshire pits and the port of Hull.

Nevertheless, it is difficult to avoid the conclusion that had it not been for the factious behaviour of many public bodies in Hull, the Hull Corporation in particular, the needed improvements in Hull port facilities might have been carried out much earlier than they were, and expenditure of millions in building the Hull & Barnsley Railway and its later branches might have been avoided. In any event, by co-operation rather than antagonism there would not have been the waste of money in fighting unceasing parliamentary battles, and the North Eastern Railway's access to and port facilities in Hull might have been improved to any extent necessary at far less cost than what was actually spent. Even allowing for the decline in coal exports between that day and this, weight is lent to the contention just expressed by the fact that since nationalisation the Hull & Barnsley system has been one of the first lines of British Railways to be almost completely abandoned – including in particular most of the main line – and without any material detriment to Hull's present railway facilities. So it was that the relations between Hull and the North Eastern Railway were not among the happier episodes of North Eastern history.

A few facts only about later happenings in Hull remain to be mentioned. One was the opening, on 12th December, 1904, of an extension to Hull Paragon Station, increasing its accommodation to nine main platforms and various docks and loading platforms; with its Royal Station Hotel it thus became one of the largest and most imposing stations on the North Eastern system. February, 1909, saw the putting into operation of a new marshalling yard, and December, 1910, of a new fish quay at the Victoria Dock. But the greatest occasion of these years was when as already described, on 26th June, 1914, King George V and Queen Mary set the seal of national approval on the *rapprochement* between the North Eastern and the Hull & Barnsley Railways by coming in person to declare open their joint King George V Dock.

CHAPTER XXII

The Last Years of Independence

By the end of the nineteenth century the North Eastern Railway network was nearly complete, though a few more lines were still to be added to it before the years of independence came to an end. Some of these were built mainly in order to tap new coalfields, and others, under the Light Railways Act of 1896, to serve agricultural districts. This Act was designed to avoid the cumbersome and expensive business of obtaining parliamentary approval for a new line; instead, Commissioners were appointed, with power, after local hearings at which opponents could state their case, to issue a Light Railways Order authorising construction if they considered this to be justified. The statutory safety precautions laid down for railway construction and operation were also somewhat relaxed, with appropriate safeguards, in the case of light railways, all of which helped to cut down both building and operating costs and so made possible the construction of lines which otherwise could not have had any expectation of profitable working.

The first light railway to be operated by the North Eastern was a line which had been built by an independent company in North Lincolnshire. It branched from the N.E.R. Hull and Doncaster main line at Marshland Junction, $1\frac{1}{2}$ miles south of Goole, and then turned eastwards for some 9 miles across the fertile Marshland region to Fockerby on the Trent. At Reedness Junction, $3\frac{1}{4}$ miles from Marshland Junction, the line forked, and a branch ran southwards from there for 3 miles to Crowle. As the Lancashire & Yorkshire Railway, with its extensive docks installation at Goole, also was interested in this area, it joined with the North Eastern in 1902 to acquire and to extend what were known as the Goole & Marshland and Isle of Axholme Railways.

By the end of 1904, the Isle of Axholme section had been extended for $9\frac{1}{4}$ miles from Crowle through Epworth to Haxey, connecting there with the Great Northern & Great Eastern Joint Line, while early in 1909 there was brought into use the Hatfield Moor Extension, a 5-mile branch to the westward from Epworth. All these additions to the joint N.E. & L. & Y. system were authorised under the Light Railways Act, as also in 1909 was the Hatfield Moor Further Extension, an $8\frac{3}{4}$-mile continuation of the Hatfield Moor branch to the complicated junctions on the Great Northern main line at Black Carr, just south of Doncaster. The last-mentioned extension, however, was never built.

Another private company in this area which had made early use of the Light Railways Act was the Cawood, Wistow & Selby, branching $\frac{1}{2}$-mile west of Selby on the Selby & Leeds line and proceeding for $4\frac{1}{2}$ miles to the northward through an agricultural district to the village of Cawood. From its opening in 1896 this was worked by the North Eastern Railway, which absorbed the small line four years later.

A new line at the turn of the century in the Selby area which was intended to be of considerably greater importance was the Selby & Goole Railway. The original idea for a direct line between these towns originated with George Hudson in 1845, as part of his battle with the London & York promoters, but nothing came of his plan at that time. It was not revived until 1899, when the North Eastern Railway was becoming concerned because of the congestion of traffic over Selby swing-bridge, used by all traffic between Doncaster and York and also between both Leeds and the Swinton & Knottingley Joint Line and Hull. It was thought that by providing a link between the Leeds & Selby line and Goole, passing to the south of Selby, the situation might be eased by diversion of much of the through freight traffic *via* Goole. These trains would still have to cross the Ouse by swing-bridge, but the average number of trains then crossing the Skelton swing-bridge north of Goole was 41 only, as compared with 141 daily over Selby swing-bridge.

Actually the Selby–Goole proposal of 1899 was by an independent company, similar to the Cawood, Wistow & Selby, for a light railway, but the North Eastern Railway took over the project in 1902, and had decided to build a line, for reasons just described, to main line standards. Construction did not begin until 1907, and the line was opened throughout for freight on 1st November, 1910. Passenger traffic was more or less an afterthought, and was never more than a sparse service of 'all stations' local trains between Selby and Goole.

The new railway took off from the Leeds & Selby line at Thorpe Gates Junction, 2 miles west of Selby, and after crossing the East Coast main line was joined on the north by a spur leaving the latter at Brayton Junction. At the Goole end $\frac{3}{4}$-mile of Lancashire & Yorkshire track was used, with the help of running powers, from Oakhill Junction, before North Eastern metals were rejoined at 'B' Junction, a mile short of Goole station. The only engineering feature of any note in the $10\frac{1}{2}$-miles length of the Selby & Goole line was the 200-ft span lattice girder bridge over the River Aire just short of Airmyn & Rawcliffe Station. After opening, a certain amount of use was made of this link by through freight and mineral trains, but as a result of the decline of freight traffic in later years the initial section between Thorpe Gates Junction and Brayton East Junction went out of operation in London & North Eastern days, and has since been abandoned and its bridges removed. Both passenger and freight trains still operate, however, between Selby and Goole.

In the Newcastle area another privately promoted railway project taken over by the North Eastern Railway was a line into agricultural and mining country to the north-west of the city from Gosforth, on the line from Newcastle to Monkseaton *via* Backworth, to Ponteland. 1st March, 1905, saw the opening of this branch for freight traffic, and 1st June of the same year for passenger traffic; an extension to Darras Hall, to reach which reversal was needed in Ponteland Station, was opened on September 27th, 1913.

During these years there were other important openings of new connecting lines in the Newcastle area, designed to facilitate the movement of freight traffic. One such, brought into use on 22nd April, 1907, was from King Edward Bridge Junction West, at the southern end of the King Edward Bridge; this dived under the main line from the south at Bensham to reach the Ouston Junction to Dunston and Blaydon line at Norwood Junction, and so provided a through route for freight trains from the Sunderland and South Shields directions to both the Team Valley marshalling yard and the Newcastle & Carlisle line without crossing the East Coast main line tracks. Of other new local connections spur lines from Swalwell Junction to Derwenthaugh (Blaydon Main Colliery Junction), and from Whickham Junction to Dunston West Junction, opened in 1907 and 1908, opened a new direct route between the Derwent Ironworks at Consett and the Redheugh and other staiths on the south bank of the Tyne.

Mention must also be made of two new developments affecting Sunderland. The one remaining stretch of the north-east coast between the Tyne and the Humber as yet without a coastal railway was that lying between Seaham Harbour and Hartlepool. The privately owned 6-mile Londonderry, Seaham & Sunderland Railway, which had been opened on 3rd August, 1854, had been worked by its own locomotives and rolling stock up to the year 1900, when it was taken over by the North Eastern Railway. In the intervening years there had been various proposals by other railways to use the Londonderry line as a part of grandiose long-distance schemes, one in particular in 1865, mentioned in Chapter XVI, for the Leeds, North Yorkshire & Durham Railway, incorporating the Londonderry Railway in a through line from Hartlepool *via* Sunderland to cross the lower Tyne and link up with the Blyth & Tyne Railway. In 1892 there came a less ambitious scheme to link West Hartlepool with Seaham Harbour, but the Bill for this, opposed both by the North Eastern Railway and the Marquis of Londonderry, was thrown out in the House of Commons.

The North Eastern Railway Board, however, was merely holding its hand until sufficient collieries had been opened up on this coastal strip to guarantee reasonable success for a new railway. By 1894 this seemed probable, and a Bill for a railway from Seaham to Hart, 3¼ miles short of West Hartlepool on the Ferryhill to Hartlepool line, received the Royal Assent on 24th July, 1894. Some time elapsed before work was begun, but on 1st April, 1905, the new coast line was opened.

As with the coastal lines in North Yorkshire, so the 10 miles of line along the coast between Seaham Harbour and Hartlepool called for some considerable engineering work in crossing the various denes carrying streams down to the sea. Of viaducts, the biggest was the nine-arch masonry structure, 800ft long, across Castle Eden Dene. With the help of earthworks of considerable size, the gradients were kept down to a figure a good deal less severe than those around the Yorkshire coast, there being nothing steeper than single miles at from 1 in 100 to 1 in 125. At its southern end the new railway reached the Ferryhill to Hartlepool line at Hart, but continued as an independent double line as far as Cemetery Junction, where the West Hartlepool through line diverged from the original line to the East Hartlepool terminus. At its northern end the new line took off from the Londonderry line just short of the latter's Seaham Harbour terminus.

Laid to main line standards, the Seaham to Hart line was destined in later years to become a main route of major consequence. The Hartlepools were becoming of such importance that they could no longer be neglected by the principal long-distance trains *via* Sunderland using the direct Wellfield route between there and Stockton, and by degrees not only were these diverted *via* West Hartlepool, but new day restaurant car and night sleeping car trains between Newcastle and King's Cross were introduced over this route, giving Sunderland, West Hartlepool and Stockton through communication with London. In course of time, also, an hourly service was brought into operation in each direction between Newcastle and Middlesbrough, with the trains calling at Gateshead, Sunderland, West Hartlepool, Stockton and Thornaby; to these, in later years still, stops have been added at Seaburn, Seaham, and Billingham-on-Tees, the last mentioned in the interest of the vast Imperial Chemical Industries plant located here. It was $3\frac{1}{4}$ miles farther from Sunderland to Stockton *via* West Hartlepool, but the diversion certainly enabled the former express trains by the Wellfield route to escape the formidable 1 in 44 ascent of Ryhope bank on their southbound journeys, and the 1 in 52 climb from Hart to Hesleden going north.

Shortly after this a development in Sunderland brought into existence one of the most notable bridges in the country, though one never seen by North Eastern passengers, for it has been used only by freight trains. In order to relieve the traffic carried by the congested line between Sunderland and Monkwearmouth, over the Wear bridge, it was decided to build a second bridge, about a mile upstream, between Millfield and Southwick, connecting the Sunderland and Durham line with the former Hylton, Southwick & Monkwearmouth Railway. The Sunderland Corporation also desired high-level road communication between these two suburbs, with their busy industries, and therefore agreed to join with the railway in building a double-deck bridge, with the railway on the upper and the road on the lower deck. The Act for the new $1\frac{3}{4}$ miles of line, bridge included, was obtained in 1900.

As there were shipyards above the site, the River Wear Commissioners insisted on a clear headroom of not less than 85ft, and also that there should be no obstruction of the river channel during the building of the bridge; these conditions not merely called for a bridge of great size, but also for novel methods of erection. The design, therefore, was for a bridge with a main lattice girder span of no less than 330ft, flanked by three 200ft spans, one on the south and two on the north side of the river. The main girders were 32ft apart centre to centre, ranging in depth from the 30ft side spans to 42ft in the centre of the main span. This last weighed no less than 2,600 tons, and a total of 9,000 tons of steel was used in all. Obstruction of the river channel was avoided at the time of building by cantilevering the two halves of the main span out from their abutments until they met above the centre of the stream, a task which took seven months to complete.

Work had begun on the line in January, 1905, and the great structure, named the Queen Alexandra Bridge as the complement of Newcastle's King Edward Bridge, was opened for traffic by the Earl of Durham on 10th June, 1909. The total cost of the bridge and approaches was £450,000, to which the Corporation contributed £146,000. Later events have proved, however, that the Corporation rather than the railway has been the ultimate beneficiary. For half-a-century later the bridge was no longer being used by the railway, nor most of the Hylton, Southwick & Monkwearmouth line on the north side of the river. Thus the railway share of the cost was largely wasted money – a sad fate for a bridge of such outstanding engineering merit.

Finally, in the realm of development, reference needs to be made to another line built early in the present century, and again primarily for the purpose of coal transport. The line in question was of particular interest, for – like the co-operation between the North Eastern Railway and the Sunderland Corporation which produced the joint Queen Alexandra Bridge – it showed a realisation at long last by the major railways that it was a more sensible and far less costly plan, where they were in pursuit of new traffic, to combine in a single joint project rather than to fight one another in and out of Parliament in order to obtain exclusive access. The traffic concerned was that of carrying coal from new pits being opened up in the Maltby district of South Yorkshire, and five different railways – the North Eastern, Great Northern, Great Central, Midland and Lancashire & Yorkshire – all were concocting plans in 1901 and 1902 to get into it.

In 1903, however, these companies had the good sense to combine and present to Parliament a Bill for a line called the South Yorkshire Joint Railway, which obtained its Act in 1903. It was for $15\frac{1}{2}$ miles of new construction beginning at Kirk Sandall Junction, midway between Doncaster and Thorne on the Great Central Doncaster–Frodingham–Grimsby line (used also, of course, by North Eastern trains from Doncaster to Hull). From here the South Yorkshire route curved round Doncaster Racecourse, to the east of the town, and crossed above the East Coast main line at Black Carr Junction, where the Great Northern & Great Eastern Joint Line and the Great Northern main line converged. A spur came up here from the Great Northern at Potteric Carr to join the South Yorkshire at Low Ellers Junction.

About the time of completion of the South Yorkshire Joint in 1909 the independent Dearne Valley Railway, extending eastwards from the Lancashire & Yorkshire Railway in the Wakefield area and worked by the latter, also had reached Black Carr, and formed part of a maze of junctions at this point, with connections going south-eastwards to the Great Northern line at Loversall Carr and the Great Northern & Great Eastern at Bessacarr Junctions, and southwards from Black Carr East and West Junctions to the South Yorkshire at St Catherine's Junction. From here the S.Y.J.R., continuing southwards, passed through Tickhill and Maltby to Dinnington, where it linked up with the existing Midland & Great Central Joint Line from Shireoaks to Braithwell and beyond.

Of the partners, therefore, the North Eastern Railway had access to the South Yorkshire Joint Line from the north end, the Great Northern and Lancashire & Yorkshire from Black Carr, the Midland from the south end, and the Great Central from both ends. In later years the S.Y.J.R. threw off a branch from Firbeck Junction, just south of Tickhill, to Firbeck Main Colliery, opened in 1926, and another and shorter branch from the latter to Harworth Colliery, opened in 1929, both authorised in North Eastern Railway days but completed after the formation of the London & North Eastern Railway. But the South Yorkshire Joint by this time had become joint London & North Eastern and London Midland & Scottish property.

By 1914, immediately before the outbreak of the First World War, the expansion of the North Eastern Railway, apart from its 1922 amalgamation with the Hull & Barnsley Railway, had come to an end. With this last exception and that of the modest North British Railway intrusion into Northumberland, it had retained its territory intact, and had absorbed all the former independent railways within its borders, save for three tiny lines that were still left. Two of them, both branching from the East Coast main line, possessed no more than a single locomotive apiece; in Yorkshire there was the 2½-mile Alne & Easingwold, opened in 1891, and in Northumberland the 4-mile North Sunderland, from Chathill to Seahouses, opened in 1892. Finally, in the very heart of things, there was the Derwent Valley Light, opened in 1907 from its York terminus at Layerthorpe for 16 miles eastwards and then southwards to a junction with the Selby and Market Weighton line at Cliff Common. At the York end there was a junction with the Foss Islands branch so that freight could be run through to the N.E.R. at both ends of the line. The Derwent Valley had its own wagons and a couple of passenger coaches, but the N.E.R. provided the motive power. All three remained independent after both the grouping in 1923 and also after nationalisation.

From the date of its incorporation in 1864, the North Eastern Railway had grown in extent from 703 to 1,698 route miles, together with 20 miles leased or worked and a share in joint lines totalling 34 miles. Expressed in miles of single track, sidings included, about 1,500 miles in 1864 had grown to 4,894 miles by 1914. The railway's seventeen docks, with their tidal harbours, basins and timber pools, by now had a total water area of over 440 acres.

The authorised capital of the company had increased in the same period from £23,000,000 to £81,000,000, and the total capital expenditure, including money raised by loans, to nearly £85,000,000. As to gross revenue, £1,600,000 in 1854 had grown by 1913 to £11,315,130. In the latter year the North Eastern Railway carried just over 68,000,000 passengers (excluding the journeys of 31,350 season ticket holders); 44,165,950 tons of coal, coke and patent fuels; 15,526,450 tons of iron ore and other minerals; 10,816,170 tons of merchandise; and 2,772,780 head of live stock – an impressive total indeed. To perform this service, 45,911,187 miles had been run by steam locomotives, in the proportion of 16,573,796 miles on passenger trains; 12,312,455 miles with freight trains; 3,283,491 miles in assisting or running light; and an estimated 13,471,445 miles when shunting. To these figures there were added 13,471,445 miles run by rail motorcars and 1,255,235 miles worked by electric traction, the introduction of which is dealt with in Chapter XXV.

Such was the impressive record of achievement that put the North Eastern into the forefront for prestige and power among the railways of Britain. On the outbreak of war in August, 1914, like all the other lines the N.E.R. came under the control of the Railway Executive Committee, and independent action came to an end. After the end of the war there was but a brief time for recovery before the North Eastern became absorbed, with the Great Northern, Great Central, Great Eastern, North British and Great North of Scotland Railways, in the London & North Eastern Railway. In this group the N.E.R. exerted no small influence, among other achievements providing the group's first Chief General Manager. But that is another story.

CHAPTER XXIII

The Locomotive Miscellany of Earlier Years

MORE than one able pen has dealt with the varied locomotives of the North Eastern Railway; for the purpose of the present volume, therefore, a more brief review of North Eastern locomotive history must suffice. Also, within the limits of space it would be impossible to go into the locomotive story of all the constituent railways that came eventually into the North Eastern fold – 53 public and 21 private companies in all, many with their own rolling stock – and we must content ourselves with what happened from the incorporation of the North Eastern Railway in 1854 onwards.

Edward Fletcher was its first Locomotive Superintendent, and the task that he faced in trying to establish some system in N.E.R. locomotive affairs, with the most heterogenous collection of locomotive power ever owned by a single railway, was no enviable one. Yet he did succeed in bringing some semblance of order out of confusion, and during a reign of no less than 28 years left a mark on North Eastern locomotive practice that was plainly visible for many years afterwards. At first Fletcher exercised no more than a general supervision. He took personal charge of the principal locomotive works at Gateshead, of what had been the York, Newcastle & Berwick Railway. At York, under the supervision of John Stephenson, were the works of the former York & North Midland Railway, while the Holbeck shops at Leeds of what had been the Leeds Northern Railway were under the supervision of an engineer named Johnson.

In 1863 the absorption of the Stockton & Darlington Railway brought in a fourth locomotive works, at Darlington, under William Bouch, together with 157 locomotives of the most extraordinary variety. Moreover, as we have seen in Chapter XVI, for ten years after this amalgamation the Act had laid it down that Stockton & Darlington affairs should be managed by an independent committee, so that for this period Fletcher had little control over the S. & D. locomotive stock; indeed, Darlington continued to design its own engines until about 1875. York and Leeds also still retained a considerable measure of independence; for years all four works had their own differences of design, external lines and even colour, before anything approaching standardisation was begun.

As to appearance, stovepipe chimneys were general, also large domes crowned with safety-valves additional to the safety-valves mounted over the fireboxes inside a variety of casings. York produced the neatest outlines, and Gateshead engines that were sent to York for rebuilding to relieve the parent works often emerged with their appearance considerably improved. The Stockton & Darlington Railway outlines for the most part were un-

gainly, their flat-topped cabs with square front windows being particularly
ugly. Leeds locomotives also were severely plain in appearance. As to
variety, many of the classes comprised no more than one to five engines;
Ahrons comments that at one time the 33 passenger engines stationed at
Leeds were from no fewer than 13 different classes. He also remarks
that as late as 1875 at least 100 photographs would have been needed to
portray all the different types stationed at the two York engine sheds.
Acworth, in his *Railways of England*, wrote that when he visited the running
shed at Gateshead he found no fewer than 200 different varieties of nuts,
bolts, pins and other fittings were needed to service the 120 locomotives
stationed there.

This almost incredible miscellany extended also to colours. Gateshead
favoured a light green with red-brown underframes, the whole lined out
with dark green and black bands and white and vermilion lines. York had
a simpler scheme, also mainly light green, with claret-coloured underframes and a lining of black bands with white lines. A lighter green was
the standard for Stockton & Darlington engines, with dark chocolate
underframes. Leeds specialised in a brilliant emerald green for the entire
engine, underframes included, lined out with yellow.

Engine crews in those days had their own engines, and apparently were
allowed a free hand in applying their own embellishments, such as brass
collars round chimneys, brass crowns, stars and other devices on smokebox
fronts, and so on. A favourite location for such displays also was the large
sandbox casing provided on many North Eastern engines in front of the
driving splasher, which by transfers many drivers decorated with portraits
of the Queen and other members of the Royal Family, or of leading
statesmen. Political bias at times proclaimed itself, as, for example, when
a Radical engine-cleaner 'improved' a likeness of Lord Beaconsfield by
providing him with a pronounced squint, while in retaliation another
cleaner of the Tory persuasion blacked Mr Gladstone's eye and otherwise
altered, not to their entire advantage, the features of that prominent
politician.

But the limit was reached when, to quote Ahrons, 'an enterprising
driver of one of the 6ft coupled engines of the "686" class turned up in
Leeds Station with his engine, on the sandbox of which was a transfer
picture depicting a classic nymph reclining in an extremely *négligé* attitude
on the greensward . . . . For some minutes the proud driver surveyed and
beamed smilingly on an enthusiastic crowd of passengers, porters and
others that collected round the engine. The nymph lasted for a few days
. . . . then she suddenly disappeared. I believe the driver was rash enough
to take her to York. Now York is, as everybody knows, not only the centre
of North Eastern official activity, but also possesses a dean and chapter
and various other distinguished ecclesiastical luminaries. Whether the
picture caught the eye of one of these dignitaries or whether one of the
superior officials of the Company came across it I do not know, but the
net result of whatever actually occurred was that the lady was promptly
and effectively expunged with the aid of a pot of green paint'. Shortly

after this all the other transfer pictures also disappeared, but not until McDonnell succeeded Fletcher was a clean sweep made of the many other unofficial locomotive decorations.

Up to the time that Fletcher took office, passenger engines were mostly of the 2-4-0 type, though there were also a number of 2-2-2 engines in service. But as far back as 1860, William Bouch, of the Stockton & Darlington, tried the 4-4-0 wheel arrangement, and as mentioned in Chapter XIV Robert Stephenson & Company built to his designs the 4-4-0 locomotives *Lowther* and *Brougham*, with 6ft coupled wheels, specially for working the Darlington to Tebay line, and very large side-windowed cabs which in those days were unique. The idea was to provide proper shelter for the enginemen when travelling in winter over the 1,370ft altitude of Stainmore, but remarkable to relate the men so disliked being boxed in, as they thought, that these cabs later were replaced by simple weatherboards.

Bouch next produced, in 1862, a curious quartette of 4-4-0 engines, with inside cylinders (as compared with the outside cylinders of *Lowther* and *Brougham*) and coupled wheels of no less than 7ft diameter – an extraordinary choice for a line with no start-to-stop runs of any length and no opportunity for speed. The upper part of the driving wheels, which were very closely spaced, was enclosed by splashers of which the remainder was completely open, the whole presenting a most singular appearance. Not content with these, Bouch built in 1871 to 1874, shortly before his retirement, 10 more 4-4-0s, outside-cylindered once again, which incorporated coupled wheels with the even larger diameter of 7ft 1in, and, among various other untried novelties, a piston-stroke of no less than 30in and piston-valves in place of slide-valves. These machines gave so much trouble that they soon earned a nickname which was the reverse of complimentary.

In 1872, a Member of Parliament, concerned at the way in which the poor were treated in his time, had written a book advocating the reform of the poor laws, and including the history of a fictional character whom he named 'Ginx'. This unfortunate pauper, expecting a further expansion of his family, had publicly declared that if the addition arrived, he or she would be promptly drowned in the water-butt, and Ginx would take the consequences. A horde of public officials, ministers of religion, philanthropists and philosophers forthwith descended on him, to deter him from his deplorable purpose, but as a result it was Ginx himself who jumped over one of the Thames bridges to his death in the river. 'Ginx's Baby' from then on became a public byword; and 'Ginx's Babies' was the nickname fastened on to Bouch's last and most eccentric production, though without the same unfortunate effect on their designer!

But the mainstay of the Stockton & Darlington locomotive stock was the 0-6-0 locomotives of that company, and amongst the most numerous of those built in the later years of its existence and after its absorption into the North Eastern Railway, was the '1001' class. The first 11 of these were turned out by the firm of Gilkes, Wilson & Company in 1852 with 4ft 2½in coupled wheels; in the next series the wheels were increased in diameter to 5ft and the cylinders to 18in by 24in, adding another 54 engines between 1860 and 1868; while a final 60, now with 17in by 26in cylinders, built between 1870 and 1875, brought the total up to 125 engines of an almost completely homogenous class, from then on extensively used over the North Eastern system.

All were of the well-known 'long-boiler' type evolved by Robert Stephenson & Company, with the middle and rear coupled wheels closely spaced, and the firebox behind the rear pair, which meant a considerable overhang at the cab end of the engine. In various ways this type of engine was as well suited to Stockton & Darlington freight service as the 7ft 4-4-0s were unsuited to its passenger trains, and the former did admirable service for many years, some of them lasting for more than half-a-century. A tribute to the class has been paid by the preservation of No. 1275 in the Railway Museum at York.

During the first years of his reign at Gateshead Edward Fletcher allowed almost as much latitude to the outside contractors who built for the North Eastern Railway as he did to the subsidiary works under his nominal control at Darlington, York and Leeds. This certainly applied to fittings, which differed considerably as between one works and another, and accounted for the multiplicity of parts, mentioned earlier, which had to be kept in stock at the locomotive depots. This must have been an expensive business, but it was in the halcyon days of North Eastern prosperity, and well before the succession of George Stegmann Gibb to the post of General Manager in 1891, when for the first time all expenditure came under close scrutiny.

For the first 16 years, from 1854 to 1870, it would seem from the variety of designs that were turned out under Gateshead auspices that Fletcher was feeling his way. During this period eight different types of passenger engine were built, the most numerous comprising 14 locomotives and the whole eight numbering no more than 76 all told. Building of odd examples of older types in several cases continued after newer types of the same wheel arrangement had begun to make their appearance. For example, of the '220' class 2-2-2s six were turned out in 1854, one in 1859 and the last in 1863 after the improved '450' class had been introduced in 1861. Most of the remainder were 2-4-0 engines, and the '25' class, the first of which appeared in 1863, may be regarded as foreshadowing Fletcher's successful '901' class of later years. The '25's were the first North Eastern engines to run through from Newcastle to Edinburgh when the N.E.R. began to exercise its running powers over the North British from the summer of 1869 onwards.

An exception to the concentration on 2-4-0 passenger engines was the 10 engines of the 'W.B.' or 'Whitby Bogie' type, built in 1864–1865, which as their name implies were of the 4-4-0 wheel arrangement. These odd-looking machines, with their short wheelbase bogies set well back from the smokebox centre-line in order to reduce their length, were designed specially for the steep gradients and sharp curvature of the Whitby & Pickering line, for which reason also their driving wheel diameter was kept down to 5ft. The 14 '686' class engines were intended for the Leeds Northern line, steeply graded similarly, though not in the same degree as the line to Whitby; these had an intermediate driving wheel diameter of 6ft. Otherwise 6ft 6in was a general driving wheel diameter for passenger engines. Inside cylinders had now become an invariable rule. Large numbers of 0-6-0 freight engines also had been built during this period, and a number of 0-6-0 saddle tanks for shunting service.

At last, in 1870, something more like standardisation began at Gateshead. First there came the '708' class of 0-6-0 freight engines (rather oddly so named, as the first example was No. 706), of which 70 were built from 1870 to 1873 inclusive. These were sturdy machines with sandwich frames and outside bearings, as was customary with most of the freight designs. Then, in 1872, there appeared No. 901, the first of a 2-4-0 series that was destined to become famous. With many locomotive engineers in the past one of their designs has stood out pre-eminently by the excellence of its performance, and the '901' class with little doubt was Fletcher's *chef d'oeuvre*. In all, 45 engines of the class were built between 1872 and 1882, and after various rebuildings a few were still in service after the formation of the London & North Eastern Railway in 1923.

With their 7ft coupled wheels, 17in by 24in cylinders, 1,209 sq ft heating surface, 16 sq ft firegrate and 39½ tons weight, the '901's combined very free running with economical performance. Ahrons records that in 1884–1885 a link of 13 '901's working Newcastle–Edinburgh trains from Gateshead shed were averaging 4,421 miles monthly on a coal consumption of 28.4 lb per mile with 160-ton trains, while a second link of 13 engines on the Newcastle–York–Leeds service was covering 4,412 miles per engine per month at 29.5 lb of coal a mile with 170-ton trains. As to speed, in the 1888 Race No. 178 is credited with having covered the 57.5 miles from Berwick to Edinburgh in 58 minutes, and both Nos. 269 and 1325 with having run the 80.6 miles from York to Newcastle, *via* Gateshead and the High Level Bridge, in 82 minutes. In much later years No. 844 was standing pilot at Darlington one day in 1907 when the engine of the 12.20 p.m. from Newcastle to York ran hot, the 2-4-0 having to take over at a moment's notice what was then the fastest train in the country. Although the flyer was made up of seven coaches instead of the more usual five, the little engine dropped no more than 4½ minutes on schedule, covering the 44.1 miles in 47½ minutes start to stop.

Fletcher's successor, McDonnell, to whom we shall come next, made some considerable changes in the external appearance of the '901's, and, it must be confessed, to their advantage, various of the unsightly parts which had rather spoiled the lines of the original engines being stowed away out of sight. The process was continued by William Worsdell, and finally Wilson Worsdell amused himself by a complete rebuild of Nos. 167 and 933 with a bigger boiler of 4ft 10in diameter, and the latter with a leading bogie in addition. No. 933 in particular was a most handsome engine, and it would have been difficult to imagine from appearances that it had ever had any connection with its Fletcher original.

One other Fletcher class needs mention – his 'BTP' or 'Bogie Tank Passenger' type, of which construction continued, with certain variations of design, from 1874 to 1883, to a total of 130 of these 0-4-4 tanks. There were many variations of design; some had 5ft, some 5ft 3in and some 5ft 6in coupled wheels, while the cylinders varied in diameter from 16in to 17in, with 22in stroke. This was another long-lived class, over 40 passing eventually into London & North Eastern ownership. Many finished their days on push-and-pull passenger work as 'Auto-cars', coupled permanently to composite bogie coaches with driving compartments at the outer ends.

Edward Fletcher retired from North Eastern Railway service early in 1883 and was succeeded by the dour Alexander McDonnell, who came to the N.E.R. after 18 years in the same capacity with the Great Southern & Western Railway of Ireland. At Inchicore Works economy had been a prime consideration, and McDonnell had pursued a steady policy of standardisation with the few hundred locomotives in his care; at Gateshead he was to take charge of something more like 1,500 locomotives, of as many and diverse types and fittings, despite the start on standardisation that Fletcher had made, as could well be imagined. The go-as-you-please atmosphere of the North Eastern locomotive world, and the traditional conservatism and suspicion of 'foreigners' that prevailed on Tyneside, all militated against McDonnell, and doubly so when he began a ruthless programme of reforms, so starting an unhappy year and a half in North Eastern locomotive history.

Everything had to be altered. Fletcher had fitted his '901' class engines with exhaust cocks, by the use of which drivers could release part of the exhaust below the cylinders and thereby soften the blast when they thought fit, an arrangement which made some contribution to more economical running. McDonnell decreed that the exhaust cocks must go, and soon they were being removed. In the following year, 1884, the first of his own engines emerged from Gateshead Works, and it broke with all the Fletcher traditions. It had a leading bogie instead of Fletcher's single pair of leading wheels with outside axleboxes; a parallel chimney with flared top compared with Fletcher's tapered stovepipe; left-hand instead of right-hand drive; no exhaust cocks, needless to say; and even a different colour, a much darker green than Fletcher had standardised. The enginemen took a violent dislike to these radical changes, and immediately decided that the new engines would not steam properly; unfortunately for McDonnell they did not, even when in the less prejudiced hands.

The McDonnell 4-4-0s, 28 in all, had easily the neatest outline of all locomotives which up till then had run over North Eastern metals, but their boilers were too small, and their performance was so markedly inferior to that of the Fletcher '901's that before long the former were barred from the principal main line duties. The 0-6-0 freight engines built under his superintendence, of which 48 in all were turned out, equally were damned in the men's eyes, because after his bad start nothing that he did could be viewed favourably by the men, or, to a large extent,

Above, the famous intersection at the east end of Newcastle Central Station, with the East Coast main line to the left and the lines to the High Level Bridge to the right. This was one of the earliest installations of cast manganese steel crossings in Great Britain. *Below*, the signal gantry at the west end of the station, carrying no fewer than 67 semaphore arms on 25 posts. Note the calling-on arms below all the stop signals.   [*Both, British Railways*

Dock installations of the North Eastern Railway at West Hartlepool. *Above*, a portion of the docks dealing with timber. *Below*, an impression of the vast scale of pit-prop handling.

[*Both, British Railways*

Above, electric coaling belts at the North Eastern Railway's Victoria Dock, Hull. *Below*, an aerial view of Hull's Alexandra Dock, built by the former Hull & Barnsley Railway.

[*Both, British Railways*

A remarkable aerial photograph of the North Eastern Railway's dock installations at Middlesbrough, with its impression of

[British Railways

by the works staff either. After his departure, however, these 0-6-0s did well, and became quite popular.

History repeats itself; and it is striking to recall how in London & North Eastern days, 60 years later, Edward Thompson, on succeeding Sir Nigel Gresley as Chief Mechanical Engineer, set about in exactly the same way undoing as much as possible of Gresley's work, only in Thompson's case with considerably less justification and with no small stimulus from personal aversion as well. Thompson suppressed any possible trouble by transferring away from Doncaster various men who had been closely in touch with Gresley; but 18 months of opposition at Gateshead was enough to decide McDonnell to give up the unequal struggle and to resign, which he did in the autumn of 1884.

This resignation left the management in a difficult position, for non-stop running over the 124½ miles between Newcastle and Edinburgh was to begin in the following year, and the McDonnell 4-4-0s would not be adequate for such an assignment. Henry Tennant, at that time General Manager, therefore brought the divisional locomotive superintendents together in committee to produce a new express passenger design, which they did with such rapidity that the first of the 'Tennants', as they became known, were on the road in ample time for the accelerated service. At a cost of no more than 3 tons increase in weight – 39·1 to 42·1 tons – they were superior in power to the Fletcher '901's by being fitted with 18in by 24in instead of 17in by 24in cylinders, and especially by having a firegrate with 18·0 instead of 16·1 sq ft area. The 2-4-0 wheel arrangement re-appeared, with a tapered chimney, right-hand drive, restored exhaust cocks, and at the same time an elegant simplicity of line equal to that of the McDonnell engines.

The reception by the men of the 'Tennants' was vastly different from that of their immediate predecessors, and soon these engines were giving good and reliable service on the principal East Coast expresses, though at scheduled speeds which in those days were no more than moderate, as, for example, 43 m.p.h. only on the non-stop Newcastle–Edinburgh run. In the 1888 Race, however, several of the 'Tennants' gave a very good account of themselves, running the 80½ miles from York to Newcastle *via* Gateshead with 115-ton trains in between 80 and 82 minutes, while on one particular night No. 1505 covered the 124½ miles from Newcastle to Edinburgh in 127 minutes. Twenty 'Tennant' 2-4-0s in all were built, and No. 1463 also has now found honoured retirement among the full-size locomotives in the York Railway Museum.

CHAPTER XXIV

Locomotive Development Under the Worsdells and Raven

THE principal assistant to McDonnell had been Wilson Worsdell, and he was probably the man chiefly responsible for the design of the 'Tennant' 2-4-0s. But when it came to the appointment of a successor to McDonnell, the choice of the North Eastern directors fell on Wilson's elder brother Thomas William, who took office in 1885. William had had a wide experience; it included several years in the United States when he was quite a young man as Master Mechanic at the celebrated Altoona Works of the Pennsylvania Railroad; then 10 years at Crewe as Works Manager for the London & North Western Railway; and finally 4 years as Locomotive Superintendent of the Great Eastern Railway at Stratford Works, from which came the transfer to Gateshead. Both Altoona and Crewe had their influence on T. W. Worsdell's work at Gateshead, as we shall see later.

In particular, the years under F. W. Webb at Crewe had given 'T.W.' a strong leaning towards compounding, though at the same time he had learned to realise the weakness of the Webb system with its two high pressure cylinders and a single low pressure cylinder which was far too small for the work it was expected to do. Instead, Worsdell adopted the German von Borries two-cylinder system, with high and low pressure cylinders of unequal size, and the valve-gear so arranged as to provide for a longer cut-off in the low pressure than in the high pressure cylinder, thus as far as possible equalising the work done in both. The first compound to appear from Gateshead Works was No. 16, of Class 'C', in 1886; 10 simple 0-6-0s, Class 'C1', were turned out at the same time, but from then on compounding set in on such a flood-tide that no fewer than 170 two-cylinder compounds of this type alone were built between 1886 and 1892.

Passenger locomotive compounding proceeded at a rather slower pace. The first such compound was a 2-4-0, No. 1324, also completed in 1886; the next 10, of Class 'F', introduced the use of a leading bogie, which from now on was to be permanent but Worsdell showed some caution in building 10 simple 4-4-0s of Class 'F1' at the same time, all turned out in 1887. The compounds were claimed by comparative trials to be more efficient than the non-compounds, but as the former had been given 175 lb pressure as compared with the beggarly 140 lb of the simples such a result was hardly surprising. One of the new compounds, No. 117, with the well-known driver Bob Nicholson of Gateshead in charge, made the best time of the 1888 Race from Newcastle to Edinburgh – 126 minutes for the 124½ miles with a load of 100 tons.

Next came an unexpected reversion to single driving wheels. The invention at the Midland Derby Works of steam sanding had made it considerably easier for single-driver locomotives to start without slipping, and it was considered that some modern locomotives of the 4-2-2 type would do well on the light express trains between Leeds and Scarborough. Worsdell, therefore, first built, between 1888 and 1890, 10 'I' class 4-2-2s with 7ft driving wheels for these secondary services, and then 10 considerably more powerful 'J' class engines with 7ft 7in wheels for main line work. The former had 18in high pressure and 26in low pressure cylinders with a common stroke of 24in; with the latter the respective diameters were 20in and 28in. The 'J's had the advantage over the 'I's of 20·7 as compared with 17·2 sq ft firegrate area.

The 'J' class engines did some notable work, and under test No. 1518 showed ability to develop an indicated horsepower of no less than 1,089 at 86 m.p.h., cutting off at 53 per cent in the low pressure and 70 per cent in the high pressure cylinder. But these single-drivers suffered in various ways from the complication of their motion, and after no more than 6 years all had been rebuilt as two-cylinder simples, as also had many other of the compounds; the longest to retain their compound cylinders were a number of the Class 'C' 0-6-0s.

As to tank engines, William Worsdell's handy Class 'E' shunters of 1886, with 16in by 22in cylinders and 4ft 6in wheels, not merely remained standard, with slight modifications (such as cutting down the coupled wheels to 4ft diameter in his brother Wilson's 'E1' class of 1898) until the end of North Eastern independence, but a few more were even built in 1948, after Nationalisation. The total reached 120 engines of this type.

Mention must also be made of T. W. Worsdell's compound tank engines, of which he turned out 51 with the 0-6-2 wheel arrangement at Gateshead between 1888 and 1890. F. W. Webb had previously built at Crewe a few experimental three-cylinder compound tanks for the London & North Western Railway, but Worsdell's were the only compound tank engines ever built in Great Britain as a numerous class. They had 18in high pressure and 26in low pressure cylinders, with a common stroke of 26in, 5ft 1in coupled wheels and 160 lb pressure. Among their duties were through workings with 285-ton coal trains of 16 wagons and a brake from Darlington over Stainmore summit right through to Cockermouth, on the Cockermouth, Keswick & Penrith line; and they could tackle the long 1 in 60 climbs west of Barnard Castle at 14 to 18 m.p.h. with these loads. Between 1902 and 1912, however, they were all converted to two-cylinder simple propulsion.

In 1890 T. W. Worsdell, whose health was not of the best, decided at the relatively early age of 53 to retire, but by now he had left a strong impression on North Eastern locomotive practice. This was seen particularly in externals; already a pronounced family likeness had begun to replace the extraordinary miscellany of earlier years. One of the most distinctive features of Worsdell's 4-4-0 engines, which he had first introduced on the Great Eastern Railway, was the combined splasher over both the coupled wheels. To this he had added a shapely flared chimney, a handsome brass casing over the safety-valves, and in particular a large and comfortable cab with a pair of windows on both sides – no doubt a product of his sojourn in the U.S.A. – now as warmly appreciated by the enginemen as Bouch's similar cab on the Stockton & Darlington Railway in earlier years had been disliked.

Wilson Worsdell now at last came into his own, and proved a more than worthy successor to his brother during the 20 years that he was destined to remain in office. He began his superintendence under the most favourable auspices. On the design side he had as his most able Chief Draughtsman Walter M. Smith, who had graduated through the Midland Railway Works at Derby. His principal assistant, ultimately to succeed him, was Vincent Raven, North Eastern through and through. Then, a year after his appointment, as we shall see in Chapter XXIX, the forceful George Stegmann Gibb was to become General Manager, and to give a solid backing to everything that would make for greater progress, efficiency and economy. For all practical purposes compounding was out; the Joy radial valve-motion that had been fitted extensively by T. W. Worsdell was to give place to the Stephenson link-motion; and a beginning was to be made with the fitting of piston-valves in place of slide-valves. Darlington from now on was to take an equal share with Gateshead, and eventually to replace Gateshead altogether, in the building of new locomotives.

First, Wilson Worsdell was responsible for turning out a succession of 4-4-0 locomotives, on a gradually ascending scale of power. It began with Class 'M', of which the pioneer, No. 1620, completed in December, 1892, was the most powerful express passenger engine built in Britain to that date. The cylinders had increased in size from the 18in by 24in of Class 'F' to 19in by 26in, mated to 7ft 1in coupled wheels, and with an enlarged boiler, having 1,341 sq ft heating surface and 19.5 sq ft firegrate area, to provide ample steam.

This was proved by No. 1621 on the culminating night of the 1895 Race, when Bob Nicholson, hero of the 1888 Race, with his fireman Tom Blades, in later years to become an equally famous driver, took the 105-ton Aberdeen sleeper over the 124½ miles from Newcastle to Edinburgh in 113 minutes. Even with the allowance for what must have been some considerable risks taken round the curves at Morpeth, Alnmouth, Berwick and Portobello, this was an amazing performance, and fully justified the place now occupied by No. 1621, with the other three early North Eastern locomotives, in the Railway Museum at York.

Next came Class 'Q', 10 in number and now with 19½in cylinders, though with no corresponding increase in boiler capacity; these were built in 1896. In the same year Wilson Worsdell, possibly anticipating yet another 'Race', built his two 'Q1' 4-4-0s, with coupled wheels of no less than 7ft 7in diameter, and 20in by 26in cylinders, but these never had the opportunity of displaying their prowess in racing conditions. All this was preliminary to the introduction of the most famous of all the Wilson Worsdell 4-4-0 engines – his Class 'R'. The relation between boiler and cylinders was altered by reducing the cylinder diameter to 19in, whereas a much bigger boiler was fitted with 1,572 sq ft of heating surface, and a fire-grate area of 20 sq ft, together with a working pressure at the unusually high figure in those days of 200 lb per sq in.

No. 2011, the first 'R', came out in August, 1899, and for two years, double-manned, ran 455 miles daily, 6 days a week, from Newcastle to Edinburgh and back (including the southbound 'Flying Scotsman'), and then from Newcastle to Leeds and back, so accumulating no less than 284,182 miles before going into the shops for her first general overhaul; indeed, in the first 16 months she ran 139,543 miles without showing any appreciable wear of valves or valve-motion. The remaining 9 engines of the first batch all averaged 163,000 miles between heavy repairs. One can well imagine the approval that such a performance as this earned in the eyes of General Manager Gibb. Not a little of its excellence was due to 8¾in diameter piston-valves and large entry and exhaust ports.

It may be added that Wilson Worsdell had built one of his 'M' class 4-4-0s as a two-cylinder compound, like its predecessors on the Worsdell–von Borries system, but in 1898 he allowed his Chief Draughtsman, W. M. Smith, to plan a complete rebuild of the engine with three cylinders, one high pressure inside and two low pressure outside. A boiler carrying 200 lb pressure was provided, with a firegrate area of 23 sq ft, and independent cut-offs for high and low pressure cylinders. In competent hands No. 1619 did well, but the two independent cut-offs – a complication previously unknown to British engine-crews – decided Wilson Worsdell against any further compound building at that time; nevertheless No. 1619 acted as a trial heat for two much larger compounds, as we shall see in a moment. In any event No. 1619 had the distinction of being the only British locomotive that has ever worked with two entirely different systems of compounding; in her rebuilt form, also, she was one of the prettiest engines that the country has ever seen.

The time had now arrived for still greater passenger power, which meant ten-wheel rather than eight-wheel locomotives. Thus it was that in 1899 Wilson Worsdell produced his Class 'S' 4-6-0 design. They were not Britain's first 4-6-0s, for that distinction belonged to David Jones of the Highland Railway; but his 4-6-0s were intended for freight service, where-as those of Wilson Worsdell were for heavy express passenger work. There were 10 of them, Nos. 2001 to 2010, but with the valve-setting methods of those days their 6ft 1in coupled wheels were on the small side for speed, and they achieved no success proportionate to their size. Neither did the 'S1' class, much more imposing 4-6-0s with 6ft 8in coupled wheels, though the latter, with their piston-valves (rather curiously Worsdell had reverted from piston-valves to slide-valves in his 'S1's) certainly were the freer-running machines of the two.

Eventually, however, the North Eastern Railway came into line with its neighbour to the south, the Great Northern Railway, by standardising the Atlantic or 4-4-2 wheel arrangement for express passenger service. Wilson Worsdell was one of the party of North Eastern officers which, as mentioned in Chapter XXIX, accompanied George Gibb in 1901 on a tour of the United States to study American railway operation. The fastest trains in the U.S.A. at that time were those of the Philadelphia & Reading Railway, of which the star turn was a flyer booked to cover the 55½ miles from Camden to Atlantic City in 55 minutes, soon after reduced to 50 minutes. The engines used were Atlantics, which with their large boilers so impressed Worsdell as to decide him to produce a similar machine with as ample dimensions as the British loading gauge would permit. The result was the appearance in November, 1903, of 'V' class 4-4-2 No. 532, by far the largest and most powerful North Eastern locomotive to be built up to that date.

As compared with the 'S1' 4-6-0s, the cylinders had been increased from 20in by 26in to 20in by 28in; the 5ft 6in boiler had a total heating surface of 2,455 as compared with 1,769 sq ft; and the firegrate area had gone up from 23 to 27 sq ft. The coupled wheels had a diameter of 6ft 10in. A considerable impression was caused at the time by the massive appearance of these engines, as is hardly surprising. Ten were built, and in the last year of Worsdell's reign another 10 were put in hand and actually were completed in 1911, after his resignation. Class 'V1' differed a good deal in appearance from Class 'V', and rather surprisingly the tractive effort came down considerably owing to a reduction in cylinder diameter from 20 to 19½in and in working pressure from 200 to 180 lb per sq in.

Mention was made a little earlier of the rebuilt compound 4-4-0 No. 1619 as providing a kind of trial heat for a design of greater power. This emerged in 1906 in the shape of two four-cylinder compound Atlantics, Nos. 730 and 731. Walter Smith, the Chief Draughtsman, whose system of compounding had been adopted by the Midland Railway and was being tried on the Great Central, was given a virtually free hand in the design of Class '4CC', and the product was probably the most advanced technically in the locomotive realm that the North Eastern Railway ever possessed. The only restraint appears to have been in the size of the boiler, which, doubtless for weight reasons, was kept down in diameter to 5ft, but though the total heating surface of 1,991 sq ft was 464 sq ft less than that of a 'V' class boiler, the compounds had the advantage of a larger firegrate, 29 sq ft in area, and a 25 lb higher working pressure – 225 lb per sq in. Their high pressure cylinders, outside, were 14¼in diameter and their low pressure, 22in, inside – a tight fit indeed between the frames for two cylinders of such size – with a common stroke of 26in.

No. 731 was the first North Eastern locomotive to be fitted with Walschaerts valve-motion; No. 730 had the customary Stephenson link-motion. Under test and in day-to-day running Nos. 730 and 731 proved themselves more than equal to the 'V' class Atlantics; their superiority was appreciable in both tractive power and economy in fuel consumption. Had they enjoyed the later benefits of superheating and bigger boilers they might have had considerable influence on the future development of compound propulsion in Great Britain. Unhappily, however, they had barely entered service when their designer, W. M. Smith, died, and without his driving force no further extension of locomotive compounding took place in the N.E.R.

Meantime a variety of other standard locomotive classes had been turned out. The year 1894 saw the emergence of the 'P' class of 0-6-0s for general freight service, with 18in by 24in cylinders and 4ft 6in coupled wheels, $7\frac{1}{4}$in less in diameter than those of their predecessors, the William Worsdell 'C1' class. Between 1894 and 1898 70 of these were turned out, to be followed, from 1898 to 1903, by 140 of the 'P1' class, with $18\frac{1}{4}$in by 26in cylinders. The next stage was the very much bigger 'P2' class, with the same cylinders as the 'P1's, but a boiler of no less than 5ft 6in diameter carrying 200 lb pressure. Of these 50 were built in 1904, and the final stage was Class 'P3', from 1906 onwards, 115 strong, with slightly bigger cylinders, of $18\frac{1}{2}$in diameter, but pressure reduced from 200 to 180 lb. By 1914, before the outbreak of war, the North Eastern Railway had in service no fewer than 797 0-6-0 tender engines.

In 1901 an eight-coupled locomotive appeared for the first time on North Eastern metals. This was the pioneer of the 'T' class for heavy freight service, with the 0-8-0 wheel arrangement, outside cylinders of 20in diameter and 26in stroke, and 4ft 8in coupled wheels. Ten of these were built, followed in 1902 by 10 of the modified 'T1' class, with slide-valves instead of piston-valves. But 30 more piston-valve 'T's followed between 1902 and 1904.

The year 1908 saw a reversion from the 4-4-2 to the 4-4-0 wheel arrangement for express passenger service, in the 'R1' class, among the most powerful engines of this wheel arrangement ever to run in Great Britain. The usual 6ft 10in driving wheel diameter was adopted, and though the cylinders were restricted in dimensions to 19in diameter by 26in stroke, the tractive effort was greatly assisted by a working pressure of 225 lb per sq in. The 5ft 6in boiler afforded a total heating surface of 1,737 sq ft, and was mated to a firebox with a grate area of 27 sq ft. For the first time the adhesion weight on two coupled axles was allowed to rise to 42 tons out of a total engine weight of $59\frac{1}{2}$ tons. Ten 'R1' 4-4-0s were built, and gave a very good account of themselves; in general their work was quite equal to that of the 'V' and 'V1' class Atlantics.

In the tank engine realm William Worsdell's 2-4-2 wheel arrangement – no doubt influenced by his years at Crewe – had given place to Wilson Worsdell's very competent Class 'O' 0-4-4 tanks on branch line passenger service. Many 0-6-0 side tank shunters also had been turned out. A novelty of 1907 was the 'W' class of 4-6-0 tanks, built specially for the coast line between Scarborough, Whitby and Middlesbrough, with its tremendous gradients; later, to increase the bunker capacity, these engines were rebuilt with the 4-6-2 wheel arrangement.

Wilson Worsdell's last design, produced in the year before his retirement, was also of a tank engine, and was of considerable importance as introducing the three-cylinder simple propulsion which from then on was to be standard in practically all new North Eastern locomotive construction. This was Class 'X' of 4-8-0 tanks for marshalling work, in which the perfectly even torque exerted by three cranks dividing up the circle into three equal parts is of particular value when pushing a rake of wagons at a very low speed over a hump. A final development of the Worsdell régime was that the 'S' class 4-6-0 design which had first appeared in 1899 had become standardised as a type for mixed traffic service, and numerous further examples had been built as a modified 'S2' class. These were the last locomotives built at Gateshead Works, which closed down in 1910.

During Wilson Worsdell's tenure of office the directors, in 1902, had changed his title from Locomotive Superintendent to Chief Mechanical Engineer (another result, no doubt, of George Gibb's American visit in the previous year), and it was to this position, when Worsdell retired in 1910, that Vincent Litchfield Raven succeeded. As we have previously seen, the latter had grown up in the North Eastern Railway, and was steeped in North Eastern traditions. His place as Assistant Mechanical Engineer was taken by A. C. Stamer, another North Eastern man through and through.

Three-cylinder simple propulsion having now been introduced – and incidentally some nine years before Gresley's first three-cylinder design, 2-8-0 No. 461, had appeared on the Great Northern Railway – Raven was so impressed by its possibilities that he decided to extend its use. Incidentally, one important respect in which the North Eastern three-cylinder engines differed from the Great Northern was in being fitted with three separate sets of Stephenson's link-motion rather than the patent derived motion for the inside cylinder fitted by Gresley.

The first Raven three-cylinder design was Class 'Y' – a powerful 4-6-2 tank type intended for short-distance runs with mineral trains over the steep gradients of County Durham. With the Class 'X' 4-8-0 tanks maximum traction effort at low speeds was needed, and for this reason they had three 18in diameter cylinders; with the Class 'Y' the diameter was reduced to $16\frac{1}{2}$in, though a considerably larger boiler was provided. These 20 Class 'Y' engines were competent and reliable machines; they could haul 1,000 ton loads on the level at 20 m.p.h., and one of them on test started a load of just over 850 tons on a rising gradient of 1 in 150 and accelerated it in half-a-mile to 10 m.p.h.

More express passenger power was now needed, and Raven decided to apply the three-cylinder principle to a new series of 4-4-2 express locomotives. The advantages of superheating by now were beginning to be realised in Great Britain, and 10 of the new Atlantics, Class 'Z1', were fitted with Schmidt superheaters, while the remaining 10, Class 'Z', were not. But the value of high temperature superheat was so soon manifest that in a relatively short time the engines using saturated steam were superheated, and the whole 20 then became Class 'Z'. The non-superheated engines had been fitted with $15\frac{1}{2}$in by 26in cylinders and boilers carrying 180 lb pressure, but with the change the cylinder diameter was increased to $16\frac{1}{2}$in and the boiler pressure dropped to 160 lb. The superiority of the 'Z's over the 'V's was very marked; tests in later years showed that the former could average 4·6 as against 6·15 lb of coal per drawbar-horsepower-hour, and 3·73 lb of water compared with 5·52 lb, and also run a considerably higher mileage between general repairs. Owing to Darlington Works being heavily occupied at the time, the first 20 'Z' class Atlantics were built by the North British Locomotive Company in 1911.

By now three-cylinder simple propulsion was well under way, and successive new three-cylinder versions of existing two-cylinder types began to make their appearance; superheating also began to be applied on an extensive scale to existing locomotives, including all the earlier 4-4-0s, of the 'F', 'M', 'Q', 'R' and 'R1' classes. The now fairly numerous 'S2' mixed traffic 4-6-0s received the same attention. As an experiment, the last of the latter, No. 825, was equipped with Stump 'Uniflow' cylinders, of double the normal cylinder length, each with two inlet ports at the outer ends, and a single central exhaust port permanently open, uncovered at the moment when the lengthy piston reached each end of its stroke. The aim of this patent was to reduce the drop in steam temperature between entry and exhaust, and thereby lessen condensation, by arranging that the steam flow should be in one direction only.

Comparative tests between No. 825 and No. 797 on some trains were decidedly in favour of No. 825 so far as coal consumption was concerned, as for example, 4.60 compared with 5.35 lb of coal per drawbar-horsepower-hour and 4.02 against 4.65; but on other turns coal and water consumptions were almost indentical. These results were too inconclusive to justify similar equipment of other 'S2' type engines; though curiously enough the last of a further series of 20 'Z' class Atlantics, No. 2212, was built in 1917 with a modified type of 'Uniflow' cylinders. Owing to the war conditions, however, the experiment was not pursued further. The 'Uniflow' engines could be heard from miles away by the staccato barks of their exhaust, much more pronounced than that of Great Western locomotives, noted for their large exhaust ports.

Similar developments were taking place in the freight realm. The first 10 'T' 0-8-0 freight class of 1901 had been succeeded from 1902 to 1904 by 30 'T1's, with slide-valves instead of piston-valves; the superheated Class 'T2' followed in 1913, with 20in by 26in cylinders and 4ft 7¼in coupled wheels – a type capable of being worked all out, even at around 70 per cent cut-off with wide open regulator, over quite appreciable distances, with a drawbar pull of 10 tons and even more, an asset of great importance with such heavy gradients as those of the mineral lines in County Durham.

Meantime, while 152 of the 'T2's were being built between 1913 and 1921, there appeared Raven's three-cylinder version, the 'T3' 0-8-0 type, the first of which, No. 901, was completed at Darlington Works in 1919. In these the three cylinders were of 18½in diameter and 26in stroke, the coupled wheels remaining at 4ft 7¼in diameter; after modification, the boiler provided a combined heating surface of 2,427 sq ft, with a firegrate area of 26.7 sq ft. Fifteen engines of this type were turned out, and once again proved to be a type which could be worked at over 70 per cent cut-off with full regulator on the hardest duties, such as the tremendous climb with ore trains from Tyne Dock up to Consett. Under test one of these engines exerted a momentary drawbar pull of no less than $16\frac{1}{4}$ tons.

Simultaneously with the first 'T3' there emerged from Darlington in 1919 the first three-cylinder mixed traffic locomotive, No. 840, of Class 'S3'. This shared with the 'T3' 0-8-0s the same boiler, cylinders and motion but with 5ft 8in coupled wheels suitable for fast freight and subsidiary passenger work, on which, later as the L.N.E.R. Class 'B16', the 'S3's achieved considerable success. Seventy in all of the 'S3' class were built.

Meantime, in 1913, Raven had designed and introduced into service one of the most handsome tank engine types ever seen on a British railway, with the unusual 4-4-4 wheel arrangement. This was his Class 'D', eventually built to a total of 45 engines. They had three $16\frac{1}{2}$in by 26in cylinders, 5ft 9in coupled wheels, 160 lb pressure, and a weight in working order of $84\frac{3}{4}$ tons, of which $39\frac{3}{4}$ tons were available for adhesion. Their first assignment was to take over from the Class 'O' 0-4-4 tanks the smartly timed local service over the busy Darlington–Middlesbrough–Saltburn route, on which this enhanced power proved valuable. In all, 45 of the class were built, 20 in 1913 and 1914 and the remainder between 1920 and 1922. In London & North Eastern days, to provide additional adhesion for working over more heavily graded lines, they were all converted to the 4-6-2 wheel arrangement.

Raven's last production was his biggest. In 1922 there had appeared from Doncaster Works of the Great Northern Railway Gresley's first Pacific locomotive, and the North Eastern did not intend to be left in the shade. So it was that just before the end of 1922 there emerged from Darlington Works No. 2400 – a massive machine with a parallel boiler of no less than 6ft diameter and the first-ever N.E.R. wide firebox. Three 19in by 26in cylinders, 6ft 8in coupled wheels and 200 lb pressure gave a nominal tractive effort of 29,920 lb; the boiler afforded a total heating surface of 2,422 sq ft and a superheating surface of 696 sq ft; and out of the engine weight of 97 tons 59 tons were available for adhesion. 'Skittle Alleys' was the nickname suggested irresistibly by the long level boiler top and the three safety-valve columns in line at the rear end.

But the North Eastern Pacifics, five in all, did not prove to be Raven's most successful design. In 1923, with the North Eastern Railway's own dynamometer car, comparative trials were carried out between No. 2400 and a Gresley Pacific, but the advantage – even though this was well before Gresley had learned his lessons in valve-setting from the exchanges of his Pacifics with Great Western 4-6-0 'Castles' – was definitely, even if slightly, in favour of the Great Northern engine. There are no records of the Raven Pacifics ever having put up performances superior to those of his 'Z' class Atlantics.

Mention in the last paragraph of the North Eastern dynamometer car recalls the fact that this was built in 1906 on the lines of the Great Western car which Wilson Worsdell borrowed in that year for the purpose of testing his first 'V' class Atlantic No. 532. After the formation of the London & North Eastern Railway, the N.E.R. car became a highly valued possession of the bigger company, and was used to record the performance on many of the most famous runs in British railway history, in particular the world record of 126 m.p.h. achieved by the Gresley 'A4' Pacific *Mallard* in July, 1938.

Sir Vincent Raven, as he had now become – the honour of K.B.E. had been conferred on him in recognition of his war work as Chief Superintendent of the Royal Ordnance Factories at Woolwich from 1915 to 1919, during which time A. C. Stamer was in charge at Darlington – continued in office until the North Eastern Railway became merged in the London & North Eastern at the beginning of 1923. Raven had worthily carried on the North Eastern tradition first established by William and Wilson Worsdell.

Among the distinctive features of North Eastern locomotive practice that continued to the end was the addiction to Stephenson's link-motion when the Walschaerts gear was making such strides in other parts of the country. One unique feature was the use, in three-cylinder engines, of an extremely complicated casting which incorporated three cylinders and three valve-chests as well as providing the direct support for the smokebox. In general, however, there were few locomotive developments on the N.E.R. which could be said to have influenced British locomotive practice as a whole – comparable, for example, to Churchward's work at Swindon or the performance of the Great Western 'Castle' class 4-6-0s – but for excellence of workmanship and beauty of line and finish the North Eastern Railway locomotives of later years can have had few rivals and certainly no superiors.

CHAPTER XXV

Electrification

ELECTRIFICATION was first introduced on Tyneside as the result of the opening of new electric tramways around Newcastle, and in particular of a new route from Gosforth through to South Shields, which made some damaging inroads on North Eastern passenger traffic in the area. On the principle that it is necessary to 'fight the devil with fire', the N.E.R. Board came to the conclusion that the only way in which to counter this competition would be to electrify their own North Tyneside lines similarly and contracts accordingly were placed for the electrification of 37 route miles of line, using current at 600 volts d.c., with third rail conduction.

The lines selected were from Newcastle Central Station to North Shields and Tynemouth, with the Riverside loop; from Tynemouth through Cullercoats and Whitley Bay to Monkseaton; and from Monkseaton back to Newcastle *via* Backworth, Benton and Gosforth. This at first brought the electric trains making the circuit into the former Blyth & Tyne terminus at New Bridge Street, ¾-mile away from their starting-point, for not until 1st January, 1909, was the ½-mile extension opened from Jesmond to a junction with the main line at Manors, so completing the circuit from Newcastle Central back to Newcastle Central again. Also the East Coast main line was electrified from Newcastle Central to Benton Cutting, where a new south-to-east spur was laid in to connect with the Gosforth–Backworth line, and so to make possible quick non-stop runs between Newcastle and Monkseaton by a shortened route for the benefit of commuters.

The line equipment was carried out with commendable speed, and electric operation of the lines concerned was introduced in stages between 29th March and 25th July, 1904. Near Benton the electric trains crossed the Killingworth wagonway on which, 90 years earlier, George Stephenson had carried out the trial run of his first steam locomotive, which was to have so revolutionary an effect on transport. A year before the death of that great engineer and inventor, he is reported as having declared that 'electricity will be the great motive power of the world'. What an accurate forecast! Incidentally, the Tyneside electrification of the North Eastern Railway was practically a dead heat with the Liverpool, Southport and Crossens electrification of the Lancashire & Yorkshire; both were the first electrified systems outside the London area.

In its next electrification, however, the North Eastern Railway was to establish a precedent in Great Britain. For it was the 1913 plan to electrify the line between the marshalling yard at Shildon, collecting point for coal from all the West Durham mines, and the Erimus marshalling yard between Thornaby and Middlesbrough, which had been brought into use at the end of 1908 as a point of distribution for coal and other supplies both for shipment and to the ironworks and steelworks of Tees-side. The line concerned was the original Stockton & Darlington as far as Simpasture, the former Clarence Railway main line from there to Carlton, from which the west curve was taken to the much later direct Ryhope–Bowesfield Junction line, and finally the freight tracks of the Darlington to Saltburn line into the Erimus yard. The route mileage to be electrified was 18 miles, but some 50 track miles required to be equipped, and it was planned to increase the single engine train loads from 900 to 1,400 tons per train.

An important decision was to use direct current at 1,500 volts, with overhead conduction. Before the line equipment was complete, the First World War had broken out, but the work was continued, and by 1st July, 1915, electrical operation began. For the period, the 12 Bo-Bo locomotives were of an advanced design, each axle being motor-driven, with a total rated output of 1,100 h.p. They proved capable of handling 1,400-ton loads on the level at 25 m.p.h., and with 800-ton trains of empties in the opposite direction were able to make four return trips, a total distance of nearly 150 miles in the day. The gradients of the route were with the load throughout; on the return journey with the empties the locomotives had to face steep gradients at several points, in particular $1\frac{1}{4}$ miles at 1 in 150 from Thornaby East Junction and $1\frac{3}{4}$ miles at 1 in 104 to Carlton South Junction, also $4\frac{1}{2}$ miles at 1 in 230 from Carlton to beyond Stillington.

On a test run with an 800-ton train of 92 empties a maximum drawbar horsepower of 16 tons was recorded, an average of 23 m.p.h. was maintained on the long 1 in 230 and the train was started without difficulty from a stop on the 1 in 104. This electrification gave efficient service for over forty years, but by then the decline in coal traffic had been such as to make it uneconomic to continue to keep the conductors energised for the reduced number of trains passing over the line, and there was a reversion to steam operation.

It was the original intention to use the experience gained from the Shildon–Newport electrification towards the far more important task of electrifying the busy 80-mile stretch of the East Coast main line between York and Newcastle. In anticipation, under the direction of Sir Vincent Raven there was built at Darlington Works Britain's first electric express locomotive, of the 4-6-4 or 2-Co-2 type, carrying the number 13 (following the 12 Bo-Bo freight units already in service). With a one-hour rating of 1,800 h.p. and a continuous rating of 1,300 h.p., the locomotive was designed to be able to haul a 450-ton train on the level at 65 m.p.h., and to be capable of maximum speeds up to 90 m.p.h.; it weighed 102 tons, out of which the weight available for adhesion was $55\frac{1}{2}$ tons. With the limited experience of electric traction then available, No. 13 was fitted with driving wheels of no less than 6ft 8in diameter, equal to those of the company's express locomotives at that time; later experience would have suggested a much smaller diameter and a proportionately higher tractive effort. But No. 13 was never destined to enter passenger service on the North Eastern Railway, for to this day the York to Newcastle main line has never been electrified.

CHAPTER XXVI

Coaches and Wagons

THE earliest passenger coaches on the constituent railways which ultimately merged to form the North Eastern Railway were little more than stage-coaches mounted on flanged wheels; this, of course, is not surprising seeing that they were in almost all cases hauled by horses rather than locomotives. They had the same single compartment, with the other passengers, the driver and guard included, riding on top. For many years afterwards guards continued to ride on seats above the coach roofs, where also luggage was stowed, and would make risky expeditions at times along the roofs from one end of a train to the other while trains were in motion.

Even by the time of the incorporation in 1854 of the North Eastern Railway, passenger travel was still of the most primitive description, in four-wheel coaches, with third class passengers, and many second class also, riding on comfortless bare boards, and illumination provided at night by nothing more than feeble oil lamps. Passenger carriage design had by no means kept up with locomotive development, and was far behind that of the same period in the United States, where already centre-corridor coaches up to 50 or 6oft long, heated by stoves, and even sleeping cars, had come into use. By the early 1860s second class passengers at last were being provided with cushioned seats. The first North Eastern six-wheel coach, so far as can be traced, was a 37ft vehicle acquired when the West Hartle-pool Harbour & Railway was taken over; it had radial axleboxes at the two ends to permit smooth travel round sharp curves.

The by-laws of all the early railways strictly forbade smoking in their carriages. The minutes of the Newcastle & North Shields Railway in 1839, so Tomlinson relates, regarded smoking as 'an evil that had caused injury to the best carriages, the parties getting lights after entering the carriages from phosphorus boxes'; the Board announced that their servants had been instructed to expel passengers who were found smoking in trains from their compartments, and to proceed against them under the by-laws. After the incorporation of the North Eastern Railway, the year 1856 saw the introduction on the Tynemouth branch of a first class coach with a special saloon compartment for smokers, and from 1868 onward, under the requirements of the Regulation of Railways Act of that year, accommodation for smokers had to be provided in every train which included more coaches than one of each class.

In the same year the Great Northern Railway built at Doncaster the first coaches which were to be owned jointly by the Great Northern, North Eastern and North British Railways for the East Coast passenger services, known as 'East Coast Joint Stock' and lettered 'E.C.J.S.' But

these were no more than six-wheelers, the use of which, even in important
Anglo-Scottish expresses, continued well into the present century. It was
some of these that figured in 1907 in Gresley's first experiments with coach
articulation, being joined together in pairs with bogies at the outer ends
and the two adjacent ends supported through the medium of a steel casting
on a centre bogie. Even the first East Coast sleeping cars, one of which was
built by the North British Railway in 1873 for service three times weekly
in each direction between Glasgow and King's Cross, as well as similar
sleeping cars that followed soon after from Doncaster, were six-wheelers.
The slowness with which the use of bogie stock spread in Great Britain was
quite astonishing, and when it did come about the North Eastern Railway
was far from taking a lead in the matter.

The first of the East Coast expresses which were able to cut the exiguous
'meal stop' at York down from 20 to 10 minutes, owing to restaurant cars
at length being introduced, were the afternoon trains between London and
Edinburgh, in 1893. These certainly were bogie cars, but the central
kitchen cars were six-wheelers, as also were the rest of the coaches in these
trains, whereas by the same date the competing West Coast trains were
composed of bogie stock throughout. In 1894, the North Eastern Railway
completed at York and contributed to the East Coast Joint Stock its first
bogie sleeping car, 52ft long, with four single-berth and two twin-berth
compartments, a smoking compartment, a pantry with gas cooker and two
lavatories.

The year 1900, however, saw a revolution. At long last the 'Flying
Scotsman' itself was provided with two brand new trains, each of eight 65-ft
cars carried on six-wheel bogies, with automatic couplers, bow ends and
Pullman vestibules of the American type, and clerestory roofs. The North
Eastern Railway's York shops were responsible for the passenger coaches
while the restaurant cars were built at Doncaster. The 'Flying Scotsman'
trains had been preceded by a similar train built by the G.N.R. for its
King's Cross–Leeds service, and the new stock set a style which was to
remain permanent with the Great Northern and North Eastern Railways
for a long time afterwards.

Early in the century, probably as an outcome of the visit of General
Manager George Gibb and his chief officers to the United States, the
York shops turned out some new twelve-wheel coaches for joint N.E. &
G.N. use, comfortable enough inside but extremely ugly outside with
vertically panelled straight sides without any waist. A similar six-coach
restaurant car set, this time of eight-wheel coaches, was produced for the
5.30 p.m. express from King's Cross to Newcastle and its return morning
service, lettered 'G.N. & N.E.' to indicate joint Great Northern and North
Eastern stock. In later years joint sleeping cars also were built to work
between London and Newcastle by the express which in much more recent
years has become the 'Tynesider'.

Apart from the different varieties of joint stock, it is curious to reflect
that the North Eastern Railway built less corridor stock for its own use
than any of the principal English railways other than the London,

Left, the attraction to juveniles of York Railway Museum; in the foreground is 'Tennant' 2-4-0 No. 1463, and behind it the Great Northern 8ft 4-2-2 No. 1.

[*British Railways*

Right, the historic 2-2-4 tank locomotive *Aerolite*, another York Railway Museum exhibit.

[*C. R. L. Coles*

Below, in the centre is seen the first G.N.R. Atlantic, No. 990, and to the left one of the Stephenson long-boiler 0-6-0s of the Stockton & Darlington Railway.

[*British Railways*

George Stephenson

George Hudson

Sir George Stegmann Gibb

Sir Alexander Kaye Butterworth

Brighton & South Coast and, possibly, the South Eastern & Chatham. In the first decade of the century a handsome corridor train, restaurant cars included, was completed at York shops for service between Newcastle and Liverpool Exchange to work turn-and-turn-about with a similar train of the Lancashire & Yorkshire Railway, and another for the Leeds–Glasgow service that later became the 'North Briton', but very little other North Eastern corridor stock was built apart from coaches with internal corridors but no end vestibules.

About the year 1900, a beginning was made with the standard and well-appointed North Eastern non-corridor bogie stock for internal use. These 52-ft coaches, of handsome external lines with distinctive clerestory roofs, gradually took over almost all the stopping main line, secondary main line and branch line services. On many of these services, as, for example, those between Newcastle and Carlisle or Newcastle and Middlesbrough, the normal formation was four coaches – third class brakes at both ends, a lavatory composite with internal corridors communicating with central lavatories, and either a further non-lavatory third or, more usually, another composite but without lavatories. So matters continued until the end of independent North Eastern history; not until after the London & North Eastern Railway had been formed did corridor trains come into wider but by no means universal use in North Eastern area territory.

A word is needed, in conclusion, about the braking system that became standard on the North Eastern. In the year 1874, an important series of experiments was begun in order to decide what type of braking to install on passenger stock in the interests of safety. Until then trains had been brought to a stand mainly by the use of hand-brakes, or by brakes worked from the engines by ropes, which were anything but reliable, though there had been trials of the Newall & Fay continuous brake, mechanically operated, on the lines between Hartlepool and both Ferryhill and Sunderland. Other types that were tried from then on were the Heberlein brake between Newcastle and Tweedmouth and the Smith vacuum brake between York and Starbeck. But the most important, and finally the most successful, of the trials were those of the Westinghouse automatic brake, which by now was coming into extensive use in the United States.

After some preliminary tests over the steeply graded circuit between Newcastle, Consett and Durham, a full-dress trial at speed was staged between Newcastle and Tweedmouth on 18th March, 1877. A train of twelve coaches had been made up, each equipped with a couple of brake blocks, and this was brought to rest from 50 m.p.h. in 203 yards down a 1 in 754 gradient and from $60\frac{1}{2}$ m.p.h. in 295 yards down 1 in 286. These and other results were far superior to those with any other type of brake that had been tested, and coupled with the behaviour of the brake on the 1 in 60 gradients of the Consett line they were sufficient to decide the North Eastern authorities to standardise the Westinghouse brake for future use on passenger trains. Not only were the passenger engines fitted from then on, but also a number of freight engines, so that they might be able to work excursion and other special passenger trains at times of pressure.

There were complications due to the fact that the East Coast joint stock was fitted with the vacuum brake from the same year onwards, and this difference persisted until the end of North Eastern history, so that N.E.R. engines had to be fitted with combination ejectors in order to be able to cope with both types of braking. It is interesting that when William Worsdell came from the Great Eastern to the North Eastern Railway in 1885, he transferred from one Westinghouse railway to another; and there are not a few locomotive engineers today who are convinced that with steadily increasing speeds it would have been better had all the railways of Britain standardised on the Westinghouse air-brake, as in most other countries, rather than on its vacuum rival.

A few words are necessary, in concluding this chapter, concerning the wagon stock of the North Eastern Railway. Just before the outbreak of war, in 1914, it had reached the formidable total of all but 118,000 vehicles – about a thousand less than the number owned by the Midland Railway but far in excess of the stock of any other British line. Also, whereas the Midland boasted 82,313 open wagons, 12,398 covered wagons and 18,309 mineral wagons, the corresponding N.E.R. figures were 34,893, 8,445 and 59,815 respectively, the vast preponderance of North Eastern mineral wagons clearly indicating the nature of the bulk of the freight traffic handled in North-Eastern England.

Of the minerals that were moved, needless to say, coal easily took the first place. In the early days the so-called 'chaldron' wagons were in universal use – primitive vehicles with outward-tapering wooden sides carried on four-wheel chassis with wooden frames, innocent of springs or buffers, and generally known as '6-ton tubs'. In the 1860s the Stockton & Darlington Railway had developed to an 8-ton wagon design, and by degrees capacity increased through 10 tons and 12 tons until by 1902 the North Eastern Railway was not merely building its first 20-ton four-wheel wagons, but also had introduced an all-steel bogie coal wagon of 40 tons capacity. Owing to greater bulk in proportion to weight, similar capacities were not possible for coke wagons; many of these were older wagons whose capacity had been increased by adding a 'crate' of wooden rails above the wagon sides.

The wagons had to be designed for different types of unloading. Discharge at ironworks and steelworks, and at the coal depots at many stations, has always been on gantries into coal dumps below, for which hopper wagons with bottom doors were needed. Ore wagons have invariably been of the same bottom discharge type. But many other wagons also have been needed with side-door or end-door discharge, the latter for lifting bodily and tilting to be emptied, particularly when coal was being shipped. The side-door coal wagons have been required, among other uses, for carrying locomotive coal to the various depots. A large proportion of the wagons for bottom unloading have been built with the floors sloping downwards from both ends towards the bottom doors, to facilitate emptying.

In an area producing so much rolled steel, there has had to be ample provision for carrying steel rails and lengthy steel sections. In the past such carriage was mainly on short four-wheel bolster wagons, many close-coupled in pairs and with four-wheel end runners for the longer loads, whereas in more recent years, and especially since 60-ft rails have become standard, this duty has been taken over by long bogie wagons. Before the First World War 40-ft bogie wagons had been introduced by the N.E.R. for the carriage of long steel plates. A great number of other special bogie wagons, mostly 40ft in length and in many cases with deep wells between the bogies, had been built for carrying heavy castings, machinery, agricultural equipment, and so on. With its various types of covered wagon, the North Eastern Railway not merely set a near-record numerically in wagon ownership, but in the variety of types also.

CHAPTER XXVII

Train Services and Speeds

IN earlier chapters various references have been made to travel conditions and train speeds over the constituent lines which merged from 1854 onwards to form the North Eastern Railway. Chapter IX related how, on the opening day of the Newcastle & Darlington Junction Railway, 18th June, 1844, the first through train in history to link London with Tyneside, leaving Euston terminus in London bright and early at 5.3 in the morning, came to a stand at Gateshead at 2.24 the same afternoon. Travelling *via* Rugby, Leicester, Derby, Chesterfield, Normanton, York and Darlington, and deducting 70 minutes spent in stoppages, it had taken an actual running time of 8 hours, 11 minutes for a distance of 303 miles, and thus had averaged 37 m.p.h.

That such a speed could have been maintained in the conditions of the time was remarkable, and the nine passengers in this special were hardly to be envied. Over the light tracks of the period the four-wheel coaches would roll and pitch; it was said that in the early 1840s on the Brandling Junction Railway the motion was 'precisely similar to that of a boat on a somewhat troubled sea', and that, worse, on the York & North Midland Railway, it 'went far to produce a similar unpleasant climax' to that suffered by queasy travellers on the water. In view of the operating conditions, also, the safety of the trains in the middle 1840s was far from being a foregone conclusion.

Working timetables were unknown; not until 1846 and 1847 had the main lines of the chief North Eastern Railway constituent companies been equipped with the electric telegraph, which needed the lapse of quite a few years before it was put to its first systematic use in controlling train movements; and the first semaphore signals were only just beginning to come into use by 1852. It was, therefore, left to enginemen to travel with all possible caution, picking up what information they could about the state of the line ahead, and prepared to stop – though without any assistance from continuous brakes in these early days – should there be any obstruction. In such conditions, needless to say, both delays and accidents were frequent, especially after dark. Mineral trains were not even provided with guards.

Further hazards were caused by mischievous members of the public, who at any time might move points, lay stones or pieces of timber on the lines, damage bridges, or otherwise misbehave to the danger of the trains. All things considered, it is remarkable that there were not more accidents. A financial hazard for the railways was that in the event of an accident involving loss of life, a 'deodand' might be assessed on the locomotive concerned. This ancient custom was first devised in the Middle Ages as a kind of expiation for the souls of those suddenly snatched away by violent death, and even as late as the 1840s there were cases of locomotives having amounts of £500 to £1,400 levied on them by coroners' juries after fatal accidents had taken place. The last of these impositions, however, were reversed on appeal by the Court of Queen's Bench, and the practice then came to an end.

From the opening of the Great North of England Railway in 1841, a service of five passenger trains in each direction daily was established between York and Darlington. Stopping trains, taking 2½ hours for the 44 miles, left Darlington at 5.45 and 8.0 a.m. and 12.30 and 6.0 p.m., and York at 6.0 and 9.35 a.m. and 2.30 and 6.0 p.m. There were also the 'Mails', calling only at Cowton, Northallerton, Thirsk and Alne and allowed 2 hours 5 minutes; these, from Darlington at 3.30 p.m. and York at 7.20 a.m., were in connection with night trains between York and London. As related in Chapter VIII, by the use of the Stockton & Darlington, Stockton & Hartlepool, Durham & Sunderland and Brandling Junction trains, with bus connections across Stockton and between Sunderland and Monkwearmouth and a change of trains at Haswell, it was possible to travel from York to Redheugh Station, opposite Newcastle, in 6½ hours, and to continue to Carlisle in an overall time of 9½ hours.

The next record run of note was one which took place in 1848. The opening of the Caledonian Railway from Carlisle throughout to Glasgow in February of that year, of the North British from Edinburgh to Berwick in 1846 and the Newcastle & Berwick as far north as Tweedmouth in 1847 were all contributories to the mounting rivalry between the West Coast and East Coast companies for the traffic between England and Scotland. The firm of W. H. Smith, the newsagents, by now had come into existence, and in November, 1847, had commissioned a special newspaper train from Euston, which had covered the 339 miles to Beattock – beyond which the Caledonian line by then had not been quite completed – in a time which, excluding stoppages, had worked out at an average speed of about 40 m.p.h.

But on the night of 19th February, 1848, this performance was soundly beaten by the East Coast partners, with a second W. H. Smith newspaper special, notwithstanding the fact that, as neither the High Level Bridge at Newcastle nor the Royal Border Bridge at Berwick were yet complete, the papers had to be carried across both the Tyne and the Tweed by road. It is said that the entire journey of 472½ miles was covered in no more than 10 hours 22 minutes, though it is difficult to imagine that with the track, locomotive power and operating conditions of the period an average running speed of 49 m.p.h. for the entire distance, stops excluded, could really have been achieved. The reason for the haste was to have the full details of Lord John Hope's Budget speech in the hands of Glasgow readers by the following day.

By the time of the incorporation of the North Eastern Railway in 1854, express trains were travelling between York, Newcastle and Berwick at average speeds of between 39 and 41 m.p.h.; the York to Newcastle 'Mail' was credited by a Parliamentary Committee of the period as being the speediest train in the country. In general, N.E.R. trains were faster than any in England other than those of the Great Western Railway. 'Parliamentary' trains carrying third class passengers could generally show an average of 18 to 23 m.p.h., considerably higher than the minimum of 12 m.p.h. demanded by law.

Over the principal main lines seven or eight trains were being run in each direction daily, two or three of them of the 'Parly' type, as the Parliamentary trains were known; the number on the branches ranged from 12 to 16 a day on busy lines such as those between Newcastle and both sides of the Tyne down to two or three only on the minor branches. Even to the end of N.E.R. history a number of branches saw no more than four passenger trains each way daily. The busiest station on the system was Newcastle Central, handling 49 departures on a normal weekday, and 63 on a Saturday, when 14 additional market trains were run; in the opposite direction 47 arrivals on weekdays and 60 on Saturdays brought the totals up to 96 and 123 respectively. Up to 1914, Sunday passenger traffic on the N.E.R. in general was less than that of most other English lines.

The development of train services over the East Coast Route, and the effects of the 'Races' from London to Edinburgh in 1888 and to Aberdeen in 1895 which were caused by fierce rivalry with the West Coast Route, were dealt with at length in Chapter XX. The 1888 Race resulted in an agreement between both sides that the times of the day trains between both King's Cross and Euston and Edinburgh should not be cut below $8\frac{1}{2}$ hours. This was well before the introduction of restaurant cars to any of the Anglo-Scottish trains; the through day trains on both sides of the country therefore made certain lengthy intermediate stops to enable passengers, at risk to their digestions and extremely high prices, to bolt hasty meals. The West Coast stop was at Preston and the East Coast at York; in each case the scanty time allowance was no more than 20 minutes.

Although the first dining car out of King's Cross had begun to operate in November, 1879, this was to Leeds; it was not until 1893 that the first restaurant cars appeared on one of the East Coast day trains, which were the afternoon service in each direction, and not the 'Flying Scotsman'. That famous train had to wait until 1900 to receive a pair of brand new trains of twelve-wheel stock, dining cars included, of a most up-to-date type. The York stop in each direction could now be cut from 20 to 5 minutes, and the minimum times of day trains agreed between the East and West Coast Companies (the latter having similarly brought restaurant cars into use) was reduced from $8\frac{1}{2}$ to $8\frac{1}{4}$ hours between London and both Edinburgh and Glasgow.

The dead hand of this agreement continued to operate to the end of North Eastern Railway history and for 10 years of that of the L.N.E.R. also, even to the absurdity of the 'Flying Scotsman', when all its stops had been cut out during the summer months from 1928 onwards, having still to spin out 8¼ hours on the run in order not to infringe the agreed minimum. Not until 1932, after acceleration had been going on apace in every other direction, was the agreement brought to an end, and in the very first summer 45 minutes was cut at one stroke from the non-stop timing. From then onwards times shrunk year by year until the 6-hour streamlined 'Coronation' express began in 1937 to operate between King's Cross and Edinburgh, while by 1962 the 'Flying Scotsman' itself, now diesel-hauled, had also become a 6-hour train.

In the early years of the present century the East Coast service between London and Scotland had settled down into a steady pattern. The 10 a.m. 'Flying Scotsman' from London reached York at 1.45 p.m., and then, not stopping at Darlington, called at Newcastle and Berwick to Edinburgh. Next out of London was a rather curious semi-fast train at 10.35 a.m., nevertheless provided eventually with restaurant cars, which called at all principal stations on the Great Northern, North Eastern and North British lines; leaving York at 3.30 p.m. it did not make its way into Edinburgh until 8.40 p.m. The afternoon service was at 2.20 p.m. out of London, and making the same stops as the 10.0 a.m., *plus* Darlington, this train ran into Edinburgh Waverley at 10.45 p.m. In the up direction the 10 a.m. 'Flying Scotsman' and the 2.20 p.m. took the same overall times, but the former also made the Darlington stop through most of its history, indeed, till after the 1939–1945 war. The up counterpart of the 10.35 a.m. down was a train out of Edinburgh at 7.50 a.m., through coaches from which were transferred at Newcastle to a 10.30 a.m. train for King's Cross, arriving at 4.10 p.m., a forerunner of the far faster 'Talisman' of modern times.

The summer months saw an interesting additional restaurant car express, which left King's Cross at 11.20 a.m., called at Doncaster, and from there made directly for Harrogate by what was the former East Coast main line from Shaftholme Junction through Knottingley to Church Fenton, and then on through Wetherby and up the tremendous climb from Spofforth into the popular spa. The East Coast line was then regained at Northallerton, where the 11.20 headed off the 10.35 a.m. from London, and Edinburgh was reached at 7.45 p.m. There was a corresponding up express at 12.25 p.m. from Edinburgh, giving a fast evening service to London from Harrogate at 5 p.m., with an arrival at 9 p.m. It should be added that Harrogate also had throughout the year its direct 1.40 p.m. luncheon car express from King's Cross by the Knottingley and Church Fenton route and a corresponding up express from Harrogate at 10.10 a.m.

About the year 1904, there was introduced what was destined to become one of the most popular of all the trains between London and Newcastle, the 5.30 p.m. down. Originally this was a train from King's Cross to Nottingham and Sheffield, to which a Newcastle portion was later attached, but the Sheffield portion soon shrunk to a single coach only, going no farther than Nottingham, whereas the Newcastle train had come to stay. With its overall time of 5¼ hours, it was with one exception the fastest train of the day, and on North Eastern metals it had one of the three first runs in Great Britain ever to be timed at over a mile-a-minute from start to stop – from York to Darlington, 44·1 miles, in 44 minutes. Initially the return service, at 7.40 a.m. from Newcastle, was nothing like as fast, but before long this was changed to an 8 a.m. departure, and with Durham, Darlington, York and Grantham stops only, as on the down run, King's Cross was reached at 1.30 instead of 2.20 p.m., a total acceleration of 70 minutes.

Reference must now be made to the night Anglo-Scottish trains. These had never been tied down in time like the day trains, and were considerably faster, particularly in the northbound direction. Indeed, the 8.15 p.m. from King's Cross, carrying sleeping cars for Glasgow, Aberdeen, Perth and Inverness, made the fastest time of all from London to Newcastle – 5 hours 12 minutes – and took $7\frac{3}{4}$ hours to Edinburgh. The 11.30 p.m. down, also with sleepers for Edinburgh, Glasgow, Perth and Aberdeen, was allowed exactly the same time. The corresponding up trains, however, were a good deal slower, being allowed 8 hours 20 minutes. There were also still slower night trains in each direction; provided with sleeping cars, making various additional stops intermediately.

In the first decade of the century, as a competitive result of the Anglo-Scottish acceleration introduced over the Midland and North British route in 1901, a morning express began to run from Leeds *via* York and Newcastle to Edinburgh, later extended to Glasgow, and returning in the evening – the forerunner of the modern 'North Briton'. Between York and Newcastle this train was timed to make one of the fastest runs in Great Britain at that time, being allowed no more than 82 minutes for the $80\frac{1}{2}$ miles, including the Durham service slack and the tortuous approach to Newcastle through Gateshead and over the High Level Bridge. From there followed the fastest run of the day or night to Edinburgh, non-stop over the $124\frac{1}{2}$ miles in 148 minutes. So, after an 8.50 a.m. start from Leeds, Edinburgh was reached at 1.30 p.m.

In later years, when the train had become corridor and restaurant car equipped throughout, these times were a little eased; also the southbound timing, at 6.25 p.m. from Edinburgh, was nothing like as fast, for Leeds was not reached until 15 minutes before midnight. When restaurant cars had been added, and had begun to run through from Leeds to Glasgow and back, these cars and their staffs were covering 555 miles in all daily, and like those on the 8 a.m. from Newcastle to King's Cross, running 537 miles daily, were among the only ones in the country on which breakfast, lunch, tea and dinner were all served in one day's shift; also probably they had no rivals in the distance covered each day.

Mention was made a little while back of the only three runs in Great Britain timed at over a mile-a-minute from start to stop in the years before the First World War, one of them the 44-minute sprint of the 5.30 p.m. express out of King's Cross from York to Darlington. A second was a Caledonian Railway run over the $32\frac{1}{2}$ miles from Perth to Forfar in 32 minutes, by the 8 p.m. night express from Euston to Aberdeen – another legacy of the 1895 Race. The third was not merely the fastest in Great Britain for many years, but also in the British Empire, and it was claimed by the North Eastern Railway. The train concerned was the 12.20 p.m. from Newcastle to York, carrying through Midland Railway coaches to Bristol. From the summer of 1902 onwards this express began to run the 44·1 miles from Darlington to York in 43 minutes, at a start-to-stop average of 61·5 m.p.h.

This run continued to hold its premier place for over twenty years until in 1923 the Great Western Railway accelerated an afternoon express from Cheltenham to London to make the run of 77·3 miles from Swindon to Paddington in 75 minutes, at 61·6 m.p.h., so securing a fractional lead. By 1932, the time of the 'Cheltenham Flyer', as it then had become known, had come down to 65 minutes, and its speed had been raised to 71·4 m.p.h. from start to stop.

While there was no North Eastern response at that time, over the same racing course the North Eastern Region of British Railways today has re-established a very handsome lead in speed over all other competitors. For today's fastest time from Darlington to York, by the diesel-hauled 'Tees–Tyne Pullman', has come down to 35 minutes, requiring a start-to-stop average of 75·6 m.p.h., and there are other runs in 36 minutes (73·5 m.p.h.) and quite a number in 37 minutes (71·5 m.p.h.). Faster still is the flying average of 82·7 m.p.h. now required of the southbound 'Flying Scotsman' and 'Talisman' between passing Darlington and passing York. So this marvellous North Eastern stretch of straight and level track between Darlington and York is still Britain's premier railway racing ground today.

There were other very fast North Eastern schedules in the years imme-diately before the 1914–1918 war, some, indeed, faster than any current timings over the same routes. Inducements were held out to businessmen and others in Leeds and Bradford to settle themselves and their families for lengthy summer periods in the Yorkshire coast resorts of Scar-borough, Bridlington and Filey, while they themselves were provided with some exceptionally fast trains to enable them to 'commute' to and fro. As far back as 1901 an early Pullman sleeping car was converted at York into a first class refreshment car to work between Leeds and Scarborough, though this amenity did not last for very long.

The 'star turn' among these flyers was the 4.45 p.m. from Bradford to Scarborough, timed to cover the 67½ miles from Leeds to Scarborough non-stop in 75 minutes. Normally three coaches sufficed for passenger accommodation, but it must be remembered that the train had to climb out of Leeds to Cross Gates, slow to little more than a walking pace through York, and negotiate at reduced speed the 5 miles of curved track in the Derwent Valley between Barton Hill and Malton, within this 54 m.p.h. average, so that speeds up to and even over 80 m.p.h. were often needed to keep time. The morning train taking the commuters to their work had a somewhat easier timing of 80 minutes. Suffice it to say that in the year of grace 1963 the fastest train between Leeds and Scarborough

in either direction is allowed 95 minutes for the run, though certainly
making intermediate stops at York and Malton.

Bridlington and Filey also had their evening flyer from Leeds during the
summer, pretty nearly as fast, allowed 73 minutes for the 63¼ miles non-
stop from Leeds to Bridlington. On this run the handicaps were the severe
slowings through Selby, Market Weighton and Driffield, and the stiff
1 in 95–100 climb up through the Wolds from Market Weighton to
Enthorpe. A very much easier 86 minutes was allowed for the return
morning journey. For one summer an even more adventurous experiment
was tried with an evening tea-car train from Sheffield to Bridlington, by
the Swinton & Knottingley line to Milford Junction and from there round
to the Leeds–Selby line, following from Gascoigne Wood the same path
as the Leeds train. But this was very poorly patronised and did not last.

Mention was made in connection with the 'fastest train in the British
Empire' from 1901 onwards that its formation included through Midland
coaches for Bristol. This is a reminder that a number of through services
between Newcastle and the Midlands, the south and the south-west,
were established in 1880 with the help of the Swinton & Knottingley Joint
Line. At the beginning of the century there had been no development of
through services between the Midland Railway and North-Eastern
England in any way comparable with those of today. By 1910, in addition
to the one Newcastle–Bristol through coach working already mentioned,
there was the night mail train in each direction, with its sorting coaches
carrying the letters 'M. & N.E.J.P.S.' which sometimes puzzled the
uninitiated; they stood for 'Midland & North Eastern Joint Postal
Service'. Also by 1910 a through restaurant car train was in operation
between Bristol and York by the Midland route.

The scope of through working to and from the north-east was greatly
increased from 1900 onwards, when the Great Central Railway, whose
London Extension had been opened in the previous year, completed the
spur from Woodford connecting with the Great Western Railway at
Banbury. This opened up a variety of new possibilities which were
promptly exploited. The first introduction, from July, 1902, was a new
through express between Newcastle and Bournemouth *via* Sheffield,
Nottingham, Leicester, Banbury, Oxford and the Reading West Curve.
Composed on alternate days of Great Central and London & South
Western rolling stock, this brought the latter's coaches for the first time
as far north as Newcastle. As mentioned in Chapter XVIII, the train took
the coast route between Northallerton and Newcastle *via* Stockton and
Sunderland, so giving through communication between the ports of
Southampton and those of the North-East Coast from the Tees round to
the Tyne; for a year or so it followed the direct Stockton–Sunderland
line *via* Wellfield, avoiding West Hartlepool, but this arrangement did not
last long.

Next came the inauguration of a second ports-to-ports express, in 1906,
this time between Newcastle and the Welsh ports of Newport, Cardiff and
Barry. The Great Central Railway worked the train from York to Ban-

bury, where the Great Western took over, using between there and Cheltenham a most unusual route – a single line branch which never before had seen an express train – by way of Chipping Norton and Stow-on-the-Wold. This brought Great Western Railway stock into Newcastle, the trains being composed of Great Western and Great Central coaches, restaurant cars included, on alternate days. Yet another new through service was one between Southampton and York *via* Oxford, Banbury and the Great Central line, connecting with the Channel Islands and other steamer services at Southampton.

Then, of course, there were the through expresses between Newcastle and Liverpool, first introduced in 1883. Again with the object of providing direct ports-to-ports facilities, the three in each direction worked in conjunction with the London & North Western Railway to and from Manchester Exchange and Liverpool Lime Street took the coast route *via* Sunderland, West Hartlepool and Stockton, from there proceeding direct through Harrogate to Leeds, whereas the two which operated by the Lancashire & Yorkshire route to and from Manchester Victoria and Liverpool Exchange used the main line from Newcastle to York, where North Eastern was exchanged for Lancashire & Yorkshire locomotive power. For years the Newcastle to Liverpool midday express by this route, after waiting at York to be passed by the 'Flying Scotsman', used to leave at precisely the same time – 2.35 p.m. – as a North Eastern express from York to Leeds, and many were the exciting races between L. & Y. and N.E. enginemen that took place over the $10\frac{3}{4}$ miles before the two lines separated at Church Fenton. These through services brought both London & North Western and Lancashire & Yorkshire stock into York daily.

The main line between York and Newcastle in the years preceding the First World War was the most colourful stretch of track in Great Britain for the variety of coaching stock colours that it saw every day – the varnished teak of the East Coast Joint, Great Northern and Great Central stock, the crimson of the North Eastern and the Midland, the so-called Windsor brown and cream of Great Western, the chocolate and white of the London & North Western, the yellowish-cream and brown of the London & South Western, and the red-brown and light brown of the Lancashire & Yorkshire.

Locomotive colours were just as varied, for they included the royal blue of the Great Eastern, which worked its through trains from both Liverpool Street and Harwich to York, the varied shades of green of the North Eastern, Great Northern and Great Central, the red of the Midland, the sober black of the Lancashire & Yorkshire, and for a short time of the London & North Western also. What a paradise York was in those days for railway 'fans' of all ages; its only rival of note was Carlisle. Even after the grouping of 1923, the only British main line over which daily the colours of all four main line railways were seen was that of the London & North Eastern Railway between York and Newcastle, with those of the Pullman Car Company also north of Northallerton.

Of other through services linking ports across the width of the country there were those between Hull, Manchester and Liverpool by three different routes, all headed out of Hull by 'foreign' locomotives. The London & North Western Railway worked expresses out of Hull Paragon three times daily *via* Leeds, Huddersfield and Manchester Exchange to Liverpool Lime Street; the Lancashire & Yorkshire twice a day *via* Goole, Wakefield and Manchester Victoria to Liverpool Exchange; and the Great Central three times each day *via* Doncaster, Sheffield, Stockport and the Cheshire Lines to Liverpool Central. All the three companies concerned exercised running powers over North Eastern metals that had been granted at various times as compensating arrangements for privileges which the N.E.R. had received in return; and the 'foreign' locomotives working the last services of the day into Hull and the first morning services out were accommodated for the night at the N.E.R. engine-sheds in Hull. From 1883 the Midland Railway began running through between Sheffield and Hull *via* Normanton, Milford Junction and Selby, but this service lasted only five years.

There were many mutual uses of each other's tracks, with the help of running powers, by the North Eastern and Midland Railways. We have seen already in Chapter XV how the two companies opened a joint line in 1865 between Otley and Ilkley, in conjunction with a new connecting Midland line from Apperley Bridge, and how the latter company in 1868 added a spur from Shipley to Guiseley, thereby providing a new direct line from Bradford to Harrogate. Over this in 1880, the North Eastern began a daily service between Harrogate and Bradford, not only for the benefit of Bradford business men living in Harrogate, but also to give a direct connection at Harrogate between Bradford and express trains to and from the North. For a short time from 1889, the Midland worked its own trains through between Colne, Skipton, Ilkley and Harrogate.

From 1882 onwards, also, the North Eastern started running through over the Midland main line between Leeds and Bradford, at first only with excursion trains, but from 1902 with daily passenger trains between Bradford and both Hull and Scarborough. It was not until 1903, however, that the Midland began working between Leeds and Harrogate with its own locomotives and stock, including through coaches between London St Pancras and the Yorkshire spa. In the previous year the Lancashire & Yorkshire Railway also started working through between Leeds and Harrogate with its own locomotives and trains from and to Liverpool *via* Manchester, Rochdale and Halifax. Finally, as we have seen, the Great Northern Railway operated express trains between King's Cross and Harrogate *via* Church Fenton, and one daily train, indeed, to and from Ripon. From July, 1893, to the end of 1904, also, the London & North Western Railway worked through between Liverpool and York; between Leeds and York for some years it used the same locomotive – 2-4-0 No. 1220 *Belted Will* of F. W. Webb's 'Newton' class.

As regards local trains, the North Eastern Railway was among the first in the country to introduce train services timed at even intervals. This was natural, of course, with the inauguration of electric working on the

Tyneside lines in 1904, but systematic timing was applied also to certain steam-worked services from quite an early date. By 1913, an even-interval hourly service had been brought into operation between Newcastle and Middlesbrough, with each train allowed 1½ hours for the run of all but 50 miles including intermediate stops at Gateshead, Sunderland, West Hartlepool, Stockton and Thornaby. Four-coach train sets were used, hauled most efficiently by the small 0-4-4 tanks of Wilson Worsdell's Class 'O', of which the first had been built in 1894; these were among the longest through runs in the country entrusted to tank engines half-a-century ago.

By the same year, 1913, various other steam-worked services in the Tyneside area had been put on to even-interval timings, such as those from Newcastle to South Shields, Newcastle to Sunderland, South Shields to Sunderland, and Newsham to Blyth. From the outbreak of war in 1914, there came the gradual curtailment and deceleration of trains that took place all over the country, and the North Eastern services, like all others, were only just beginning to recover when North Eastern history came to an end with the formation of the London & North Eastern Railway group.

CHAPTER XXVIII

Signalling

REFERENCE was made at the beginning of Chapter XXVII to the almost complete absence of proper signalling at the time of the incorporation of the North Eastern Railway in 1854. In the earliest days of its constituent companies there were nothing but signals by hand or flag in the daytime and some kind of light at night. The first record of any systematic form of signalling at a junction was where the Brandling Junction and Stanhope & Tyne Railways crossed one another on the level at Brockley Whins. At the approach to the crossing there were three posts in succession on each line. On reaching the first post, a driver had to whistle; at the second he reduced speed; at the third, if a white flag were hoisted at the crossing a Brandling Junction train could pass at half speed, and if a red flag, a Stanhope & Tyne train. If both flags were hoisted together and waved, or if no flag was shown, the driver had to stop at the third post, clear of the crossing. At night lamps replaced flags.

The first installation of semaphore signals in North-East England appears to have been about the year 1852, but only for the protection of junctions. It is on record, however, that when one of these was erected in that year at Norton Junction, near Stockton-on-Tees, to control the convergence of the Leeds Northern and Clarence lines, the signalman, who also had to work the points, found the business so complicated that he fell back on the old signals, with the result that on 21st July, 1852, there was a collision in which the Engineer of the Leeds Northern was killed.

About the same period the electric telegraph was beginning to come into use. The York & North Midland, York & Newcastle and Newcastle & Berwick Railways installed electric communication in 1846 and 1847, the Leeds Northern in 1852 and the Newcastle & Carlisle between 1852 and 1853, but it was a long time before the stationmasters, and particularly those at the smaller stations, had mastered the telegraph sufficiently for them to put it to any regular use in controlling the movement of trains. Only on the single-track Middlesbrough & Guisborough Railway, which had installed the electric telegraph by the time of its opening in 1853, had a simple form of block system of operating come into use.

In general, until the end of the 1860s, the signalling, even on main lines, was in the form of rotating disc signals, which indicated danger by exhibiting a red face, with a red lamp below it at night, but were invisible when turned end on, for clear, when the light changed to white. Auxiliary or distant signal discs, rectangular in shape, were provided on some lines. These signals were so low, however, that the drivers of non-stopping trains had difficulty in seeing them from any distance. Indeed, as late as

August, 1873, 65 North Eastern Railway enginemen signed a petition to Edward Fletcher, then Locomotive Superintendent, complaining that the distant signals seldom worked properly, owing to slack wires, and demanding sufficient additional time in their schedules to permit them to stop, if necessary, at any station or signalbox to assure themselves that it was safe to proceed.

Up to that date there had been nothing in the nature of block signalling on the North Eastern Railway. As far back as 1869 the Board of Trade had recommended serious consideration of block working to all the railways in the country, and also in 1869 T. E. Harrison, the N.E.R. Engineer, had recommended the provision of facing-point locks at all junctions, but very little had been done by the N.E.R. Indeed, the only block working on the entire system until then was through Shildon Tunnel, from 1865 onwards. When an estimate was prepared, after receipt of the Board of Trade recommendation, of the cost of installing block signalling on the N.E.R., it amounted to £12,173 for the 276 miles of the principal main line from Normanton to Berwick, £10,666 for 229 miles of secondary main lines, and £37,780 for the 871 miles of the entire system; and Henry Tennant, the then General Manager, refused to contemplate expenditure on such a scale. In 1871 a very limited installation was authorised, from Leeds to Milford Junction, Leeds to Harrogate, Darlington to Penshaw, Stockton to West Hartlepool and Norton Junction to Ferryhill only.

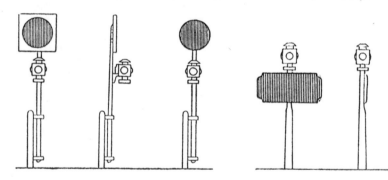

HOME SIGNALS   DISTANT SIGNALS
EARLY NORTH EASTERN RAILWAY SIGNALS, *circa* 1854

[*Andrew Reid & Co., Ltd.*

But the enginemen's petition of 1873, which got into print in the *Leeds Mercury* and other papers, brought the matter prominently to the notice of the public. It led to a Board of Trade enquiry, and also to a letter from H. S. Thompson, the Chairman of the Company, to the next Board Meeting (which he was unable to attend), expressing in the strongest terms his view that the petition was no ground for disciplinary action against the men, but an urgent matter of public safety, and that something must be done without delay. His fellow directors agreed, and Tennant, the General Manager, was instructed by the Board to take action. In 1875 a second petition, this time signed by 600 drivers, complained that the hand-signalling which still persisted at a number of junctions was unsafe, and this added further fuel to the fire. At last the work of installing the block system, with semaphore signals, was taken in hand, including classes for the instruction of signalmen, but not until 1878 had the whole of the North Eastern system been equipped.

By contrast, when North Eastern independence came to an end in 1922 the North Eastern must have been the most lavishly signalled railway in the entire country. In charge of signalling it had an engineer named Hurst, who thought it necessary to provide a separate signal to control every conceivable movement that a train or locomotive might be called on to make. Moreover, Hurst was no believer in ground signals of the disc type, and considered it essential that practically every signal authorising movement should be a semaphore arm mounted on a post. Further, whereas on other railways the 'calling-on' arms which permitted limited movement beyond a stop signal were pulled off only when such a movement had to be made, the North Eastern calling-on arms, of which there was a vast number, had to be pulled off also whenever the stop arms above them were off, which added greatly to the work of the signalmen.

Even at relatively modest junctions on the N.E.R., the profusion of semaphore signals was almost unbelievable, and when it came to the larger stations, like Newcastle, the signal gantries could have had few rivals in the country for their complexity. That at the west end of Newcastle Central Station mounted no fewer than 67 semaphore arms! It is small wonder that the three signalboxes controlling the working of this station required between them the massive total of 613 levers to operate all the points and signals; and it must have been no small relief to the men when in 1909 electro-pneumatic power took over from manual operation. One could hardly envy the driver of a North Eastern express passing at speed a junction like Darlington, and having to pick out his signals from the forest of posts on the gantries ahead of him, and still worse from the maze of lights at night. It is related of A. E. Tattersall, who took over the position of Signal Engineer to the North Eastern Area in London & North Eastern days, that he claimed to have removed one of Hurst's semaphores, on the average, for every day of his occupancy of that office!

Another curiosity about North Eastern signalling of those days was the tenacious adherence to the archaic type of signal post on which the semaphores worked in a slot in the post instead of being pivoted to the outside. This practice had long been abandoned by most other railways both because of the cost of slotting the post and also the risk of the slot getting choked with snow in severe winter weather – a hazard which in the past had resulted in serious accidents because a stop signal arm, held by packed snow, had not returned to danger when the signalman had put the lever back in the frame. However, although the North Eastern Railway had its quota of bad collisions caused by signalling errors, there is no record of any such arising out of the use of slotted signal posts. Nevertheless, Hurst's reign over North Eastern Railway signalling must have been a costly one for the company, and as just mentioned, his successor for years devoted a considerable amount of energy to the removal of the many semaphore signals that he regarded as superfluous.

There was, however, some modernisation during the early years of the present century. One important step, taken as far back as 1905, was the second earliest main line installation in Great Britain of completely automatic signalling. This was brought into operation on 4th June, 1905, over the 11 miles between Alne and Thirsk, with electro-pneumatically operated semaphore signals. In the same month electro-pneumatic signalling came into use at Tyne Dock, preceding by 4 years the far more extensive and complicated electro-pneumatic signalling installation at Newcastle already mentioned.

Reference should be made here to the important junction at the east end of Newcastle Central Station, not so much from the signalling as from the track point of view. The sharp divergence of the multi-track East Coast main and High Level Bridge lines developed eventually into a very complicated layout, with no fewer than 24 diamond crossings, many of them almost right-angled, which are of the type to give the most trouble by wear. In September, 1924, what has proved to be a very successful experiment was the installation of a completely new layout entirely in cast manganese steel; notwithstanding an average of 1,000 daily train movements these have proved capable, with the help of electric welding, of lasting for 14 years, and to date have required no more than two replacements. The castings are laid down on timbers which themselves are supported on tar macadam, and this provides efficient drainage.

It may not be generally realised that Britain's first installation of cab signalling, in the interests of safe running, was on the North Eastern Railway, as far back as 1896. Vincent Raven (who 14 years later was to become Chief Mechanical Engineer) at that time held a position similar to that of the Locomotive Running Superintendents of later years, and he began to fit N.E.R. locomotives with pendulum levers which came into action when struck by lineside stops. The stops co-acted with the signals to which they referred; if any signal was at danger or caution, the stop was raised – like one of the stops installed on London's electric Underground lines – and by intercepting the locomotive pendulum, caused the latter to sound a whistle in the cab. The warning was audible only, and did not cause any brake application; also the stops were installed at every running signal on the principal main lines, distants, homes and starters alike. During his term as Chief Mechanical Engineer, Raven devised an elaborate electrical development of this simple mechanical device, using centrally mounted track ramps, but the advent of the Grouping in 1923 brought this cab signalling to an end, which was a distinctly retrograde step. So in these various ways signalling in the later North Eastern Railway years was a curious mixture of the ancient and the ultra-modern.

CHAPTER XXIX

The Men and the Management

THE later years of North Eastern Railway history were troubled at various periods by labour unrest. Chapters XVII and XIX described the first of these outbreaks, from 1867 onwards; then, after several disputes had been settled, between 1879 and 1889 comparative peace descended for a decade. By the latter year, however, the first trade unions had come into existence, and in pursuit of their aims the men now had behind them the Amalgamated Society of Railway Servants. Trouble which broke out in 1889 proved to be the precursor of a long period of difficulty, though so far as concerns the N.E.R. more from external than from internal causes.

The men's first demand, known as the 'Darlington Programme', was for a 10-hour day; it was also claimed that overtime should be paid at the rate of time-and-a-quarter and Sunday duty at time-and-a-half, and that a day's pay should be granted to every man who was called out for duty, whether he had to work the full day or not. As yet there had been no recognition by the directors of the union as entitled to represent the men, and the first deputation to wait on the directors was composed of railway servants only. The Board made certain concessions, but not all for which the men had asked, and agitation continued.

In December of the same year the men employed at Newcastle and Gateshead goods stations made a further demand, now for a 9-hour day, and backed their claim by handing in their notices. A strike was averted by the N.E.R. offering to submit the dispute to arbitration, to which the A.S.R.S., on behalf of the men, agreed. The arbitrator awarded a 9-hour day to the men actually handling goods in the two stations, but not to the outside workers such as the vanmen and trolleymen. This was the first use of arbitration in any North Eastern Railway dispute.

With the year 1890 came a demand that all future negotiations between the men and the railway companies should be carried out by their trade union representatives, and to this the North Eastern Railway, first among British railways to do so, agreed. Whereas in Scotland the railways refused to recognise such representation, and disturbances and even riots occurred in consequence, the N.E.R., because of its action, for a time at least was free from internal trouble. In December, 1890, the railway settled various questions with the General Secretary of the Amalgamated Society, cutting the hours of shunters at the busy yards to 8 a day, and the week for the passenger staff to 6 days; also the permanent way staff received a pay advance.

The next labour troubles were external, but badly affected North Eastern Railway traffic. In 1892 there arose one of the ridiculous demarcation disputes which have plagued labour relations even to the present day; it caused a 13-week strike of Tyneside and Wearside engineers and threw 23,000 men out of employment. A week's strike of South Yorkshire miners followed, but much more serious was the strike of Durham miners that began on 14th March, 1892, against a reduction in wages. All the Durham mines closed down, and most of the blast-furnaces throughout the area in consequence had to be damped down; many other works were affected; and Tyne Dock and other docks around the coast were practically at a standstill until the strike was settled 12 weeks later. During this time N.E.R. passenger train services had to be greatly reduced and mineral traffic practically ceased.

The next strike of note, oddly enough, was of some benefit to the North Eastern Railway rather than the reverse. It was of miners in Yorkshire and the Midlands, and it led to an urgent demand from these areas for coal from Durham and Northumberland. To the normal short-haul west-to-east traffic of coal for shipment there was now added a great volume of north-to-south traffic, which strained North Eastern resources to the utmost; wagons had to be borrowed from the Great Northern and Midland Railways to cope with it. Such was the congestion of traffic over the High Level Bridge at Newcastle that some of the coal trains from Northumberland had to be worked through the Central Station and over the Scotswood Bridge of the Newcastle & Carlisle line, and from there back to the main line by the Dunston Extension. This strike lasted from 1st August to 18th November, 1893.

Four years later came the railway unrest of 1897. The Amalgamated Society of Railway Servants had negotiated with the North Eastern Railway better conditions of employment for certain grades of the staff – a reduction from a 10-hour day to an 8-hour day for signalmen in the busier boxes, for example – but jealousy among other grades of the staff caused a number of railwaymen to come out on unofficial strike on 20th February of that year. This was contrary both to agreements with the company and also to union instructions, and the railway refused any discussion of the matter until the men first returned to work. This they did on 1st March.

Various other minor disputes in 1897 headed up to a programme of improved conditions of service which, if agreed to in full, would have proved very expensive to the company. It led to the North Eastern Railway Board coming to a decision which would have an important effect on the future relations between itself and its staff. This was that in the event of the directors being unable to find justification for agreeing to any future demand that might be made by the men concerning hours or wages, the Board would be prepared to submit the matter to arbitration and to abide by the arbitrator's decision. The only matters excluded from this undertaking were the demand of the locomotive men for a reduction in their hours to an 8-hour day, with pay at the rate of time-and-a-quarter for any excess over 8 hours, and questions of discipline or staff control. The arbitrator was to be appointed by agreement between both parties and in the event of failure to agree, some judical authority should make the appointment. The first arbitrator so appointed was Lord James of Hereford, and during 1897, 1898, 1899 and 1900 various deputations put their case to him and secured certain concessions. The most comprehensive settlement was the one reached after a lengthy conference lasting from 1899 to 1900.

In August, 1908, an important step in staff relations was taken by the formation of a Conciliation Conference to settle disputes between the company and its staff. There were minor strikes in 1910 and 1911, of freight men at Newcastle, Hull and Thirsk, in each case due to relatively trivial causes, but none lasting more than 3 days. It was another matter in 1919, however, when without notice there was an 8-day strike, from 27th September to 5th October, of a large part of the staff in sympathy with a general railway strike in the country, though the N.E.R. men had no grievance of their own. The national coal strike of 1912 badly affected North Eastern operation, as that of all the other railways in the country, for between 6 and 7 weeks, from 26th February to 6th April.

A much more serious occurrence in the same year, after concessions to the advantage of nearly 9,000 members of the staff had been granted at a meeting of the Conciliation Conference in June, was a strike of 7,000 men on 7th December, 1912, because an engine-driver who had been convicted and fined in Newcastle for drunkenness had been reduced in position. A full week elapsed before this unjustifiable strike was settled. It is difficult to avoid the conclusion that after having led the country in its recognition of a trade union – the Amalgamated Society of Railway Servants – the North Eastern Railway suffered more from strike action, and in several cases without notice, than any other British railway.

A short description is now needed of the men who played the major part in the development and management of the North Eastern Railway throughout its history. No family had a closer connection, from the days of the Stockton & Darlington Railway, than the Quaker Pease family of Darlington. In the index of W. W. Tomlinson's book *The North Eastern Railway*, no fewer than 16 gentlemen bearing the name of Pease, and representing at least 4 generations, are listed. Edward Pease was one of the principal brains behind the Stockton & Darlington project; as described in Chapter II, it was he who sent for George Stephenson in 1821, and it was as the result of this meeting that the Stockton & Darlington Committee appointed Stephenson as Engineer of the railway-to-be, thereby launching that eminent Northumbrian on the career which was to have so profound an effect on the evolution of railway traction.

With Edward Pease on the Stockton & Darlington Board was his son Joseph; before many years had passed the latter assumed the control of the railway's affairs, and it was in recognition of his outstanding work that a part of the Stockton & Darlington Jubilee Celebrations in 1875 was the unveiling in Darlington of a statue to his memory. Then, when by the 1863 Amalgamation Act the Stockton & Darlington Railway became merged in the North Eastern, it was a grandson of Edward and a son of Joseph who joined the N.E.R. Board – Joseph Whitwell Pease, later to be knighted.

By 1888 he had succeeded Lord Derwent as Deputy Chairman of the Company, and in 1895, on the death of John Dent Dent, he became Chairman. But this honourable association was to end under a cloud.

In August, 1902, North-Eastern England was startled by the announcement that the banking firm of J. & J. W. Pease, of Darlington, was unable to meet its financial obligations and was compelled to suspend payment. This firm was banker to the North Eastern Railway, which at the time had £230,000 to its credit at the bank. Certain friends of the Pease family rallied round and between them contributed £140,000 to reduce the deficiency, but the failure cost the N.E.R. about £125,000. The directors of the railway had previously established a fund to meet contingencies, and were able to draw on this to rectify matters, but Sir Joseph Pease, as he had now become, felt that in the circumstances he could not possibly continue in office, and therefore resigned. Other members of the Pease family who had seats on the North Eastern Board were Henry, from 1861 until his death in 1881; John William, from 1883 until his death in 1901; Francis Richard, from 1890 until his resignation in 1905; and Arthur Francis, of the fourth generation, who took his seat in 1906 and remained in office until the end of independent North Eastern history, during the whole of which one or more of the Pease family had been on the directorate.

Chapter XV has described the notable part played by Harry Stephen Thompson as Chairman in the earliest years of the North Eastern Railway; barely a year after the incorporation he assumed this responsible post, and retained it for 19 of the most difficult years in the Company's history, at the end of which his Deputy Chairman, George Leeman, another very able man, succeeded him. John Dent Dent then occupied the Chair until Joseph Whitwell Pease became Chairman in 1895. On his resignation, for reasons just described, Viscount Ridley took over, but for two years only, from 1902 and 1904, and the tenure of his successor was even briefer, from 1904 to 1905. This was none other than Sir Edward Grey, Bart., whose resignation in 1905 was due to his appointment as Secretary of State for Foreign Affairs in the Asquith Government. Sir Edward's estate at Fallodon, in the County of Northumberland, had the distinction of possessing its own private station on the East Coast main line.

The two last Chairmen, John Lloyd Wharton from 1906 to 1912 and then finally Lord Knaresborough, were overshadowed by their General Managers. During its entire history, if we except the few months at the beginning when Thomas Elliott Harrison, was in office, the North Eastern Railway had four General Managers only, and they were all masterful men. Why Harrison was chosen at the outset was because, as General Manager and Engineer of the York, Newcastle & Berwick Railway, he had been the first to propose the amalgamation of that Company with the York & North Midland and Leeds Northern to form the North Eastern Railway. As with the Y.N. & B.R., he tried on the N.E.R. to hold down the same joint appointments, but this was too much, and as his *forte* was engineering, before many months had passed he resigned the General Managership in order to devote himself exclusively to engineering. This he did with great distinction, as Chief Engineer, for no less than 34 years, until his death in harness in 1888.

From that time onwards, for purposes of supervision, the North Eastern Railway was split into three divisions, each with its own Chief Engineer – Northern, Central and Southern – and it is of interest that T. E. Harrison's nephew, Charles Augustus Harrison, was appointed to take charge of the Southern Division. Among notable tasks for which the latter was responsible was the enlargement of Newcastle Central Station, completed in 1894. From 1908 Dr C. A. Harrison, as he had now become, became Consulting Engineer, a newly created post, for the entire system.

The successor to T. E. Harrison as General Manager in the autumn of 1854 was Captain William O'Brien. This capable Irishman had been Secretary of the Great North of England Railway from 1841 to 1845, and then moved south to occupy a similar position on the Wiltshire, Somerset & Weymouth Railway. But he returned in 1850 to become Secretary of the York, Newcastle & Berwick Railway, and so was well equipped for the N.E.R. managerial appointment. It was during his term as General Manager that the North Eastern Railway successfully fought off a whole series of attempted invasions of its territory by other railways, as described in Chapter XV, and, as W. W. Tomlinson remarks in his book *The North Eastern Railway*, 'it was with no ordinary satisfaction that Captain O'Brien, and those who with him had organised the defence of the North Eastern Railway during the most perilous part of its existence, could contemplate the results of their work. Not a position of importance had been surrendered, not an inch of territory lost'. Before Captain O'Brien's resignation in 1871, also, all the independent railways within the North Eastern borders with the exception of the Blyth & Tyne had been absorbed, as described in Chapter XVI, into the 'Greater North Eastern'.

Following O'Brien came Henry Tennant and his term of office lasted through the troubled 1870s and 1880s, from 1871 to 1891. He had had a lifelong railway connection, having entered the service of the Brandling Junction Railway as far back as 1844. At the conference in 1852 between the York, Newcastle & Berwick, York & North Midland and Leeds Northern Railways that resulted in the amalgamation two years later of the three companies and the formation of the North Eastern Railway, Henry Tennant, Accountant and Traffic Manager of the Leeds Northern, represented that company.

Tennant was General Manager throughout the difficult period when the competitive Hull & Barnsley Railway succeeded in penetrating North Eastern territory, and by the time of his retirement in 1891 the Hull difficulties had not been fully resolved. But this was no fault of his; on the contrary, a tribute was paid by the directors to his 'ability, knowledge and tact' and his 'remarkable skill in matters of railway policy', and he was offered and accepted a well-deserved seat on the Board, which he occupied until his death in May, 1910. It was at the end of Tennant's term as General Manager that the decision was reached to allow a trade union to represent the men in their negotiations with the company.

Another famous name in North Eastern Railway history was that of George Stegmann Gibb, Tennant's successor. Mention was made in Chapter V of the remarkable Victoria Bridge over the River Wear, completed in 1838 as part of the Durham Junction Railway, and boasting a central masonry arch of no less than 160ft span. This was built by the firm of John Gibb & Son, of Aberdeen, grandfather and father respectively of George Stegmann Gibb. The latter had been Solicitor to the N.E.R. from 1882 until he succeeded to the managerial chair in 1891.

Gibb was no conservative. He had not been long in office before he came to the conclusion that a complete reorganisation of the traffic department was necessary. British railways, the North Eastern included, annually compiled various traffic statistics, but none of them until then had attempted such compilation on a passenger-mile or freight ton-mile basis. W. W. Tomlinson, in *The North Eastern Railway*, relates how Gibb declared that the main use of such statistics was 'practical, not theoretical. They do not enable persons bent on pursuing some unsound theory of railway rates to establish economic heresies. But they do enable a railway manager to test the work done in carrying passengers and merchandise on any part of the railway, to measure the work performed in relation to many important items of cost incurred in performing it, to compare period with period and district with district, to supervise local staff with a full knowledge of results, to control train mileage, and to enforce economy in train working'.

Gibb's next step was to take a party of his officers to the United States to study American traffic handling methods, which they did during a month's tour covering some 4,500 miles. After their return, an analysis of current figures showed that on the average North Eastern freight trains were carrying no more than 44·2 tons of merchandise and live stock and 185 tons of minerals (or 92·5 tons if empty wagon mileage be included) over a mean distance of 22·2 miles; the freight earnings were averaging 6s. 10½d. per train mile. The average complement of each passenger train was 62·1 persons, travelling an average of 13·9 miles apiece, which meant that passengers were bringing in an average of 3s. 2½d. per train-mile, while total earnings by passenger trains were 3s. 10d. per train-mile. These figures were compiled in 1900.

A complete reorganisation was therefore devised and became effective from January, 1902, largely on the American pattern. Handling and moving the traffic, from now on known as the 'operating' side, was separated from the 'commercial' business of obtaining and charging for it. For operating purposes a General Superintendent was appointed, the first occupant of this office being Henry Angus Watson, assisted by three Divisional Superintendents and nine District Superintendents. On the commercial side there was now a Chief Passenger Agent, assisted by two District Passenger Agents. The commercial side of freight traffic came under the control of a Chief Goods Manager, and under him five District Goods Managers.

In order that every aspect of traffic, both operating and commercial, should be under a single direction, the office of Chief Traffic Manager, dormant since 1856, was revived, and to it there was appointed in 1900, two years before the full scheme was initiated, Philip Burtt, himself directly responsible to the General Manager. It says a good deal for Gibb's management that in 5 years, from 1900 to 1905, average loads of mineral trains rose from 92·5 to 139 tons (including empty wagon trains; for loaded trains only the figure had grown to more than 250 tons), and average receipts per train-mile from 3s. 9¼d. to 9s. 7¾d. for trains carrying miscellaneous freight, and from 7s. 7½d. to 11s. 1½d. for mineral trains. By 1912, these figures had increased further to 11s. 1d. and 17s. 5½d. respectively, but the rate of increase slowed down considerably after Gibb had resigned his office in 1905. In 1901, the rise in the percentage of working expenses to gross revenue, which had been steadily growing for years past, was checked, and by 1906 had fallen from 65·01 to 62·66 per cent.

In carrying out his reorganisation, Gibb decided to train a few young men of a more educated type and wider outlook than those who had risen from the ranks to the higher posts and found it hard to break away from tradition. The men whom he thus introduced, however, had to gain their experience in the hard way, by also working up from the ranks – a *sine qua non*, Gibb declared, if these young entrants were to be able to work amicably with the rest of the staff. But the education with which they started was bound to be an asset during these years of training.

Men with revolutionary ideas are seldom universally popular, and in the Quaker atmosphere that had persisted in higher North Eastern circles from Stockton & Darlington days onwards, under the influence of the Pease family, and especially in a city with such Quaker traditions as York, Gibb's relations were not all of the happiest. A section of the North Eastern Railway Board, headed by his predecessor as General Manager, Henry Tennant, became jealous of his success and increasing power, and a happening in 1905 gave them the opportunity of dispensing with his services. This was an invitation to Gibb from Charles Tyson Yerkes, an American financier who had obtained control of the Metropolitan District Railway and of various London tube lines that were then under construction, to become Chairman and Managing Director of the District line and Deputy Chairman and Managing Director of the Underground Electric Railways.

The financial bait offered was a tempting one, but Gibb was loath to leave the North Eastern Railway. He felt, however, that in view of all that he had done for the N.E.R., and this new assessment of his value that had come from the south, he was entitled to ask the N.E.R. Board for some increase in his not immoderately high salary. Had this happened during the Chairmanship of Viscount Ridley, he might well have received the advance and remained with the N.E.R. for some years longer, but Sir Edward Grey had just succeeded as Chairman, and was disinclined to exercise any casting vote in the matter. Gibb, therefore, resigned on 11th January, 1906, though rather curiously, in view of the circumstances, he was offered and accepted a seat on the N.E.R. Board, which he held until he resigned this appointment also in October, 1910.

Yet once again the directors drew on the legal profession for their choice of a chief executive to follow George Stegmann Gibb. This was Alexander Kaye Butterworth, who had gained his experience in the legal department of the Great Western Railway and after that as Clerk to the Bedfordshire County Council, and had joined the North Eastern Railway as Solicitor in 1891, to succeed Gibb on the latter's appointment as General Manager. His reign extended through the difficult war years, from 1914 to 1918, after which he received the honour of knighthood; it came to an end in the last year but one of independent North Eastern history, 1921.

During this last period the team spirit which had been built up under Sir George Gibb had somewhat disintegrated. There was little love lost between Philip Burtt and H. A. Watson, especially from 1911 onwards, when Burtt suffered a distinct demotion from his position as General Traffic Manager to that of merely Passenger Manager, with Watson now securely in the saddle as General Superintendent. The former office had been abolished, and though the blow to Burtt was somewhat softened by his being appointed Deputy General Manager, this did not mean very much, and it was little surprise when Burtt, receiving compensation with what today is known as the 'golden handshake', left the North Eastern service in 1914.

Meantime other stars had been rising rapidly in the North Eastern firmament. In 1904, after gaining experience on the Baltimore & Ohio Railroad in the United States, and later on certain Indian railways, Eric Campbell Geddes (who had been born in India) joined the N.E.R. to take up the newly-created post of Claims Agent. His rise from then on was meteoric – to Deputy Chief Goods Manager in 1906, Chief Goods Manager in 1907, and Deputy General Manager in 1911. Soon after the outbreak of the 1914–1918 war, Lloyd George, who had become Minister of Munitions, picked on Geddes in 1915 to become Deputy Director General of Munitions Supply, and in 1916, though a civilian, the latter became Director General of Transportation, in which post he succeeded in bringing the British lines of communication in France to a high degree of efficiency. In 1917, though with no political experience, Geddes entered the Government as First Lord of the Admiralty, but his connection with railways had not ceased, for later, as Minister of Transport from January, 1919, onwards, he was the chief architect of the Railways Act of 1921, which resulted in the absorption of the N.E.R. into the London & North Eastern Railway on 1st January, 1923.

Meantime the North Eastern Railway had one last General Manager. Among the university graduates whom Sir George Gibb had selected to train for one of the higher posts in the North Eastern Railway was Ralph Lewis Wedgwood, who entered the N.E.R. service in 1896. After training in various departments, Wedgwood became District Superintendent at Middlesbrough, in the great reorganisation of 1902, but two years later was transferred to York to become Secretary to the company. Nevertheless, his heart was in traffic, and at his own request he returned to traffic in 1905 as Northern Divisional Goods Manager at Newcastle. By October, 1911, he had become Chief Goods Manager at York, in succession to Eric Geddes, while on the retirement in February, 1914, of Philip Burtt, he assumed the position of Passenger Manager also.

After distinguished war service in various capacities, Wedgwood came back to the North Eastern Railway in June, 1919, as Deputy General Manager, eventually to succeed to the chief executive position – a purpose which the farseeing Sir George Gibb had had in mind from the first, and saw accomplished three years before his death – on the retirement of Sir Alexander Butterworth from the General Manager's chair at the end of 1921. But this appointment was the stepping-stone to one considerably higher. For on the formation of the London & North Eastern Railway in 1923 it was the North Eastern Railway which proudly provided its first Chief General Manager, in the person of Sir Ralph Wedgwood, as he became by the well-deserved honour of knighthood in 1924. It is interesting to note that three successive North Eastern General Managers thus received the *accolade* – in striking contrast to the present day, when railway service, no matter how meritorious, seems the most certain way of avoiding any grateful recognition by the nation in the form of a decoration.

In the grouping of 1923, the North Eastern Railway was practically the only railway in the country – with the possible exception of the Great Western, which was, however, considerably enlarged by the absorption of numerous lines in Wales – to retain its identity, as the North Eastern Area, practically without alteration. In the far greater transformation that took place with the formation in 1948 of the nationalised British Railways there was the same retention of identity, though some years later this was changed by additions on a considerable scale to the area now controlled by the North Eastern Region.

Little could it have been dreamed in the past that the day would come when government from York would become supreme over much of the West Riding of Yorkshire, including the whole of the Leeds and Bradford area, the former Midland main line from Cudworth to Skipton, the former Great Northern main line from Leeds almost to Doncaster, the former London & North Western Liverpool to Leeds main line as far west as Standedge Tunnel and the former Lancashire & Yorkshire main line as far west as Hebden Bridge. The wheel has come full circle indeed from the days when all these railways had tried so hard to invade North Eastern territory! In its history the N.E.R. had its ups-and-downs, as we have seen; but there was far more success than failure, and through it all, to the present day, North Eastern *esprit de corps* remains unimpaired.

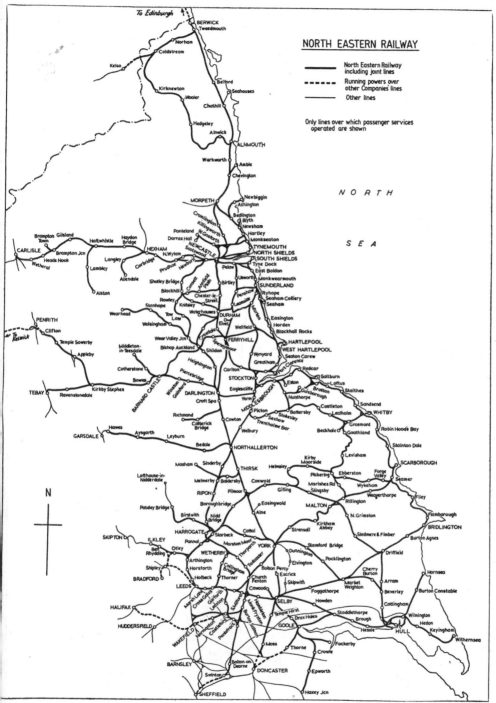

(For detailed area maps see following page)

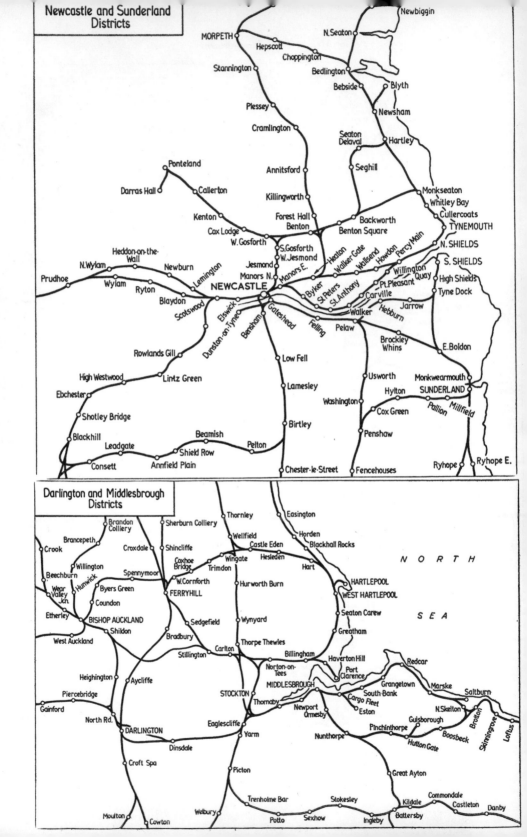

Index

NOTTINGHAM UNIVERSITY LIBRARY

6601